$1,50

THE
SPECTATOR
ANNUAL

Other *Spectator* books

Views from Abroad: *The Spectator* Book of Travel Writing
Articles of War: *The Spectator* Book of World War II
Britain in the Eighties: *The Spectator*'s View of the Thatcher Decade

THE SPECTATOR ANNUAL

Edited by Fiona Glass

Foreword by Dominic Lawson

GRAFTON BOOKS

A Division of the Collins Publishing Group

LONDON GLASGOW
TORONTO SYDNEY AUCKLAND

Grafton Books
A Division of the Collins Publishing Group
8 Grafton Street, London W1X 3LA

Published by Grafton Books 1990

Copyright © *The Spectator* 1990

British Library Cataloguing in Publication Data

The Spectator annual.
1990–
1. General serials in English
052

ISBN 0–246–13697–9

Printed in Great Britain by
Hartnolls Ltd, Bodmin, Cornwall

CONTENTS

FOREWORD

Dominic Lawson

'It was the worst of times: it was the best.' Thus, turning Dickens upside down for *The Spectator*, Sir Alfred Ayer – Freddie to almost everyone – concluded his final article before his death. Freddie was assessing the French Revolution of 1789, but there were no such ambiguities in Timothy Garton Ash's reporting of the peaceful revolutions of Central Europe two centuries later. His despatches from Warsaw, Prague and Berlin in this collection have all the breathless excitement of a man in the front stalls of history. In his piece of 27 May 1989, 'Communism gives up the ghost', Timothy Garton Ash warned that 'this does not mean that the ruling groups calling themselves Communist parties will cease to wield power tomorrow, next year, next decade'. That may yet prove a prescient analysis, but by 2 December, in 'Ten days that stirred the world', Timothy, a personal friend of Vaclav Havel and Lech Walesa, was dancing on the graves of those he had feared would rule Eastern Europe for years to come.

There are tears of sadness in this book as well as tears of joy: Jock Bruce-Gardyne's article, 'Intimations of Mortality', recounts his feelings on being told he would die in months from an incurable brain tumour. Nine months later in April 1990 Jock did die, and many of our readers asked us to reprint Jock's agonisingly dispassionate account of coming to terms with death. We do so here.

Jock had a fine gift for seeing the comedy in misfortune. This, if nothing else, he had in common with our Low Life columnist, Jeffrey Bernard. Perhaps the same could be said of the cartoons, which each week lie subversively at the foot of our writers' columns. Although the examples in the collection represent the best work of a wide range of cartoonists from Britain and America, you might sense a certain mordant style of humour which links them together. If so, that represents the taste of Michael Heath, *The Spectator*'s cartoon editor, and author of our strip 'The Suits'.

If 1989 becomes known as the year in which Mrs Thatcher finally ceased to be unassailable, then I suppose A. N. Wilson will claim much of the credit. Rather unfairly caricatured in the past as a leader of the 'reactionary young fogey' movement, A. N. Wilson began our year with the announcement of his conversion to the Labour Cause: 'Time to turn to Labour'. Thatcherism, Mr Wilson decided, was like the Duke of Norfolk's assessment of the 'rhythm' method of birth control: 'It doesn't bloody work.' When A. N. Wilson wrote these words he was accused of eccentricity, but by the end of the year it seemed that most of the population of the country had joined his crusade. This, I suppose, is the essence of a good anthology: a collection of articles which are even more illuminating in retrospect than they were when first written.

EDITORIAL NOTE

Fiona Glass

A preliminary selection of pieces from the last twelve months of *The Spectator* yielded three times as much material as there was space for. This was the year that communism died in Eastern Europe, and that subject alone could have filled a book. An anthology of this type is to some extent a personal choice, which often proved very difficult. It seemed, however, that it should contain a selection of the most interesting and best-written pieces, and give some sense overall of the year that has passed – without including too much essentially ephemeral commentary. The book should entertain as well as inform and illuminate. I have tried to choose those articles, columns and reviews which regular *Spectator* readers will come upon again with pleasure, having perhaps mislaid their original copies, and new readers will enjoy for the first time. I have also included as many cartoons as possible, since one of the great strengths of the magazine is its capacity to balance serious writing with the ability to make the reader laugh. As it is an Annual, the pieces are arranged chronologically to follow the unfolding events of the year.

10 May 1990

TIME TO TURN TO LABOUR

A. N. Wilson

English politics are excruciatingly boring, English politicians even more so. 'A plague on both your houses' has been my political creed for years; and when supposed alternatives to the Conservative or Labour parties arose, I wished a plague on them as well. I am sure that this indifferentism is not unusual, and it partly accounts for Mrs Thatcher's extraordinary success. The thundering dullness of her Cabinet is matched by the greyness of the Shadow Cabinet. The choice between Mr Lawson and Mr Smith, or between Mr Hattersley and Mr Hurd, is about as exciting as the choice on the menu at a McDonald's take-away.

Given this, it has been obvious who would win the last three elections. That is to say, it would be the party who fiddled the figures to provide the lowest rate of income tax. And it is these two facts alone, in my opinion, the dullness of the policitians and the apparently low rates of tax, which have allowed Mrs Thatcher to get away with her so-called social revolution.

But since the last election, I have changed my mind about the whole matter, and I suspect that I am not alone. It now seems to me quite essential, regardless of their personal unattractiveness, to support the leadership of the Labour party.

The trouble with Thatcherism could be summed up in the words of the Duke of Norfolk when, on a notorious public occasion, he offered some reflections on the 'rhythm' method of birth control: *it doesn't bloody work*. The illusion has been that it is possible, or desirable, to dismantle the semi-socialist state set up by Attlee's administration and supported, more or less ineptly, by every government until 1979. Every civil servant and public administrator must have known from the beginning that this was an illusion, but Mrs Thatcher's public relations advisers have allowed the public to believe otherwise.

The illusion may be summarised in this sort of way. In an 'enterprise' economy, it will eventually be possible to reduce public expenditure and discard the notion of 'public' services. Taxes will be cut. There will be more money in the hands of private individuals. They will then be 'free' to choose whether they wish to spend their money on transport, motorways, airports, education, health, art, or any other desirable commodity. Nationalised industries will be sold off. The burden on the individual will be lifted and the socialist tyranny will have been destroyed forever.

The trouble is that none of these public services can actually be paid for by private individuals. All that happens when you privatise British Telecom is that for a publicly owned company, answerable (at least notionally) to Parliament and people, you substitute a hopelessly inefficient 'private' company answerable, it would seem, to nobody. The Government knows this really, and is therefore incapable of living up to its supposed convictions. It has therefore increased public expenditure in most areas, but done so in a mean-spirited way which has resulted in a decline in quality in almost every area of public life.

Anybody who travels regularly by rail is aware of the fact that the railways are markedly less efficient than they were a decade ago. Even allowing for the fact that 'engine failure', like *Private Eye*'s 'tired and emotional', is a euphemism used by railway guards to cover the personal shortcomings of their colleagues, it is astonishing how many railway journeys are delayed by the creaking obsolescence of the engines. I would reckon that ten per cent of my extensive railway journeys in the last year have been delayed by the need to change engines in the middle of the journey.

This principle is extended by the Government into every area of life. They have not been prepared to make the necessary capital outlay to overhaul the railways. Speak to any librarian, museum curator, keeper of an art gallery or of a building in public ownership. Rather than allowing adequate funds to these bodies, the Government has relentlessly refused to increase the money as required. So, we have to face the prospect of artefacts falling into disrepair, books not being replaced or added to, museums closing off their exhibits. The classic 'monetarist' response to all this is that the idea of patronage should be reintroduced into the arts and 'heritage'. The simple fact is that, however generous rich patrons may wish to be to opera companies or museums, there is not enough money to keep these things going without government help. Insidiously, the argument turns from the rich patron to the less rich member of the public: museum charges, public library charges, and the exclusion of those who cannot pay.

The same is true of universities. Since Mrs Thatcher failed to become a Doctor of Civil Law at Oxford, we have witnessed a positive Ice Age as far as the 'freezing' of academic jobs is in question. Universities are kept going by the money placed in the Vice-Chancellor's begging-bowl by businessmen from Hong Kong or the United States. The oldest copyright library in the world, the Bodleian, is engaged in such a begging exercise, and it will almost certainly fail to raise enough even to repair its existing stock of priceless books, let alone expand to house the boundless flood of new ones. Oxford has been through a period of having no Professor of French and no Professor of German. There was even talk of 'freezing' the Regius Chair of Greek. In less famous universities the situation has been more parlous and the anti-intellectuals (right-wing dons among them) have been conspicuously gleeful at the prospect of reducing these seats of learning to a position in which they can no longer properly function. There is then the inevitable cry of 'close them down'.

If this has been true of the universities, it has been even truer of the National Health Service. And now we have a Secretary of State for Health who is only half committed to running the Health Service in the way that the vast majority of patients wish it to continue – and have paid for it to continue.

Wherever you choose to examine it, the Thatcherite idea has failed to work. It is not in a position to withdraw public spending altogether, though its extreme proponents would perhaps like to do so. Instead, it opts for the worst possible alternative, where bits of money are offered and everyone is in the red. Its attitude is that of a mean old friend of mine, now dead, who had the habit of 'taking' friends to meals. Everyone would eat their fill at his table. He would then airily offer a pound note to the waiter, and his 'guests' would be obliged to make up the shortfall out of their own purses.

It is an illusion to suppose that the Welfare State and the idea of a beneficent government committed to public spending are designed solely for the poor or the socially inadequate. They are meant for all of us. Trains, museums, operas, hospitals, universities cannot exist without public funding and those of us who pay high rates of tax have a right to expect something better than the present government offers.

Those who do not pay high rates of tax, or who pay no tax at all, or who are poor and depend on state assistance, are of course the worst affected of any of us by the Thatcherite experiment. And it is impossible to resist a feeling of distaste and shame at the sheer unimaginative meanness of this administration where the poor are concerned. It is all the more nauseating since the majority of the new Right would appear to come from modest backgrounds, and the likes of Mrs Thatcher and Mr Parkinson should be able to remember what poverty is like. One could mention their attitude to child benefit, their refusal to pay the dole to unemployed teenagers, their woeful record on housing. Two things which particularly outrage me, for some reason, are the introduction of charges for eye tests and false teeth, and the proposal for student loans.

If you are moderately well-off, it is possible to be persuaded that these schemes are fair, with ample provision for a means-tested poor. The reality of the situation is that by increasing dental charges the Government will deter the poor from ever visiting the dentist. We shall revert to being like our parents' generation, a nation of rotting gums and bad breath and people having false teeth by the time they are 40.

Similarly, the principle whereby higher education was freely available to anyone clever enough to take it has now been altered. This will in effect remove the chance of a university or polytechnic career from anyone whose parents are not in a position to help with the repayment of the loan in later life. We shall also, almost certainly, be welcoming in an undesirable system such as that which obtains in the United States, whereby graduates flood into the more swindling and superfluous branches of professional life, such as the law, in order to command the salaries which will help them with their loan repayments. (There is a direct correlation between the absurd costs of American litigation and the need for pushy young graduates to repay their loans to the state.)

The unlikely spectre of a socialist state bossing our lives and confiscating our property gave Mrs Thatcher's Pooterite dream of the small share-holder buying his own council house a sort of quaint charm, though since the collapse of the stock market and the rise of interest rates the charm has lost its glow. Besides, as Auberon Waugh never tires of saying in these pages, this government is far more interfering and bossy than any previous British administration this century. Whether you are a broadcaster, or a motorist, or a trade unionist, your liberties are markedly more restrained than they were ten years ago.

We need to return to the simple idea that public services require public spending and it is the responsibility of governments to administer this spending. The Conservative Government does not display such a responsibility. Of all the parties on offer, only the Labour party is fully committed to this idea of a government's role, and the fact that previous Labour governments were incompetent does not invalidate the principle of responsible government. Mrs Thatcher with her famous Gladstonian dictum that governments have no money (it all belongs to the tax-payer) has subtly evaded her fiscal and social responsibilities in almost every area until a crisis forces her to throw in money too late. It was truly scandalous, after two administrations of neglect, to watch her jumping on the Prince of Wales's bandwagon in her announcement that she would make 'inner cities' her priority. In some inner cities it is already too late to repair the damage caused directly by the wilful negligence of Conservative governments from 1979 onwards, and their belief that it was more important to biff Labour councils than to look after the interests of the people.

How have they managed to get away with it? Not because a majority of voters have ever supported them, but perhaps partly because apolitical figures (myself included) were unwilling to align ourselves with the Opposition. They were also helped by the fact that the Opposition party chose this moment to fragment into absurd Lilliputian factions. It is quite obvious that Dr Owen and the Other Man, leader of the Whatever It's Called Party, will never be in a position to throw the Conservatives out. The only way to bring about the electoral miracle next time round is for everyone who sees the awfulness of this government to vote Labour. Greens. Tory Wets. Liberals. Everyone.

I think there should even be electoral pacts before the next polling day in which these other individuals stand down instead of the Labour party. Cynics would say that there is no evidence that the Labour party would do any better. But Labour are at least committed to the idea that they ought to govern, rather than allow a free-for-all in which we are dependent on whims of multi-national companies and the security provided by private insurance schemes. Unless we all decide to vote Labour — we the majority who are not committed to Conservatism come what may — we face a future with dud trains, dud libraries, dud museums, dud hospitals, and the poor getting poorer — sans eyes, sans teeth, sans everything.

11 March 1989

SORRY, WRONG TITLE

Jaspistos

In Competition No. 1563 you were asked for the blurb that might have been written for a well-known book had the title been slightly different — by the alteration, addition or subtraction of one letter.

Nearly 200 entries — and what a joy the wrong titles were! *Flaubert's Carrot, Madame Ovary, A Tale of Two Cuties, Wein Kampf* (Hitler's account of his life-long struggle against alcoholism), *The Canterbury Tapes, Under the Vet, Burmese Lays, The Dairy of a Nobody, The Oxford Book of English Erse, The Valley of Jones* ('at last we have a truly Welsh novel by Mr Powell'), *The Perfect Strangler, Mr Norris Changes Brains, Old Possum's Book of Practical Mats*, Rider Haggard's *The* ('a highly personalised deconstruction of the bourgeois narrative form'), *The Nuns of Navarone, Oliver Twit* and *Edwin Drool*, and my favourite, offered by Cornelius Kavanagh, Laurie Lee's reminiscences of his youthful friendship with the aged Lord Alfred Douglas, *Cider with Bosie.*

Not a Peony More, Not a Peony Less

Jeffrey Archer's 500-page blockbuster blasts open the secrets surrounding the ruthlessly competitive world of flower-arranging where winners make — and break — the rules, where hothouse passions burst into bloom as ambition is nipped in the bud, where one peony over the limit can mean . . . disqualification.

Read about one man's determination to take a firm stand against cheating competitors and judges as corrupt as any Mafiosi; one man whose standards are high, and whose principles can't be bought — and why he's so nearly a loser. It's a hard world where fragrance and high finance clash head-on, and there is no oasis. Where it's a matter of honour to be first among equals.

And every peony counts.

(D. A. Prince)

The Heart of the Master

This is the story of an obsession. Pilkington, a bitter and ageing classics master at a Catholic public school, is stirred by the winning innocence of Bartholomew, altar-boy in the chapel. He feels his faith renewed, but cannot escape his own suspicion that his interest is sexual in origin. To continue seeing Bartholomew in the 'white purity of his vestment' he must attend mass, and to do this he must confess. But has he sinned? And if not, is the surge of wistful regret at his absence of sin not itself a greater sin? Pilkington is increasingly paralysed by introspection and guilt, but Bartholomew has understood all, and, in a striking dénouement, releases Pilkington by an extraordinary sacrificial act.

(Noel Petty)

Put Out More Fags pictures a personal pilgrimage profounder even than that chronicled in the author's acclaimed *Helena*.

'Put out more fags, Jocelyn,' cries Jacintha, a steady seventy-a-day girl, as they prepare for yet another of their brittle parties. Suddenly — while casually inspecting a dead smoker's lungs in a mortuary — she sees the light. 'Put out more fags' has acquired an urgent new meaning.

Mr Waugh shows her soaring swiftly up the scale of anti-smoking fanaticism from merely assaulting railway smokers (even those in compartments designated for their use) to fire-bombing cigarette manufactories. The climax — her astounding coup at the Lord Mayor's Banquet, amid the fumes of a hundred Havanas — has to be read to be believed.

(Jon Fernside)

Judy the Obscure

The origins of Mr Punch, the Beadle and the Crocodile have been the subject of countless books, dissertations and theses, but few scholars have delved into the background of Punch's shadowy consort, Judy.

In what will surely become the standard work on the subject, running to 510 pages in paperback, Hardy traces Judy's rise from Babylonian temple image through virgin goddess of seashores, force-fed suffragette — the sausages assume a momentous significance during this period — to the patron saint of battered wives and symbol of modern heterosexual feminism triumphant.

A must for every social service office bookshelf.

(Ella Hatfield)

The Pothouse by the East River

'Oh, Paul, would you like me to boil you a telephone or something?'

Why does Elsa's husband think she's crazy? Is it because she keeps having conversations with people who died in World War II? Is Elsa a victim of urban unreality, or . . . is she stoned out of her tiny mind?

Addicts of Miss Spark's special brand of Gothic shock-horror will be pleasantly surprised by her latest offering . . . The frantic attempts of Elsa and her pill-popping chums to make a sandwich, put on their clothes the right way round and construct normal sentences will linger on in the mind like a curious odour in the dark kitchenette of the soul.

(Philip Marriott)

4 March 1989

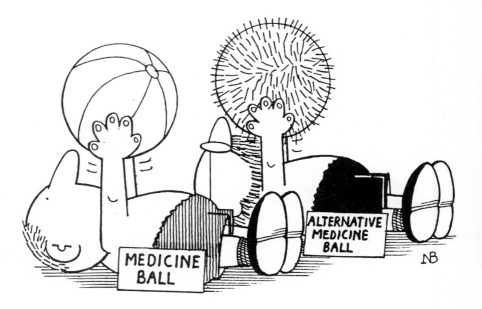

TELEVISION

STOMACH-TURNING

Wendy Cope

When P. J. Kavanagh expressed the opinion, a few weeks ago, that television critics should review the programmes that people actually watch, it reminded me that I must have another go at *Neighbours* (BBC 1) some time soon. Though I have never got as far as writing about this programme, I have frequently taped a whole run of episodes and, somewhat less frequently, forced myself to watch one or two. The challenge was to find some kind of answer to the question, 'Why is *Neighbours* so popular?' Normally, however dreadful the rubbish, I have some inkling as to its appeal. But the popularity of *Neighbours* has remained, for me, an impenetrable mystery.

Last week I taped four episodes and watched three of them. The main plot, at present, concerns a big bust-up between Scott and Charlene, the young married couple played by Kylie Minogue and Jason Donovan. In real life Minogue and Donovan have both become pop stars. In *Neighbours* they continue to lead lives of stupefying dullness on a horrible modern housing estate. One striking thing about them, to a person of my generation, is that they show no inclination whatever to get away from their parents. The cause of their quarrel was not existential agony at the prospect of five or six decades of married life in the suburbs but the fact that Charlene saw Scott kissing another girl. Whether the kiss was lustful or brotherly, I cannot tell you. But I do know that Scott is very sorry and wishes Charlene would forgive him. The entire population of the street shares this wish and people talk of little else but their plans to bring Charlene and Scott together again. Male and female, young and old are united in platitudinous concern, observing that all marriages go through rocky patches, and that things have got to be talked through because that's what marriage is all about, mate − communicating with each other.

'It's philosophy, isn't it?' commented the friend who was prevailed upon to keep me company during Friday's episode. 'It ranks with the meditations of Marcus Aurelius. Is that any help? Can I stop watching it now?'

Actually, I think there may be hope for Charlene. She seems genuinely interested in her work as an apprentice garage mechanic. And she responds to all the neighbourly nosiness with healthy irritation. If they push her any harder, perhaps she'll tell them all to go to hell, preferably in foul language, before taking off for the big city and abandoning bourgeois respectability for ever.

Channel 4's screening of *Prick Up Your Ears*, the film about Joe Orton, provided a welcome change. There's nothing like a week of *Neighbours* to enhance one's enjoyment of a homosexual seduction scene that takes place while the television at the end of the bed is broadcasting the Coronation. Or to help one appreciate the scurrilous plot summary, involving a lesbian policewoman, that Orton and his friend Kenneth Halliwell wrote in a library copy of a novel by Dorothy Sayers. Of course, the film will have shocked a few viewers and some scenes were a bit much for me. In one of them Halliwell is preparing supper. 'Do you want rice pudding *with* the sardines,' he asks, 'or separate?' 'With', replies Orton. There's a close-up of the unconventional meal and then the two stand side by side at the window, eating it up with relish. Seeing that kind of thing on television, honestly, it turns your stomach.

25 March 1989

'*Bad news, Mr Greer — it's a sheila.*'

LEAVES FROM THE COMMONPLACE
BOOK OF WALLACE ARNOLD

AFORE YE GO

While never denying my penchant — surely not peculiar even in this 'gay' (dread word) age — for the company of comely young lovelies of the female variety, I feel it incumbent upon me to stress that my acquaintance with Miss Bordes was entirely professional. It is the mark of a successful columnist that his every word should appear as effortless as the morning breeze, but it is an open secret among my fellow *écrivistes* that the high standards maintained by this particular column owe as much to sheer hard slog as to inspiration, and, for a short time, Miss Bordes provided that hard slog.

She is an acknowledged expert on herbaceous borders, and she had agreed to provide valuable research into this area for a series of ruminations on gardening that I had scheduled for the late spring. Occasionally, I would jokingly refer to her in conversation with colleagues as 'My Herbaceous Bordes', but that is as far as our intimacy went. I have neither seen nor heard from the aforesaid person since I last settled up with him or her, and so let this be an end to all further speculation.

Clearing the air

My name is often bandied about when one wordsmith partakes of snuff with another, but I must admit that I am unused to hearing it blasting loud and clear from the Big Screen. Though I barely met Miss Keeler during my frequent sojourns at Cliveden, the makers of a new motion picture called, if memory serves, *Sandal!* (misleading, as footwear plays little or no part in the proceedings) have seen fit to drag my reputation through the dirt by constant reference to 'leading society figures' implicated in the so-called sandal. They nowhere mention W. Arnold by name, courage not being high on their list of credentials, but when Miss Keeler says, 'The only man who ever made me truly happy in this whole extraordinary affair which led to the downfall of a Government is a well respected literary figure who is a frequent guest and confidant in the highest political circles', it takes no detective to divine at whom the finger points. But I have made it a rule never to pass comment on this sorry episode, and it is a rule I have no intention of breaking.

But for that episode (how unnecessary it is to bring up the name of John Profumo) my memories of Cliveden are of civilised people from all walks of life hobnobbing with one another. On one lawn, the young Imelda Marcos might be sharing small talk with the First Lord of the Treasury, whilst on another Mr Frankie Vaughan would be getting to grips with the Suez Crisis with the then Quintin Hogg, and, on the Upper Terrace, Rab would be testing his mettle in a hand of gin rummy with Mr Norman Wisdom and two of the Beverley Sisters. Golden days indeed, but then Astor went ahead with his plans for building a swimming pool, against my repeated advice, and the allure of bathing togs was too much for some people to withstand. A sad end to a glorious summer.

25 March 1989

'Would you mind stepping out of the light? I've got a solar-powered pacemaker.'

BUFFING UP MANNERS

James Michie

Good manners are easy to define. They are considerateness, the less obtrusive the better, towards other people — seeing that a guest's glass doesn't stay empty, offering a seat to the old or the pregnant, turning up to an appointment on time. The same goes for bad manners — continually interrupting someone else, jumping a queue, filling in one's weekend host's crossword puzzle. In this sense, manners are only morals, and one might imagine that from Tooting to Tierra del Fuego there would be general agreement on what's good and what's bad. I wonder. There's another, morally neutral side of manners: etiquette. For this to work, a code has to be generally accepted. Is there now any generally accepted English middle-class ('we're all middle-class now') consensus about etiquette? I doubt it.

Here are a few acts of behaviour which I personally regard as breaches of considerateness, but which are common enough: playing tapes in cars without consulting the wishes of the passengers; talking during dinner only to the person on one side; taking photographs of other guests without asking whether they mind; turning up at a friend's house unannounced; smoking between courses, whether you are host or guest (and I speak as a heavy smoker); writing letters in what you must have often been told is an indecipherable hand; reading, for however short a time, in a room in a private house in which there is general conversation; bringing an uninvited guest to a party without first telephoning the host; driving faster than elderly passengers find comfortable; using a telephone without your host's permission; going to the theatre with a hacking cough.

Whether or not these offences strike my readers as clear, nothing seems clear in the realm of etiquette. Do you still use 'Esquire' on your envelopes, or even 'Mr'? (I've given them up, unless I think the addressee would mind, which is surprisingly often.) Do you still walk on the traffic side of the pavement when accompanying a woman? (I don't, because I thought it was all about hansom cabs and flying mud, but I know a girl who finds it charming.) Is it cheeky to mend your host's fire? (In parts of Ireland it's acceptable after seven years' acquaintance.) Is it rude not to write a 'bread-and-butter' letter after staying the night with anyone not family or close friend? (Yes. And guilty, my lord.) Is it *brutta figura* to make up one's face or comb one's hair in public? (Irrationally I disapprove because it was one of my mother's *bêtes noires*. Easier to defend is my dislike of the un-hand-covered yawn: it's not so much the implication of boredom as the revelation of fillings that jars.)

Nowhere is social uncertainty so evident as in the rituals of arrival and departure. On being introduced, some shake hands, others don't. I have watched uncertain young men enter a room like gun-slingers, hands dangling at holster-level, ready for any contingency. Some say,

'See? The son-of-a-bitch did have Mr Bun the Baker.'

'How do you do?', others 'Hello', others 'Hi', and yet others 'Pleased to meet you', a strange assumption. A small school of thought follows the Continental practice of always shaking hands on meeting and parting. Then there are the kissers and the non-kissers, the former dividing into the one-cheekers and the both-cheekers (in one region of France you even find thrice-kissing folk, who negotiate each other's hair-styles and spectacles with great adroitness). For myself, I wish that 'the kissing had to stop' − it's like tipping, very difficult to lay off once you've started. To complicate matters, people variously introduce each other by title or by first and surname or by first name only, and if the second method is used nobody seems confident about the state of intimacy, or liking, or toleration at which it's all right to use the Christian name. They order this matter better in France, where formality prevails but *tu* and *vous* are free to do their subtle work. Finally, when a group is sitting in a room and a stranger enters, does everybody rise to greet him or her, or only the men? If there's to be a convention, it should surely relate to age, not sex.

Now for a few random observations. As a guest I prefer to bring flowers rather than a bottle; first, because there's no chance of the flowers being either too good or too bad, and secondly, because they're more likely to reflect the taste of the entertainer who's put in the major effort, the hostess. I think it's uncouth to telephone before 8.30 in the morning, and wise to begin all calls with a conventional 'How are you?' (I once rang a friend and launched into a comic monologue only to learn at its end that his mother had died that day.) My pet hatred is people who suffer from 'vestibulitis', departing guests who linger interminably in the porch, bantering and reconfirming arrange-ments, while the baby wakes and cold air streams in, and then drives off with a series of valedictory hoots.

Confusion rules, but does it rule OK? Does it all matter, or is it a typically English hangover from the stale U and non-U preoccupation of the Fifties, sparked off by a learned article by my old tutor, Alan Ross? An accepted code of etiquette saves time and thought, if not embarrassment any more. We don't need a new Lady Troubridge to tell us which way to tip our soup-plates while spooning, but we do need a rough consensus to get us effortlessly through the simple mechanics of social life. Yet these days it would be a bold author who risked a 'What to do' book. How reviewers would relish their one-upmanship!

1 April 1989

MOSCOW DIARY

Charles Moore

It is 30 years ago this week that British European Airways, as it then was, opened its first service to Moscow. On board the first Viscount to arrive in Moscow was a British parliamentary delegation, including Captain Henry Kerby MP, a blimpish Tory who later turned out to be a Russian spy. This week the chairman of British Airways, Lord King, took Concorde here to celebrate. On board was Mr Cecil Parkinson (who was opening the British trade fair), Mrs Parkinson, various editors, including myself, and Captain Nicholas Soames MP, who is not a spy so far as I know, and would anyway be thoroughly unsuited for that calling, as he is the most conspicuous man of my acquaint-

ance. A few weeks ago I rang Mr Soames (he does not use his military rank) to ask him if he would go to Hungary at short notice to speak on behalf of G. M. Tamas and the political movement with which he is associated. Mr Soames was tempted, but firm. 'Dear boy,' he said, 'it is Cheltenham.' Indeed, for this visit behind the Iron Curtain Mr Soames is dressed as for a National Hunt meeting. He wears a heavy brown coat, modelled, he tells me, on Sargent's portrait of Lord Ribblesdale, and a brown trilby. He also has the satisfied look of one who has done well on the turf. A few days before Aintree, Mr Soames was fishing on the Dee and caught a six-pound salmon in the Polveir pool, so when it came to betting he made a sentimental punt and got the winner.

Because we are a VIP party, we were given special treatment on arrival. Much worse treatment, it turned out, than that normally arranged by Intourist. Mr Parkinson's coat was left on the aeroplane, Mr Parkinson's luggage vanished for a long period, there were no cars to collect us. When we finally reached the hotel, a monster with literally thousands of rooms, we were confronted with a form of architecture new to me: to get from one part of the building to the other you have to go outdoors. So we went out of reception to the bit where you hand in your passports. There we got a piece of paper which told us what our room numbers were. Then we went out again and then in and up to a desk where we got our keys. To get our passports back the following day, we needed to pay one rouble and forty kopecks. To change pounds into roubles, you need to have your passport. . . .

Some of our party were rather disheartened by this vivid and immediate demonstration of the limits of *perestroika*, but it did not in the least perturb our most senior representative of the press, Sir John Junor. The Sage of Auchtermuchty understands human nature. Observing that drinks at the bar had to be paid for in roubles, and that we had no roubles, Sir John ordered Georgian champagne for me and himself and made sure that we drank it before the question of payment arose, and then exercised all his septuagenarian charm on the pretty barmaid, giving her two pound coins. Finding, at breakfast the following day, that we still lacked roubles, Sir John summoned the waitress, changed money for all of us on the black market and arranged for two pots of caviar (now officially unobtainable) to be furnished for himself on the same basis.

After our first four hours of tribulation, things improved. We reached the British embassy and its reception for Mr Parkinson. The building, secured by the Foreign Office before the revolution, is of unspeakable grandeur, and looks across the Moscow river to the Kremlin. I met an editor who told me that Russians loved coming to parties at the British embassy because, as they entered the first of the public rooms, they confronted what they imagined to be a full-length portrait of Tsar Nicholas II. In fact, of course, it is a picture of his virtually identical cousin, King George V. The plan to succumb to Soviet wishes and move out of the present building should be resisted at all costs. I can think of no more catastrophic blow to our prestige here.

Lord King took our party on to dinner where we tasted for the first time a benefit of Mr Gorbachev's rule. The Lasagne Restaurant is one of the new 'co-operative' restaurants which are allowed to run independently. The food was good, but we had to bring our own drink, since Mr Gorbachev is actually more repressive than his predecessors about alcohol, and Lord King had caviar flown in from London for the occasion, perhaps the ultimate example of coals to Newcastle. Opposite me was a young producer from Moscow Radio. He said that the most admired and taught English authors in Russia now were Dickens (which I had heard) and Evelyn Waugh, especially *Brideshead Revisited* (which surprised me). I asked him if he was a Marxist, since he said that he was a Party member. He said that he was 'interested in the insights of Marx', which reminded me of an occasion on which I asked Mr Tony Benn if he was a Christian and he replied that he was 'a student of the teachings of Jesus'. I asked the man from Moscow Radio if he were baptised and he said yes, 'but by my grandparents'. Then I asked him if his own children were baptised and he smiled and said they were. A British government minister told me last year that when he was first in London Mr Gorbachev confided in him that he too was baptised, even though both his parents and grandparents were firm communists. It is an insurance policy, I suppose, the only one that provides for acts of God.

We left the restaurant noisily, throwing a few muddy snowballs, and went and walked in the emptiness of Red Square. People had not prepared me for its extraordinary beauty. Its cobbles curve as if one is on the arched spine of some great animal. Above the darkness, the Red Flag is lit up and billows incessantly in an artificial wind blown upon it from a turret of the Kremlin. We went and admired the still soldiers by Lenin's tomb — 'the second best guard in the world,' said Mr Soames. 'You can see their boots didn't come from Lobb's,' said Lord King.

Then we walked back past St Basil's Cathedral. Lord King recalled the fact that Ivan the Terrible had put out the eyes of the architects so that they would not build anything so lovely again: 'thorough, eh?' he said.

15 April 1989

'CAN YOU DRAW PROPERLY IF YOU WANT TO?'

Nicholas Garland

Cartoonists are not always comical in daily life — but I know two who are. Michael Heath and David Austin both sprinkle their conversation with dry one-liners and, in Heath's case, sudden rambling monologues during which he assumes the accent and character of a type which for some reason or other has irritated or amused him.

I watched them greet each other recently at a *Spectator* party, mimicking the daft questions cartoonists are sometimes asked.

'You're that cartoonist aren't you? What's 'is name?'

'Do you have a proper job then?'

'Do you know Gerald Scarfe?'

'I don't like that one either.'

'Do you write your own captions?'

'Can you draw properly if you want to?'

They amused each other like this for some time and then the three of us were approached by a lady guest. 'Oh,' she said, 'you're Michael Heath, aren't you? Tell me, do you write your own captions?'

Michael replied that we'd been through all that, but went on to answer her questions politely until she laughingly asked, 'Tell me, why was there such a fuss when that Mark Boxer died? – I mean, what was it about him?'

In one way or another, we simultaneously replied that Boxer had been a distinguished artist, implying that once that was understood her question, while remaining offensive, required no further answer.

I cannot be absolutely certain but I don't think the lady would have asked in such a frivolous way about the death of a so-called fine or serious artist. 'Why was there such a fuss when that Henry Moore died?' The work – and even the deaths – of comic artists tend to be considered lightly in this country. This is not true of other art forms: it is quite common for serious or classical actors to acknowledge the debt they owe to a comedian. 'I learned everything I know, laddie, about timing, projecting, handling props, character acting, etc from Max Miller . . . Frankie Howerd . . . Ted Ray . . . Jack Benny,' and so on. Such tributes may be more than a little condescending, but they are genuine nevertheless.

But I do not remember any artist, other than another cartoonist, ever paying such a tribute to Leach for example or Vicky or Rowlandson. A sort of class distinction exists in art, by whose rules comic art is seen as an amusing sideshow or light relief to the main drama of life rather than as a serious art form in its own right. By this definition it is seen as trivial. Even when one artist is a master of both fine and comic art there is a tendency to separate his two styles and think of them as independent of each other. The comic art is perhaps seen as inspired mucking about, but the fine art is the really serious stuff.

In fact something closer to the opposite may be true. Take the work of Edward Lear. He was a good conventional artist but a comic artist of genius. His two styles could scarcely look more different but the one is by no means independent of the other. All his comic drawings, the owly owls and the grasshoppery grasshoppers and the strange little ladies and gentlemen which illustrate his nonsense verse, were drawn by a hand guided by hours and hours of patient study from nature. The briefest glance at his work reveals this to be true. You have to know a great deal about geese to be able to draw one as simply and accurately as he could. His comical animals are brilliant caricatures of whole species. The simplification and distortions all depend on a profound knowledge of the real creatures.

This hinterland of learning gives his slightest scribble its strength. But what raises this work so far above the rest is something that comes from another source and which does not contribute at all to his more conventional work. Indeed it is perhaps deliberately excluded.

In his nonsense verse and in their lively illustrations he taps straight into his own emotions and preoccupations. Themes such as loneliness, loss, love, regret and hope delicately enrich the apparently inconsequential antics of his touching and perplexed heroes. His jokes, whether he intended it or not, are unmistakably sad as well as funny. Even with as humorous an artist as Lear the word 'comic' does not seem entirely satisfactory to describe this aspect of his work. I do not know how consciously he included the melancholy side of his personality in his comic work. I would guess that somewhere he had a very shrewd idea of what he was doing, and if I'm right and he was consciously expressing his true feelings through his nonsense drawings and verses, then he was doing something very ambitious and rather advanced for his time. . . .

15 April 1989

CEAUSESCU'S MEMORIAL

James de Candole

Twenty-four hours after arriving in Rumania, I was told to leave. The Sicuritatea, Rumania's secret police and the country's largest employer by far, came to my hotel in Bucharest. They were well-dressed and polite, and claimed to be from the state passport office. They asked me what I thought of the city and then recommended that I leave Rumania on the morning plane. Oddly, they assured me that Tarom, the Rumanian airline, was very comfortable. I asked them why I was being expelled and they said that I was not being expelled; they were recommending that I leave. Why? 'For activities incompatible with your status as a tourist.' And if I didn't leave? They frowned and shrugged their shoulders: 'It could be a problem for you. Please tell your master in London to stop this unfriendly activity.'

I did not leave and it was a problem: my passport and plane ticket were stolen from my hotel after I had 'lost' my room key in a cavernous and very crowded restaurant (Rumanians live in a murky yellow half-light because of electricity shortages). In the official police statement it was written that the 'Englishman had returned to hotel in a state of inebriation after losing his key'. At no time did they show any interest in the two youths who I had been squeezed up against in the restaurant.

For four days and nights I was closely followed by three Sicuritatea: their faces and habits became familiar to me. The foulest of them chain-smoked and dressed in black. Concealed in a bag under his arm was a walkie-talkie into which he would speak by inclining his head and lifting his shoulder. He was suffering from a wry-neck as a result of this too frequent contortion. Another was short and fat, and wore a leatherette trilby − there were thousands like him. The third was young and had a friendly enough face. He disturbed me the most because of this. The others were obviously the dregs of their society but he was freshfaced and keen.

The latest edition of the official *History of Bucharest* shows for the first time a great white hole on the map of the city. This is where the mediaeval heart of the capital stood five years ago. Since 1985 almost a third of Bucharest has been razed to the ground. Hundreds of slave-workmen are dying in the creation of Nicolae Ceausescu's harrowing architectural schemes.

In the north-west of the city, near Piata Victorei, I found a street being bulldozed. By the time you read this it will have vanished. There was an old couple standing at the end of their garden, watching a neighbour's house being demolished: they were waiting their turn. Across the street piled high with rubble and broken furniture, a family stood silently in front of their home, surrounded by possessions – a bedstead, a cupboard, table and chairs. Towering over this scene of state vandalism were the pitted concrete blocks into which these people will be moved.

They will have already been forced to sign the standard letter requesting that their own house be demolished and that they be re-housed in a modern flat. A vicious twist of the knife is the money the state demands from them to cover the demolition costs.

I went into a shop and was sickened by the scene there: weary people peering into big metal buckets of cooked offal and turning away in disgust. There is very little food in Bucharest. In the market peasants stand behind tables on which they have spread little piles of nettles, sunflower seeds and bruised apples.

I visited an historian whose address I had been given. I knocked on the door and a lady leant out of a window above and asked who I was: 'A friend from England,' I replied. The door was opened and she demanded to see my passport: 'I'm sorry. I'm like a customs official,' and explained that I had not looked English. Her eyes were weeping from an infection caused by the dust. I handed over some provisions – aspirin, coffee and grapefruit.

The flat was beautiful, filled with books and furniture gathered over many generations. The whole house had been theirs once, she explained, but it had been taken from them. For a time, even the flat they had had to share with two other families. She had a grubby paper which declared her right of ownership. It is worth as much or as little as the authorities like: 'They could throw us out or demolish the whole street next week if they wanted to.'

Her husband, she said, was returning in an hour with a colleague from work and I must leave before then so as not to compromise the friend. The law on foreigners makes it a crime to speak with foreigners and all conversations must be reported to the police: 'It would terrify him to find you here.'

Rumania's National History Museum has a permanent exhibition paying homage to a married couple 'blind with covetousness of ruling'. The walls are covered in pictures of Nicolae and Elena Ceausescu opening factories and surveying fields of wheat. There is a photographic record of them together with the world's leaders; in 1978 they visited the Queen and Duke of Edinburgh, Mrs Thatcher, then leader of the Opposition, the Prime Minister of Canada, the Presidents of the United States and France, and the King of Spain. Ten years later the truth about Rumania had been revealed and the international appeal of Ceausescu sunk to nothing. Today he is forced to practise his skills of diplomacy on the likes of Gaddafi and Arafat, and on a regiment of African terrorist leaders − company better suited to a man responsible for the destruction of his country and for the misery of several millions of people.

There is a giant map of the world, with Rumania at the centre. From it beams of light shoot along tubes of glass to every continent the couple have visited. There are two large rooms chock-full of *Ceausesceana* − birthday baubles offered in fear by the people of Rumania in celebration of the achievements of 40 years. There are many grotesquely crude paintings of the diminutive couple − waving, smiling, kissing and embracing. The most ridiculous shows a flight of doves springing from Elena's head. The last room of the exhibition displays the medals and trophies, the robes and certificates given to the couple by foreign governments and institutions. Here is the copy of Elena's notorious Honorary Doctorate from the Polytechnic of Central London.

The Homage exhibition is the abominable façade behind which trembles an utterly demoralised population. It is worse now than ever before − worse even than the Fifties. People disappear so suddenly and so completely that it is as if they had fallen off the edge of the world. In winter they freeze because there is no fuel. And they go hungry all year round.

On Sunday, I went to the Morning Service at Bucharest's Anglican Church. The priest, Father Sherwood, read from Exodus, Chapter iii: 'I have surely seen the affliction of my people which are in Egypt . . . I know their sorrows.' His congregation was a mixture of diplomats and elderly Rumanians. Young Rumanians had come in the past but they were photographed leaving the church and later beaten up. Father Ian distributes food from the church door; he came back from abroad recently to discover his supply of frozen meat rotting on the floor and his crucifix beside it.

I walked up the hill to the Cathedral, followed by the wheezing hunchback Sicuritatea, and tiptoed in. I stood for an hour wondering at the beauty of the place and at the devotion of the old women who spring up and down so often and so lightly on such little food. The dignified, ponderous movements of the priests looked over-fed by comparison. I turned to leave and surprised my tail who, in a half-hearted attempt to blend into unfamiliar surroundings, quickly bowed his head and crossed himself.

By then it was dusk and I walked the full length of the Boulevard to the Victory of Socialism – an experience I shall never forget. The façade of Ceausescu's monstrous Palace of Justice is nearly finished and looks down onto a regiment of faceless acolytes, block after block stretching far into the distance. It will soon be ready; the millions of coloured paving stones have been laid and trees planted; the water pipes in the fountains are being concealed in concrete fish; and 500 lei fines (two weeks' wages) are being imposed on those who walk across the grass.

There were very few people about and the whole area was silent and devoid of human significance: 'concrete, glass and steel girders/in the space from which God has fled' (Mircea Dinescu: *Exile on a Pepper-corn*). With the passing of Nicolae Ceausescu's brief but bloody 'dynasty', the Boulevard will remain as a monument to an extremity of human wickedness.

15 April 1989

CHERCHEZ LA FEMME

Minette Marrin

Trying to have things both ways, commonly ascribed to women, is much more typical of politicians. Either way, politician and woman, Mrs Thatcher certainly does it. In particular, she plays the card of her gender both ways. She insists on being seen as a woman, with a woman's mind, but she also insists, at other times, that the difference makes no difference.

As a result she presents an irritating conundrum. Both in public and in private she very obviously displays a rather awesome femininity, none the less real for having been embellished by public relations men. Her enthusiasm for discussing the finer points of ironing and the price of apples appears, though it may serve her well with women voters, to be quite genuine. On the other hand her most striking qualities are not peculiarly female; a description of a politician as courageous, resilient, single-minded and a bit of a bully would not immediately suggest a woman. Yet many people who know Mrs Thatcher are convinced that her gender is very important, without being able (or willing) to say clearly what they mean.

It seems to me rather trivial to talk (as many do) about her feminine charm, her exploitation of her sexual appeal and her flirtatiousness. All successful people need some form of charm, some form of animal charisma, and overworked charm is just the politician's *déformation professionelle* − marked but superficial. Equally the extensive discussion in newspapers and on television of Mrs Thatcher's hair, teeth, clothes and diet seems empty. Obviously, in a conventional sense Mrs Thatcher is (on this evidence) very feminine. She enjoys being a girl. She likes pretty underwear, she knows how to keep the bows on her frocks puffed up with tissue paper and she wears Denis's pearls to flatter her good complexion. She is a good-looking and, latterly, an elegant woman. If all this is relevant to her success or failure as a prime minister, it can only be in the sympathetic impression it makes on some voters.

However, among her peers it has not mattered one way or the other; Golda Meir and Shirley Williams were not held back by their lack of conventional chic, nor was Barbara Castle advanced by her possession of it. The point about femininity, as distinct from femaleness, is that it is so obviously conventional. I am sure Mrs Thatcher would adopt a Mao suit and a cultural revolution bob, if she thought it suitable, or if it answered her purposes. As it is, she has tinkered with her hair and her voice and her manner to create a softer, less aggressive persona.

The question of appeasement is the only interesting aspect of the public manipulation of Mrs Thatcher's femininity. The difficulty with being a woman in power in a society like this is that you cannot afford to seem either too strong or too weak, a problem with stereotypes that would not confront a male prime minister. Mrs Thatcher's particular feminine style is almost successful at impressing and appeasing at the same time. The combination of rather severe suits with noticeably high heels, giving conflicting messages of decisiveness and helplessness, is a classic ploy. Mrs Thatcher's real interest in domestic detail must genuinely endear her to some women who might otherwise resent her Olympian competence. So may her occasional performances as Mrs Average, as in, 'It hasn't worn me down – no, no, no. Mums take a lot of wearing down, thank goodness.' (*Woman's Own*, 1987.)

In this sense Mrs Thatcher's femininity has simply been a superficial means of dealing with the disadvantage of being female. The interesting question about her gender is how, less superficially, being female has worked for or against her.

In one way it has helped. Mrs Thatcher may say she owes nothing to contemporary feminism, but surely the fact is that she owed her rapid early rise to tokenism, to reverse discrimination. She would not have been able to get into position for the leadership had there not been a shortage of Conservative women; she became a junior spokesman almost as soon as she had been elected, for that reason. It was clever of her to have taken advantage of this, and to have been one of those few, able Tory women. But the fact remains that her male-dominated party and Britain's voters would have felt no need and little inclination to support her had it not been for years of persistent pressure from feminists.

There is a rather more nebulous advantage in being a rare bird, one that she has instinctively exploited by remaining rare and protecting her territory. She has had very few prominent women around her, whether through lack of choice or out of the misogyny common among powerful females. This is clear in photographs: in the absence of other women, she stands out distinctly, at summits, at press conferences and in every picture where she is alone among her penguins in dinner jackets, brightly coloured among the black and white, cloven among the lesser crested.

She is often visually alone of all her sex, suggesting an almost mythic role. Much ink has been spilt on the theme of Mrs Thatcher as an invader of the nation's consciousness as some awesome female archetype – nanny, matron or bossy mummy.

However, it is unclear how myths and fantasies affect our political life. Who can presume to say what deep-seated desires and animosities are touched by the very idea of Mrs Thatcher? Tempting though it might be to discuss her as Britannia or the Witch of Endor, this must all be pure speculation.

Mrs Thatcher's imposing figure, symbolic or not, may dominate the group photographs, but she is still isolated from the groups. As a woman she cannot be clubbable, cannot be part of the old-boy network; she would be as welcome at White's as a male nurse on an obstetrical ward. She does not fit well into the male-dominated House of Commons. She cannot be part of the male establishment web of loyalty and convention. Someone else might have found this subtle exclusion a disadvantage; Mrs Thatcher positively makes the most of her apartness; she would not want to belong. Unimpeded by such ties, she seems (and is said) to have a deeper loyalty to her own convictions than to the continuing compromises of the old-boy network. 'She won't put up with it,' said one observer. 'That's why we've had so many people broken and rolled over, sackings on the *telephone.* . . . I've lived through years of prevarication based on the old-boy network. She's the negation of all the Carlton Club is supposed to stand for. That's her greatest strength.'

If it is a strength it is one in which the accident of gender comes together with something more essentially female. Even if Mrs Thatcher were magically to appear in clubland in perfect male disguise, she would still be entirely out of place, because of her many traditionally female qualities. Like many housewives, she has few (if any) interests outside her job, few intellectual or artistic pleasures and very little sense of repose. Like the great majority of women she is not witty or even humorous. She cannot, reportedly, tell a funny story and I do not think she has ever made a really memorable remark in public. Her single-minded intensity would not go well with the educated establishment's love of word-play and jokes, of disengaged verbal sparring and double meanings.

As Mrs Thatcher might well agree, these verbal games underlie one of the foremost vices of the British establishment; they can lead to a temptation to mistake rhetoric for action, or at least to think that others will, and to flannel. Mrs Thatcher was not brought up to this. She is a person who will call a nettle a nettle and grasp it resolutely. Perhaps this is what John Vincent meant when he wrote in 1982 that she had the great benefit of not having spent her formative years before the age of 40 in the company of very clever men.

I suspect Mrs Thatcher, like many women, is impatient of masculine cleverness. When asked once about a joke she had inadvertently made in the House of Commons, she replied that 'men are more conscious of double meanings than women. Women are slow to see double meanings.' She proved this recently in her own case, in her delightful tribute to Lord Whitelaw: 'Every prime minister needs a Willie.' This insensitivity to ambiguity might to some suggest a limitation in female thinking, but not to Mrs Thatcher. Doesn't a double meaning come very close to a forked tongue, after all? Don't double meanings – and Oxford rhetoric – have a lot to do with doubt and indecision, ambivalence and prevarication?

It is quite plain that Mrs Thatcher thinks single-mindedness, decisiveness and practicality are some of the greatest virtues of her approach to life, as they are of the good housewife's. Her posture as house-keeper to the nation may have become one of her greatest clichés but it is none the less genuine for all that; she clearly believes in her housewife's homilies – cut your coat according to your cloth, save up for a rainy day, the labourer is worthy of his hire, mind your manners, fine words butter no parsnips, a woman's work is never done, take care of the pence, if you want something done properly do it yourself. She lives by all this. 'Her most interesting, her most unusual quality is a real zest for detail,' according to one dispassionate observer. 'Her positive dissatisfaction with compromise, with forms of words is not so much single-mindedness, or being blinkered, as her insistence on coming back to details. She doesn't forget a thing.' She is a mistress

'If it were the Holy Grail, Mrs Robinson, it wouldn't have a hole in the bottom.'

of minutiae, from remembering a cake for some child to astonishing her civil servants with her command of facts, from making her name at the committee stage of a finance bill by her remarkable grasp of detail to her bossy, restless fussing about domestic trivia at Downing Street.

What drives her, it seems, is an inability to leave things alone, a reluctance to delegate, a need to keep everything under control, an impatience, amidst her own ceaseless activity, with playfulness or other possibilities, as if people were metaphorically threatening to muddy her nice clean floor. It is all too common to see this in the minds of other less remarkable women, who have lived more limited lives; it is odd to see it in someone who has been so free to choose her own life. Is it possible that Mrs Thatcher's perspective doesn't really extend beyond the practical and the domestic? Is it possible that mind and soul she is the housewife rampant? For all her triumphs in a man's world, Mrs Thatcher corresponds oddly closely to the old-fashioned female of the conventional stereotype. In particular her thinking seems to display the narrowness and reductiveness of which women have always been accused.

Reductive or not, female or not, this cast of mind has served her well in the past, when the obstacles in front of her were clear and concrete. She has unswervingly faced and overcome opposition from her party, from her ministers, from civil servants and from the unions, in a way that no mere man has been able to do. She has been immensely practical in her achievements. Having a certain simplicity, or crudity of concept, has made her enormously effective.

But now having ticked many of the major practical problems off her list she has got down to the more nebulous ones, as she is well aware. They mostly have to do with the question of 'society', a concept which, absolutely typically, she has found hard to deal with. Indeed until recently she couldn't be doing with it at all. But now in the midst of all her successes she is forced to ask herself intractable questions about it. Richer and nastier? Why more crime? Censorship for television porn but a free market for television drivel? The limitations of individual freedom?

Moralising on these subjects shows Mrs Thatcher in a poor light. She has often been unimpressive on the subject of broadcasting, for instance, and her remarks to the nation from Edinburgh on her religious faith did not reveal her mind at its most admirable; for instance, as Enoch Powell pointed out at the time, 'only someone whose view of life is highly simplified and conventional could assert that "we simply cannot delegate the exercise of mercy to others" '. (Mrs Thatcher in this vein is an embarrassment to her supporters.)

Muddled, limited thinking, attached to unswerving convictions, is not peculiar to women. But it is surely recognisably female. Previous prime ministers have either been more intellectually aware, or less moralistic. That is probably why in important ways they have done less well than Mrs Thatcher. But the tide, as Mrs Thatcher senses, has been turning. The questions facing her demand qualities she has not shown much of so far – a capacity for doubt, for unconventional responses, for compromise, letting be and the wider view. If she does not find these strengths, her great achievements may be eclipsed by the qualities that made them possible.

15 April 1989

LOW LIFE

BUTTON-HOLED

Jeffrey Bernard

Last week I was astonished to read that Brigham Young had 55 wives. He must have been mad. Did he manage, I wonder, to call them all by their right names in the dark or did he play safe and address them all as darling? I wonder about these little things. How amazing to come home at night to an oven containing 55 dinners. My own modest tally of four wives palls beside this magnificent and vast tapestry of life on the farm that I can see in my head. Perhaps he was showing off, but most people will marry you if you ask them nicely enough. Just think of the alimony.

Anyway, this piece of information about Young has been very disconcerting and I have even been dreaming about my wives, which gives rise to a great deal of anxiety and causes sweating in the middle of the night. Not a pretty picture that: a crumpled and damp duvet, the glow of a cigarette and a glass of horribly warm vodka left over from the previous evening. My nights seethe with devils. The days seethe with bores.

Last Monday I went into the pub and a total stranger began eavesdropping on us and then actually barged into the conversation and talked us through last week's Grand National and his Sunday lunch. Very rarely can unsolicited chat be rewarding. Sometimes it can be all right on trains. I had to go to Blackpool once and from Euston to the end a woman told me all about her various suicide attempts. She seemed quite jolly about them so it didn't depress me. I suppose the man in the pub waffling about the National was lonely and frightened but you need to be a little braver than that.

But it's those who are in town for the day who crown it all and make me want to scream when they tell you about their grown-up children. 'We went down to Eastbourne last week. Ever such a nice place they've got. Her husband is a sales executive for Birds Eye peas. Doing very well. They say he'll go right to the top. Don't they dear?' Charlie from the market is quite ruthless with these people. They have only to tell him that it is slightly colder today than it was yesterday and he says, 'Don't talk to me. I've come in here for a drink. Piss off.'

There is also one nice but extremely irritating man who will walk up to strangers and announce, 'Hallo, I'm a homosexual poet.' Why? I can easily resist informing people that I am a heterosexual hack. But where do these crowds of banal button-holers come from? Now, because of the new licensing laws, when they are spewed up from their offices at

'Reader, I married him. A quiet wedding we
had, followed by an evening disco.'

5 p.m. they know they can have a drink so they linger. Pubs in Soho are now unbearable after 6.30.

Betting shops are awful places too for being accosted by strangers who assume you are up to your neck in financial shit just as they are. Afternoon clubs for losers is what they seem to be. Depressing places. In hospital wards too there is always some old twit who will shuffle over to your bed to ask what is wrong with you. I am extremely rude to those and thereafter get left alone. Save us from strangers.

Just about the only nice ones I come across are *Spectator* readers who introduce themselves in the pub. Sometimes they fall by the wayside and stay all day. One poor sod did just that the other day and Norman had to bar him after five hours, so I was told. A very friendly lot, our readers.

15 April 1989

LIFE AND LETTERS

LET US SALUTE THEM

P. J. Kavanagh

Published biographies are usually about successful people and therefore have a predetermined shape – background, early struggles, achievement, death. Interest often fades round about achievement-time, either because we know about that, it is why we are reading the biography, or because success can seem to have a dehumanising effect, the subject sinks beneath the weight of medals, *Festschrift*, brilliant friends. Curiosity perks up again towards the end; we want to see how they will cope with enfeeblement, glad that (for the moment) it isn't ours. But, if we are most eager to know the story pre-vigour and post-vigour, the uncertain first steps, the faltering last ones, it would seem to follow that the most interesting biographies would be the ones with no successful middle period at all? Perhaps these are the biographies we would prefer to read, but it would be difficult to convince publishers.

One way round the dearth is somehow to get hold of lovingly

compiled, often locally published, accounts of the lives of people still remembered in their neighbourhoods who perhaps never quite 'made it', and whose lack of success can make that phrase, even the word 'success', seem vulgar. One such book, recently published (Alan Sutton, Gloucester) is *F. W. Harvey, Soldier, Poet*, by Alan Boden.

Harvey is best known now for his poem 'Ducks' — 'From troubles of the world/I turn to ducks . . .' which is still one of the most frequently requested poems on BBC radio poetry programmes; it seems to cheer people up. Fascinating, therefore, to learn that he wrote it in a Prisoner of War Camp in 1917, having just emerged from a period of solitary confinement, after an escape attempt. A fellow-prisoner had done a drawing of some ducks on the hut wall above Harvey's bed, and one night Harvey began to laugh at the very idea of the birds. Next morning he wrote the poem.

After two years' imprisonment he returned to Gloucestershire, to the disappointments of the Peace, and to his friend Ivor Gurney going mad. Without enthusiasm he became a solicitor in the Forest of Dean, defending poor men. His practice did not prosper and he came eventually to live with his Irish wife in what seems almost to have been a hut in the Forest. He turned Roman Catholic, neglected his appearance, and became (his biographer is gentle with his hints) over-dependent on what he had at first celebrated with a Georgian poet's ritual joviality, the local pub. He continued to publish books of

'He may be petit, but he's not bourgeois.'

poems, but not every man who sets out to be a poet becomes one; there is no 'successful' middle period for us to skip. Gurney had earlier noted what was wrong; his friend Harvey did not reach his reader because he wanted to help his reader too much, wanted to inspire him. But Gurney believed there were better things to come: 'So fine a footballer, cricketer, man, cannot wait many years after the war for his fulfilment. *This* is not it, anyway. It will do as a source of quotation for Bishop Frodsham, who will also obtain a pleasurable glow of satisfaction at his great work of Uplifting the People by Literature. Obelise him!' But Harvey continued with the Uplift for 20 more years, until publishers deserted him. MacNeice notes some of the things that can go wrong, in his 'Elegy for Minor Poets':

Who were lost in many ways, through
    comfort, lack of knowledge,
Or between women's breasts, who thought
    too little, too much,
Who were the world's best talkers, in tone
    and rhythm
Superb, yet as writers lacked a sense of
    touch,
So either gave up or just went on and on —
Let us salute them now their time is gone.

Harvey did not give up, but he did go on and on, and there is courage in that.

Leonard Clark describes his last sight of him, probably in the late 1940s. Harvey read him one of Shakespeare's sonnets from the book he had had with him in the POW camp. ' "He had everything," he said, "and they'll never better him" . . . Then he quietly bowed his head, looked at me over the top of his spectacles, and put his hand on my shoulder with the words, "Well, after all, I did write *Ducks* and they can't take *that* from me." '

22 April 1989

SETTING OFF ON THE GRAND TOUR WITH A EURODOGGLE FOR ALL SEASONS

Christopher Fildes

I am looking for an award to offer for the Eurodoggle of the year. What should it be? A mint-new European Currency Unit? The memoirs and menus of Lord Jenkins of Hillhead? Perhaps just a membership of the European Parliament? (That cannot be difficult to get, and you could bank the salary and live on the expenses.) Whatever it is, Jacques Delors must now have claims to it, but my quest began, improbably enough, in the pages of *Country Life*. I turn first to Pat Cutter's magisterial bridge column. Opposite, inside the back cover, is a full-page advertisement in colour – purple and yellow, mostly. It shows an outline of the European Community countries, which seem to have swallowed Switzerland. It is headed 'Europe for all seasons', and it urges us to travel to these countries in the off season for low prices, traditional culture, and a warm welcome from our EC partners. It reads, not surprisingly, as though it has been drafted by a committee. At its foot, marked 'ask advice of these offices', is a list of national tourist boards – 12, including the British Tourist Authority, whose baby this certainly is not. The advertisement, so it says, has been placed by the Tourism Service of the Community, and is appearing simultaneously in all 12 countries. Perhaps it will read better in Portuguese or Greek. The EC has a budget of a million ecus (about £600,000) for the campaign, as a precursor for 1990, which Brussels has decreed to be European Tourism Year. This is meant to foster greater understanding of lifestyles and cultures in good time for 1992 and the single market, and the budget for this is £3 million. I will bet an ecu to a hot cross bun that these budgets are left miles behind. They do not include the grants, which, of course, are to be agreed later. As for the advertising, it is absurd to imagine that a professionally managed and effective campaign spreading from end to end of the Community could be mounted for £50,000 a country. The whole sequence of events bears the signs of a boondoggle, which is what the Americans call a factitious project dreamed up by those who wish to benefit from it.

What we have here is a Eurodoggle. I suppose there was bound to be a Tourism Service somewhere down a Brussels corridor, working towards harmonisation of the Eurotouring experience, in such time as it can spare from long fact-finding missions to Cannes, Venice, Puerto Banus and Acapulco (for comparison). Its first mistake may have been to admit its existence. I provisionally award it a signed portrait photograph of Sir Leon Brittan.

22 April 1989

THE NIGHT OUR HOUSE BURNT DOWN

Murray Sayle

Aikawa, near Tokyo

The night of 19 December last was cold and starry. Our house stood in a clearing in a pine forest half-way up a mountainside, and the flames could be seen a good ten miles away, down by the Nissan factory. Some of them even downed tools for a moment or two, we heard, wondering what the bright light was.

Not that fires are unusual in Japan. Before the days of concrete cliffs they were called 'The Flowers of Edo', the old name of Toyko. Traditional Japanese houses are built of massive wooden beams to sway with earthquakes (ours came through the great quake of 1923 without a scratch) with two-inch-thick straw mats on the floors, papered room dividers, thatched roofs and wooden shutters to keep out the rain. You have to heat them somehow, and the choice is electricity, charcoal or paraffin — we had a full 200-litre tank in the garden. Add pots of paint and varnish, a 15-year accumulation of books and files, records, children's and adults' toys, winter clothes, bamboo furniture and three television sets and we have, or rather had, a dwelling as flammable as a box of matches.

The fire started in the children's room (boy ten, girl seven, boy two) at supper-time, around 7.30 p.m. An electric blanket had been switched on minutes before; nothing more is known of its cause. My wife,

Jenny (who hails, incidentally, from Woodford in Essex), went to investigate, found a bunkbed ablaze, emptied a fire extinguisher on it, pitched the smouldering remains of a *futon*, a kind of quilt, out the back door and returned to see flames already in the rafters. Correctly assessing her priorities (I was away at the time) she took the children to a neighbour's and returned to find the house alight from end to end.

The fire brigade, informed by telephone that a house (*uchi* in Japanese) was on fire, cruised the village looking for a non-existent Mr Uchida until it was suggested that the fiery beacon on the hillside might interest them. Some kind soul had dumped builder's rubble on the nearest fire hydrant (our water came from a spring) and by the time the amateur firemen found another, 34 minutes later, nothing of the house was standing. Jenny drove the family car out of the blazing garage moments before it too went up. The fire melted aluminium, twisted stainless steel and welded a kettle to the remains of the kitchen stove. Apart from a word-processor grabbed from our office by a brave neighbour and some emergency funds Jenny kept in the refrigerator, nothing usable was saved from the house. It was, the firemen told our neighbour, the hottest house fire they had ever seen.

In the olden days, we were told, a bronze gong would have sounded at our local Buddhist temple to inform the people that something of general concern was afoot. Our village is moving with the times, and now we have a loudspeaker system installed on trees and telephone poles which summons the part-time firemen, announces delays in school hours caused by typhoons, floods or deep snow, calls for volunteers to clear the roads, reports traffic accidents, tells children when it's time to go home for supper and generally keeps everyone in touch. For households out of earshot the local farmers' co-operative runs a similar systematised gossip network based on telephone calls with half-hourly bulletins on local news, lost cats and dogs, music for morning exercises, calls for baby-sitters and so on. Our local electronic media, we later learnt, got an early news break on the fire at the foreigner Sayru-San's house and called the *buraku-kai*, the village association, into action.

The *buraku-kai* is not exactly an official organisation. It holds no elections, appoints its officers by Buggins' turn among the old families and admits new members only after long inspection. *Buraku-kai* have run the affairs of Japanese villages since long before the days of the Shoguns and, apart from the unregretted war years when they were pressed into government service to inform on grumblers and dissidents, they bring a purely village consensus to bear on quarrels, family disputes and minor misadventures. Japanese villages as a result have no lawyers, and no use for them.

The village association runs sports days and festivals at shrines and temples and organises things like basic garbage collection, snow-clearing and cutting the grass beside the roads. We can't remember ever actually joining it, but one day there was the name Sayru on a wooden tablet hung up to indicate we were next to sort the recyclable garbage. It looked, even to us, odd among all the Suzukis and Watanabes brushed in neat Chinese characters, but somehow, without anyone ever actually saying so, we had been accepted.

Over the years, we have often been asked to village funerals and weddings, to the blessings of babies and the opening of new businesses. These outings can be expensive as the guests are expected to bring gifts of money, and we often see the sidekicks of local politicians making good fellows of their bosses by handing out well-stuffed envelopes, the constant haemorrhage of cash that leads many an ambitious Japanese legislator into corruption and scandal. We have, of course, never asked anyone for a vote ourselves, but we have tried to be good neighbours, to the best of our understanding.

As a result, we knew by sight many but by no means all of the people who gathered within minutes around the flickering embers of our house, and not out of curiosity. The women brought rice, soybean cakes and bottles of saké, the all-purpose Japanese emergency rations, and explained soothingly that everyone could do with a drink and a bite to eat, particularly the victims and the firemen. After several bids had been put in, Jenny and the children were escorted to the house of a neighbour whose children go to the local primary school with ours — where they are by way of being star pupils, being the first and only non-Japanese ever enrolled there.

About 10 p.m. the deputy headmaster of the school, no less, arrived to check that our two older children had clean underwear and school bags (other neighbours had arrived with both) and would be ready to join their group for the normal walk to school (compulsory in Japan) at the usual time, 7.45 a.m. the next morning. The police and firemen called and took statements while everybody's mind was fresh, and it was suggested that we get a good night's sleep as we all had a big day tomorrow.

The ruins of 15 years looked especially forlorn on a bright, clear winter morning. By 10 a.m. 50 people had assembled with trucks, a bulldozer and a portable generator. From the village clubhouse others had brought a tent, folding tables and chairs and more riceballs, saké and bean cakes. A volunteer salvage crew was soon at work picking through the wreckage, shoving aside the charred remains of 1,000 books – no time for frivolities at a serious moment like this – and pouncing on really useful items like blackened and buckled cooking pots and a pan that might conceivably fry again.

Roughly cleared, the site looked like a small section of wartime Berlin, Beirut or, for that matter, Tokyo. Neighbours with power saws moved in to cut down the blackened stumps of the house while the bulldozer man filled in the sewage and water tanks and dug a large hole for another, controlled fire of wreckage. As the winter afternoon faded, floodlights powered by the generator lit a busy, happy scene, all the happier for beer and saké served by beaming housewives to the workers. The clearance, we were told, had a dual purpose; partly to remove any possibility of still-smouldering fire spreading, partly to show that life goes on, starting right now.

Meanwhile, a steady procession of villagers had been arriving all day with gifts of goods and money, all listed and ticketed by two ladies at the folding tables. People we could and could not recall seeing before brought radishes, apples, ten-kilo bags of rice, schoolbooks, pencils, old clothes, new clothes, towels, blankets, more frying pans, five-kilo packets of instant curry (curry, anybody?), two television sets, shoes, scarves and hats. Most of them also left money, folded in the special envelopes sold in Japan for the purpose with the name of the giver outside and the sum written under a flap which folds over for privacy. One neighbour tallied the total while another separately listed the names, and both kept an eye open for *kajidorobo*, or 'fire-thieves', who set up their own tables at well-attended fires and funerals, collect condolences and money and decamp with the proceeds. None were sighted and more than £1,000 had been contributed by lunch-time.

The site secured and the children home from school (where the classmates of our daughter Malindi passed a resolution calling on all of us to *gambatte*, or 'hang in there', undoubtedly the most-proffered advice in Japan), it was time, we were told, for the big party, held at yet another neighbour's house. Here beer, wine, more saké, whisky, *sushi* and rice balls had been set out and, it was stressed, we were the hosts, thanking the workers for their efforts and paying for the clean-up and the party — no problem, as Jenny now had a gift handbag stuffed with banknotes. Well, everyone said, it could have been worse and, our children around us, we agreed.

The keynote speech (Japanese love public speaking) was delivered by Yukio Narui, recently retired from the silk business and the current head of the *buraku-kai*, who got a laugh by recalling that a Japanese family who suffered a fire used to be expected to move away for five generations — the time it took for the obligations they had incurred by inevitably setting the houses next door on fire to be repaid. We had, however, caused no such damage, and as the people of the village felt that we should be treated exactly as Japanese would be they wanted us to stay among them for as long as we liked. Seconding, a lady told Jenny, 'You behaved like an old-fashioned Japanese woman,' a compliment which brought applause and more drinks.

Responding, Jenny (whose command of gracious Japanese is several hundred times better than mine) said that we had been deeply impressed by seeing one of Japan's *bifu*, or 'beautiful customs', and we could understand better now why Japanese liked being Japanese when they got such support from each other in a time of trouble. Her speech went down well, and during the evening she got useful advice: bank the surplus of funds several villages away to foil envious gossipers and dump unwearable clothes at a similar discreet distance.

That night we signed 152 thank-you cards in flowery Japanese composed by a committee of neighbours versed in protocol. With these delivered before the end of the year, all our obligations (except good villagership) are, by Japanese notions, fully discharged, the slate cleared for a fresh start. Several of the guests suggested houses in various states of repair and disrepair into which we might move, and indeed we are happily re-established in one now.

Not all our friends live in one small Japanese village. The word spread, and two of them in London all unbeknownst to us started an international whipround. Letters and cheques — we were told — arrived from Britain, from the United States, from Australia, from France, from Africa and points east and west, the addresses of friends lost track of even more welcome than their contributions. Charity is, among us, a deeply ambivalent operation, it being more blessed to give than to receive which can leave us receivers feeling rather left out (a useful

insight into the plight of the refugee); simultaneously grateful, indebted and impostors in pocketing anything at all in a world with so
many more deserving claimants.

The formalised Japanese approach to misfortune acknowledges the
victims' dilemma, and perhaps suggested a response. We have started
up a fund of our own in Tokyo which, we hope, might one day help
someone here similarly touched by fate's fickle finger to give fate the
same reply. It's called the J Fund and the last time we asked it had
something like £5,000 in it. We Westerners have our own odd but
perhaps not altogether unattractive customs.

13 May 1989

LITTLE BROWN MISS AND HER AUNTY SWEETS

Richard West

TAP-TAPS TO TRINIDAD: A CARIBBEAN JOURNEY
by Zenga Longmore
A John Curtis Book/Hodder & Stoughton

The author of this delightful West Indies travel book is called on the
jacket 'a black English writer who is also an actress and blues singer'.
The adjective 'black' and her choice of a subject might give the
impression that Zenga Longmore hails from the West Indies and went
there to rediscover her roots. The same conclusion was reached by
some of the people she met on her journey, including the old men
boozing during the carnival in Dominica:

'So I spec' you be staying for the jumping tomorrow,
little brown miss.'
'Jumping?'
'Ehgh! See how she ignorant about her own isle. When
floats come long down the roads, everybody follows
them and jumps in the streets. Lord Jesus! Jus' because

you live in England for a while, doesn't mean to say
that you shouldn't — hic — learn bout the country that
you are or-ig-in-ally from . . . Oh, darlin'. Don't be so
shame of your roots.'

Although Zenga Longmore has in-laws and friends in the West
Indies, including some memorable 'aunts', she has no blood connec-
tion. Her father is a West African, and her mother a Russian Jewess
who, by her first husband, produced another *Spectator* writer, Roy
Kerridge. Half sister and brother share many gifts, including a sense of
the comic, a keen ear for the spoken language and some artistic talent.
Like many travel writers, Zenga Longmore has added her own illustrations. Unlike most such illustrations, hers are pleasing.

Whereas most people in England, especially those in the Race
Relations Industry, tend to lump all West Indian (and even Asian)
people together as 'blacks', Miss Longmore soon discovered that every
island is quite distinct from the next, not least with regard to race and
colour.

In sad, self-deprecating Jamaica, Miss Longmore found that her 'gold'
or 'fair' skin meant she was pushed to the front of a queue, given a seat
on the bus, and forbidden to wash the dishes. 'Nearly everyone I met
had a touching love of England. I began to hate England after a few days
in Jamaica, but that's not to say I liked Jamaica. I could never come to
terms with vacant faces mumbling "foreigner" at me wherever I went.'

In opulent and pretentious Guadeloupe, where the rich intellectuals
prate about *idéologie nègre*, Miss Longmore was lionised because of
her African father. A Rastafarian writer took off his gold-rimmed
spectacles and tilted his head to get a better look:

> 'Where exactly are you from?'
> 'Oh, a little village near Worthing.'
> 'Worthing?' asked one of the lecturers, 'which part of
> Africa is Worthing?' . . .
> 'Nigeria,' I mumbled softly.
> From that moment on I could do no wrong. Béarnaise
> sauce was eased over to my plate by obliging hands,
> cream was poured unsparingly into my tea, and my lead
> crystal glass was never empty of fine red claret.

Neither England nor Africa impressed the fearsome Aunty Sweets, with whom Miss Longmore stayed in Trinidad:

> 'So how your family doing? Heh heeh! I remember your uncle, that fat ugly one! What a man he was, an' how he could talk. That man put shit in your mouth, call it sugar and expec' you to swallow it! African men are crazy!'
>
> 'I happen to be particularly fond of my uncle.'
>
> 'What! That damn ignorant nigger-man? Don' look so shock up, sweetheart. I'm not saying that you're a nigger. You're a negro, an' that's another ting.'

When Miss Longmore protests that she hates the words 'nigger' and 'negro', and calls herself black,

> 'Black! Woooo! You are a red skin negro, so don't try to pretend otherwise. You as bad as my cousin. He marry a Indian woman who tink she sweeter than honey an' better than money jus' because she got long straight hair and custard-coloured skin. So now my cousin tink he sweet because he married the Indian girl. What they don' know is that she just a damn meddlesome Coolie bitch.'

Such passages should not suggest that Miss Longmore has an obsession or grievance about her colour. She is sorry for those who do, whether Jamaicans ashamed of their blackness or light-skinned French Guadeloupians praising *négritude*. It soon becomes evident that the elaborate and exotic racial insults spoken by Aunty Sweets are part of the verbal mock-warfare which is the favourite pastime of Trinidad. In fact, as Miss Longmore observes, the people of African, Indian, European and Chinese origin get on well together.

Although Zenga Longmore does not pass political judgements, she makes us wonder why all these places have turned out so differently. Like the Victorian travel writers, Charles Kingsley and Anthony Trollope, she grieves over Jamaica, 'land of religious, careworn people. . . . Somebody has to do something to make Jamaicans love Jamaica.' Like everyone she is amazed that another small island should house two utterly different countries, Haiti and the Dominican Republic. She wonders why Martinique is both so rich and so unpleasant. Or would it have been more friendly if she had known more French?

Although she is both discreet and modest, Miss Longmore has an eye for a handsome face, and tells us about her flirtations and one romance, on Dominica. She has a weakness for Rastas. To male readers, this is almost as odd as her having written a book on the West Indies without mentioning cricket.

Only in Trinidad did Zenga Longmore lose, for a term, her liberty. When she said 'hello' in reply to a good-looking stranger:

> A sharp slap stung my wrist.
> 'Keep your eyes away from the mens!' shrieked Aunty Sweets.
> I turned back to the man with an embarrassed titter, and WHAM, another slap caught me square on the back of the head.
> 'You keep your eyes on the road straight in front of you, or you get more licks and slaps from me, chile.'

To get away from her Aunty Sweets, Miss Longmore has to invent an important friend, a science professor living across the island. Then she discovers a rascal willing to act the professor's part. His smooth talk tames even Aunty Sweets. Trinidad grows as delicious as Dominica, or even St Lucia, so that Miss Longmore indulges in one of her rare moments of gush, quickly banished:

> I clung to a fern-like palm with both arms, and prayed that time would stand still; that I would hold this tree in the tropical evening for ever and never grow old, and never feel another drop of icy sleet upon my face again. It was a crystal moment suspended in infinite poetry, rudely broken by the high-pitched tones of an Indian man shouting, 'You wan' hole onto something nice an' big, lady? Den leave go de tree, man, an' let me give you somet'ing plenty more sweet!'

This extraordinary first book stands up to comparison with the classic accounts of the West Indies, Patrick Leigh Fermor's *The*

Traveller's Tree and V. S. Naipaul's *The Middle Passage*. For although her purpose is to amuse, Miss Longmore also conveys much truth concerning a part of the world obscured by the ignorance and prejudice of outsiders, especially those whites devoted to 'anti-racism'.

Most of the people who live in the former British West Indies cling to the values that most of the British themselves have dropped. The proportion who go to church on Sunday is about the same as for those who do *not* go to church in England. Parents demand and obtain schools that turn out children with good manners as well as plentiful 'O' and 'A' levels. West Indians are zealots for law and order: 200 people wait in Death Row; on some islands, you can be jailed for using bad language.

Even in poor Jamaica, the problem island, Miss Longmore met only a few Rastas, heard little reggae music, and did not fear for her safety. Even there, public opinion as well as the law is hard against drug users.

Whereas in England the Race Relations Act bans even insulting 'body language', most West Indians air their opinions boldly. They know how to handle their differences with the result that race relations are better in Port of Spain than in Brixton or Southall.

As Zenga Longmore often and rightly says, the British do not deserve the loyalty and affection of those whose ancestors they took into slavery; still less so, now that we in the 'Mother Country' have discarded the principles and the traditions that West Indians admire.

13 May 1989

THEY SHALL NOT GROW OLD

Vernon Scannell

Logic, grammar, each grey vocable
Broke into pieces when the telegram
Fell from her faint fingers, dainty bomb
Exploding on the carpet like a bubble.

No punctuation, though beyond the glass
Of veiled french-windows could be seen a few

Dark circumflexes printed on the sky
And yellow commas scattered on the grass.

Mummy was distraught and Daddy proud,
Each isolated in parentheses.
Silent exclamations marked her cheeks,
But he stood staring at a distant cloud.

Private, pleasurable to contemplate.
He almost smiled. Never had she felt
Such hatred for the man, or so much guilt
Remembering her son and her delight

And pride reflecting his exuberant joy
In those twin asterisks that gleamed upon
Each epaulette: her own sweet subaltern,
Unchangeably her gentle, aureate boy.

At least she cannot see him now he lies,
A black full-stop punched neat between white eyes.

HOME LIFE

DOG'S DINNER

Alice Thomas Ellis

I never used to have very strong views about dogs in the dining-room. I know cats who sleep on the dining-table. You sweep them off before meals and polish the surface. As long, I feel, as they are not shedding fur in the soup or dipping their paws in the salad dressing it doesn't matter. Not much. Dogs, I now realise, are a different matter. They don't *look* hygienic, and when you come to think of it they don't behave in a hygienic fashion. They don't watch where they're walking and they don't wash their feet as cats do. Some, I am sure, are acceptably clean but others are not.

We met such a one in a boarding house we recently spent a night in. It was a very small dog; perhaps the smallest dog I've ever seen except for those rat-like things that people keep up their sleeves. It had hair on its head but the rest of it was bald; it wore a tartan waistcoat in an attempt to disguise this deficiency and was quite the most revolting thing I've ever seen outside a jar of formaldehyde. The sort of dog it was is supposed to have longish hair all over and when in health resembles a hairy caterpillar. This one resembled a slug going to a Burns Night with its sporran on its head. Even Janet, who is all for animal rights, had to concur in my opinion. It was deeply horrible, and, of course, it took a fancy to us.

The nice owner of both boarding house and dog was under the impression that she'd given us *boeuf stroganoff* for dinner. At the most charitable estimate it was beef stew — chewy chunks of meat in grey gravy — but what it really looked like was dog's dinner. The dog thought so too, and sat at our feet going yap, yap, yap in an aggrieved and proprietorial way, while we pushed it round the plate. 'Oh, isn't she naughty,' said its owner. 'She knows she's not allowed in the dining-room.' So kick her out, I thought, but was too polite to say so. As we toyed with the kind of coffee they advertise on television — i.e. so disgusting the makers have to spend millions to persuade you to drink the muck — the animal's protests increased. 'That's because you're drinking coffee,' said the owner. 'She can't bear to see anyone drinking coffee unless she has some too.' I thought that if this was really the case and the owner habitually gave in to its demands it would probably account for the fact that all its hair had fallen out, but she gave it a saucer of milk which it slurped up, making even more unpleasant noises. Janet asked how old it was, because you have to say something, and we learned it was 15. Doing a laborious bit of mental arithmetic I figured that that made it 105 in human terms.

Next morning we opted for the cooked breakfast because we were paying for it anyway and bacon and egg is always and only bacon and egg. Unfortunately a sausage was generously added to this simple repast, and as I regarded it the ancient beast tottered into the dining-room and sat at my feet. I directed hurtful and rejecting vibes at it, but it wasn't psychic − or if it was it didn't care − and it went on sitting there, its pink-brown baldness only ill-concealed by its clothes. I looked from sausage to dog and from dog to sausage and ended up pushing breakfast round the plate.

For a moment I wondered whether the owner kept her pet simply for

A calendar for 1989 by Posy Simmonds

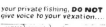

JUNE

Etiquette for the New Landed Gintry
Part 6: Dealing with Trespassers

There is no situation more freighted with angst for the new owners of a country place than the intrusion of trespassers upon their property. Traditional respect for *Seignority* allows the GENTRY a certain *insouciance* when turfing people off their land, but the GINTRY, (*parvenu, novus homo*), must exercise EXTREME CAUTION, or else risk appalling loss of face and damage to their social aspirations.
Thus, when you espy a party of trespassers invading

your private fishing, DO NOT give voice to your vexation....

This is especially important, if the intruders are dressed in any kind of waxen-wear. From a distance, it is IMPOSSIBLE to tell if the wearers are just *Joe Public* in chain store Barbour-gear, or local GENTRY in the *real* thing. Two ill-chosen words to the latter, could utterly ruin your ambitions of being welcomed into their social circle.

Have NO TRUCK, either, with ANYTHING carrying an Ordnance Survey map and wearing fell boots, serious anoraks, Alpine breeches etc.

These people will have NO respect for private ownership and will make you look foolish when they point out an ancient Right of Way on their map.
In both these cases, the DONE THING is to remain hidden, whilst your dog pack does the harassment. Etiquette demands that your voice MUST be heard reprimanding the animals for being such silly boys.

You may, however, personally approach any party whose demeanour suggests a want for forelock-tugging.

In your most courtly and patrician manner, you may *hint* at the trespass they commit. They will then offer obeisance. This exchange will be satisfying to both sides: they will be giving you full endorsement of your new social position. You will give them the rich experience of having met a real, old-style English GENTLEPERSON, such as is rarely to be found beyond the confines of television drama.

economical reasons — just to make the customers so nauseated they left everything for the next guest — but she swooped in, picked it up and cuddled it. Love, I reflected, is not merely blind but quite impervious to hygienic considerations. I could no sooner have nuzzled that dog than the banger cooling amidst egg yolk on the plate. I hate bossy restaurants where they won't let you smoke, but I now have every sympathy with the interdict NO DOGS ALLOWED IN THE DINING-ROOM — especially not naked ones in waistcoats.

13 May 1989

COMMUNISM GIVES UP THE GHOST

Timothy Garton Ash

One day, someone will write a marvellous history book. It will explain why communism gave up the ghost. Why communism gave up the ghost in the 1980s rather than the 1970s or the 1990s. And why communism gave up the ghost at more or less the same time across the whole vast Eurasian land mass, from Wittenberg to Vladivostok and from the Arctic to the China Seas.

I say 'gave up the ghost' advisedly. This does not mean that ruling groups calling themselves communist parties will cease to wield power tomorrow, next year, next decade. It does not mean that, when you read these words, those brave, idealistic Chinese students — demanding 'democracy' in fluent English — will not have been driven by force from the Square of Heavenly Peace. It does not mean that there will be no reversal in the Soviet Union. It does not mean that Western-style prosperity and liberty will come to most of Eurasia in our lifetime.

It means only that those ruling groups calling themselves communist parties have lost the battle of ideas. They have made, or had extracted from them, certain fundamental admissions that cannot be unmade. They have ceased to represent a future. Of course there has always been change inside communist systems. But the change between 1979 and 1989 is different, and not only in degree, from the change in any previous decade, certainly since 1949, and probably since 1917. In 1979, it seemed inconceivable that within ten years crowds would be on the streets not merely of Warsaw and Budapest but of Moscow and Peking, demanding, simply, democracy and liberty. The working assumption of virtually everyone in the West was that, for as long ahead as we could foresee, that quarter of mankind would continue to live under a system, described as 'communist' or 'social-ist', which was different in its essential political and economic foundations from the systems (or lack of system) we knew in the developed West, in non-communist Asia, Africa or Latin America.

There might be growing national differences. There might be further crises. The socialist world might fall further behind economically and technologically. Great reforms would be necessary. Clever political scientists told us how they could be done. There might be — indeed, some Sovietologists assured us, there already was — 'socialist plural-ism'. There might be a 'socialist market economy'. But in any case, one way or another, by reform or by repression, by hook or by crook, there would still be something that was recognisably a communist system. In its political and economic fundamentals any communist state would be more like any other communist state, however remote, than like any non-communist state, however near. In terms of the political and economic *system* it was still (just) true in 1979 that Hungary was more like China than it was like Austria. At the great universities of the West, men and women would continue to teach subjects called 'communist economics' and 'communist politics'.

Those were the days. For today, we need a new intellectual tool-kit, or perhaps merely an old one, with concepts like representative government, the rule of law, the separation of powers, but also populism, nationalist demagogy, military dictatorship. In Poland they talk musingly of the Spanish model, the Chilean model, the South Korean, the Iranian. . . .

Why the change? The near-simultaneity diminishes particular ex-planations. For the recent break-through in Poland I might be inclined to say Solidarity and the Pope. But in Hungary there was no massive social movement, and the churches played a very minor role. Gor-bachev? Deng Xiao-ping? But why Gorbachev? And where is Deng? What all have in common is relative economic and technological failure — relative to the West and non-communist Far East. One curiosity in my library is an East German school atlas published in 1978. As an endpaper it has an evenly ascending block graph headed 'The Development of Productive Forces 1917 to 1975: the scientific-technical revolution' and underneath: 'The period of transition to socialism/communism'. Each year is inscribed with landmarks of scientific-technical progress, capitalist ones in black, socialist ones in pink. As we approach the present, the pink takes over from the black, with such triumphs as 'First woman (W. Tereschkowa) in space' and 'Beginning of Comecon gas pipeline "Drushba-Trasse" '. But the East German schoolboy has only to look out of his window and compare a Trabant with a Mercedes. Those that live by science will die by science.

Provided, of course, that their people can see the Mercedes. Hence two other explanations: détente and television. The whole web of ties with the West, spun since the 1960s in pursuit of very diverse Western strategies or simply of profit or pleasure, has undermined the system. Whether Hungarian politburo members or Chinese students, they have seen the capitalist-imperialist past and it works. And if they have not seen it by coming here, or as a result of Westerners going there, they have heard it on radio or seen it on television: the anti-communist revolution as a function of the information revolution. One day someone should write the history of the V-for-Victory sign. How did it spread from Churchill to the workers in Gdansk, to the students in Tiananmen Square. By television?

But what you see of the West – even on television – is not all milk and honey. People are not usually ready to admit that their sufferings have been entirely pointless. Nations are not generally prepared just to copy other nations. So what about a Third Way? What about some 'socialism with a human face'? 'We are saying: there is no third way. There is no credible alternative between Eastern socialism and Western capitalism.' Thus an activist of a liberal opposition party in Budapest last month. Not the answer you would necessarily receive in Moscow, of course, let alone in Peking. Yet what is striking is how, by contrast with 1968, no alternative 'model' has emerged from all this turmoil. At the moment, there seems to be no natural stopping-point (although there are many side-tracks) on the road from the command economy to the free-market one, and from dictatorship to democracy. No country, not even Hungary, seems very likely to arrive safely, without mishap or diversion. Most will probably get bogged down

half-way. One and a half billion people are falling between two stools. But few seem inclined to mistake that for arrival.

Perhaps one reason for this is the intellectual crisis of the Left elsewhere in the world. For two centuries since 1789 there has been a recognisable something called the Left. It was always to be found on the left bank of the Seine. But where is it now? What's left of the Left? In search of an answer to that question, my good friend Dr Steven Lukes has gone out from Balliol into the world, and we must await his conclusions. I met him pursuing his quest in Warsaw last year. Yes, we were told by a clever Polish oppositionist, there is still hope for the Left in Poland. In fact, there are two hopes. Their names are Envy and Mother Church. Because of the legacy of 'socialist' socialisation, and because of the corrupt profiteering and conspicuous consumption that you inevitably get in a part-liberalised economy, we can expect an egalitarian backlash. The social teaching of the present Pope will make 'leftist' ideas of social justice palatable to a wider audience. So the Catholic Church is the last best hope of the Left in Poland. One wonders who would be more insulted.

Yet there is something a little uncanny in this sudden, comprehensive, ideological triumph of the West. For there can be few, if any, moments in history when one set of ideas has so thoroughly routed its rivals across so vast a field. Somewhere, one feels, there must be some great, new, rival ideology struggling to be born. Fundamentalist Islam? But that has limited appeal even to Muslims, and − the Rushdie affair and international terrorism notwithstanding − the possibilities of spreading it on the blade of the scimitar are rather less than in the middle ages. Perhaps something green? Something female? Eco-feminism? Somehow, with the best will in the world, one doubts it. But this much seems certain: whoever and wherever the new Marx and Engels are, they are unlikely to waste their time writing a new *Manifesto*. No, they will make a television programme.

27 May 1989

THE GREAT FALL OF CHINA

Stephen Handelman

Peking

Near the Wuxing Ting Teahouse in old Shanghai, there are dozens of young people looking for foreigners on whom they can practise their English. One rainy afternoon this month, I was the willing target of a petite graduate student. Our conversation inevitably turned to the 'democracy demonstrations' which had begun the previous month. 'I support the students,' she said a little sadly. 'But actually I find their protests useless. They never achieve anything.'

I am thinking of her as I write this in Peking, three weeks later, in the midst of what we all have begun to call China's second revolution. I wonder what she would say now. I even wonder if she may still be right.

There can be no doubt that in less than a fortnight Chinese politics and Chinese people have passed through one of those rare moments in history when the desire for change and the ability to act on that desire converge in one dramatic explosion. No one who has lived through the tumultuous events on the streets of China's capital this spring could fail to be moved. Comparisons can be distorting, but think of the exhilaration of Czechoslovakia in 1968 and the sense of liberation − without the violence − of St Petersburg in 1917, and you begin to approach what it feels like to be caught in smiling crowds swelling to a million or more.

Although an end to the crisis is still not in sight as this article goes to press, the students have clearly won a moral victory. They have shattered the complacency of one of the world's most authoritarian and highly disciplined societies. Yet the usefulness, as my Shanghai friend might put it, of Peking's Spring remains open to question. The temporary breakdown of order is as likely to lead to a new, rough hand at the helm and a slowdown in economic reform and investment, as to the emergence of genuine democratic institutions.

One wants, of course, to believe in miracles. As I write, the remarkable confrontation between the Chinese people and their government is deteriorating into a kind of peaceful, amiable chaos. Youths and workers, with red flags and banners reading 'Peking belongs to the people', march in ragged columns up and down the main streets. Elderly women in their distinctive pyjamas offer them money. Shop clerks, hotel bellhops and taxi drivers insist on knowing your opinion of the demonstrations. A journalist colleague placed a hunger striker's red bandana he had been given as a gift on the lampshade in his hotel room. He returned later that night to find an extra bar of chocolate left there as a silent gesture of approval.

Eight of the capital's 16 districts have been placed under martial law, but it must be one of the only impositions of martial law in history where the military are as helpless to influence events as the dazed tourists making their way through the crowds. Young men in red armbands direct traffic, occasionally stopping cars to demand rides to the centre of town. Food and gasoline are running short. Factory production lines have slowed to a crawl. There is hardly any city transport system. Underground attendants have walked off their jobs and locked the entrances, and bus drivers have 'donated' their vehicles for use as barricades against the army. The broad boulevards of the city have been turned into an obstacle course. The police, when they are there at all, pretend not to notice.

It is a painless revolution for an outside observer. You can begin your day by taking tea in one of the modern, Western-financed hotels on Changan Street, listening to Verdi performed by an orchestra in evening dress. Stepping outside, you may take your bike or hired pedi-cab — the modern version of the rickshaw — the five leisurely kilometres to the Square of the Gate of Heavenly Peace — Tiananmen

— currently occupied by tens of thousands of youths, and where you are likely to spend the remaining hours until dawn listening to rhetoric that unashamedly mixes Abraham Lincoln and Karl Marx.

Meanwhile, the army troops who have been poised in the suburbs since Saturday have a comic opera quality. Immobolised in a human net of citizens who will not let them pass, they can move neither forwards nor backwards, reversing Mao's famous image of soldiers moving freely among the people 'like fish in water'. The harassed government of Premier Li Peng is not far wrong when it describes the situation as being close to anarchy.

Perhaps Mao would understand the importance of what has happened. But the authorities, including the elderly men who once served at his side, clearly do not. As a result, authority — both of the moral and coercive kind — is non-existent.

The lack of authority is cause as well as effect of the present crisis. A few hundred thousand students, an élite handful by Chinese standards, should ordinarily not have expected to awaken the conscience of a nation which is still for the most part pre-industrial. Yet they have skilfully exposed the incompetence of a leadership unsure of its goals and unable to manage the process of reform. All the precedents for popular unrest in China do not seem to apply here. From the Boxer Rebellion to the Cultural Revolution, they were inspired and led from the top, and discarded when they no longer served their political purpose. The current 'insurrection' has been a grassroots one, and it has extended upwards into the party apparatus. Young journalists, scientists and party cadres have gradually joined the marching students, and given the event its special character as a conflict between young and old.

'The most remarkable element of the demonstrations is how they have gone against Chinese traditions,' a Western diplomat said as we sat in his comfortable flat in one of Peking's foreign compounds. 'There have always been official court critics, but it has never been easy to express real feelings about the rulers. Whatever happens, people realise they can do this again, come out on the streets, and the army won't intervene. It's a kind of liberation never seen in Chinese history.' But none of this, he adds, could have occurred without the change in China's economic landscape. The revolution of 1989 is both a product of China's 11-year-old experiment in economic liberalisation, and a proof of its limitations.

Since 1978, China has been embarked on an extraordinary transition from orthodox Marxism to entrepreneurial consumerism. The students who launched a hunger strike on Tiananmen Square on 12 May were as notable for their Japanese watches and American running shoes as for their commitment to democracy and free speech. Economic reform has revived Chinese political as well as commercial instincts, while offending the Chinese sense of fair play. Corruption and political patronage are rife. The quantity of goods available for sale — astonishing to someone who lives in the other Communist monolith in Moscow — is not matched by the ability to buy them. 'Ten years ago,' my Shanghai friend told me, 'we had nothing to buy so we didn't know what we couldn't afford; that's why some people are so angry.' Now, there is inflation and unemployment, which officials disguise in statistics under the heading of those 'looking for work'.

It is a logical step to look to political reform as a way of compensating for economic powerlessness. 'Truth is more important than rice,' read one slogan on the square. Ironically, Chinese youth take the politicised Soviet Union of Mikhail Gorbachev as a model of what they want. They have seized on glasnost and the new Moscow political climate, in the same way Russians have cast an envious eye on China's entrepreneurial success. When I pointed out to one student that a similar demonstration would probably not last ten minutes on Red Square she smiled engagingly and said, 'I guess we don't know enough.' Most students, asked to define what they want, retreat to a vague notion of democratising the Communist Party. Of course, there is a great deal of sophistication along with their naïveté. Not a small part of their trumpeting of glasnost slogans this month was a calculated effort to cause their government discomfort during the Sino-Soviet summit. What was surprising was that the government made itself a willing victim.

The initial demands at the start of the student movement in April were relatively mild, centring on a promise to involve the students in dialogue over future political reforms. The leadership, under the 84-year-old Deng Xiao-ping, disdainfully ignored them. Deng's own experience as a victim of youth anarchy during the Cultural Revolution may have had something to do with this. But China's one-billion-plus population is hampered by a government alliance of technocrats and battle-scarred veterans of 1949. Only a minority in the ageing councils of state appears to have any sense of the ferment which their economic revolution has inspired. 'They are used to pushing buttons and getting answers,' commented one observer. 'They were probably stunned to discover that none of the buttons worked this time.' They were not prepared for the idealism of teenagers and youths in their early twenties prepared to starve themselves for vague notions of political democracy. 'The country needs you. Why are you risking your health?' government spokesmen asked with numbing persistence.

As the crisis grew day by day, so did the mutual incomprehension. Even a week ago, a puzzled Chinese official asked a few Westerners over lunch why the Americans were behind the unrest. 'What do they hope to gain by this?' he wondered. By the time the government was ready to grant that the students shared some of its declared goals, the slogans in the street were calling for the overthrow of senior leaders. 'You really don't understand,' Wuer Kaiki, one of the student leaders, told Li Peng in a notable televised confrontation. 'It is not students who have created the problem, but the general political situation.'

He was right, of course, but that has made the search for compromise immeasurably harder. In some ways it is a tribute to Chinese civilisation and restraint that the affair contains so many soft edges. Few governments in the world would have tolerated such a lengthy disruption of public life without bringing all the force of their authority to bear. When the protesters and hunger strikers first marched into the square, the authorities seemed prepared to shrug them off. Although there was apparently an unsuccessful attempt to involve the army in clearing the area on the eve of Mr Gorbachev's visit, the demonstrators were handled with kid gloves until martial law was declared a week later. Perhaps the government was already uncertain of its ability to count on the military, an increasingly important factor in the struggle for power in the leadership. One story making the rounds is revealing. The commander of one unit is said to have flatly refused to lead his troops against the students, claiming a 'conflict of interest': his daughter was among the strikers in Tiananmen Square.

The failure of martial law suggests that the Chinese government is locked in a crisis of legitimacy as well as 'face'. At the very least, this month's events have accelerated the sickness at the heart of the system. 'It's not really the leadership we're fighting,' another earnest student told me. 'It's our 1,000 years of feudalism.' That's the sort of battle, however, which will not be won on Tiananmen Square alone.

27 May 1989

'Piles playing you up again?'

'Isn't that just typical? You wait half the day . . .'

'It's Meryl Streep's latest.'

IRAN'S PROPHET

Amit Roy

There are few things that Iran's ayatollahs relish more than a malicious joke, especially about one of their own number. The crack about Ayatollah Montazeri was the first indication I had that in the eyes of his fellow clergymen, at least, he lacked the stature to succeed Ayatollah Khomeini as *Vali-e-fagih* – Iran's high religious authority. Over lunch with a gathering of ayatollahs during a visit to Urumieh in north-west Iran in 1980, the conversation turned to Montazeri, who, according to this joke, was visiting the Louvre museum in Paris. The attendant there handed him a shoe: 'This is a Louis XIV.' Montazeri tried it on and complained: 'It's a bit tight – can you give me a Louis XV?' The assembled ayatollahs chuckled. Then, one fixed me with a keen eye, and asked: 'And what do you think of our Imam?'

A joke about Khomeini was unthinkable. I would bracket him, I ventured, with the three great revolutionary leaders of the 20th century: Lenin, Gandhi and Mao Tse-tung. They interpreted the reply to be an approval and thankfully quizzed me no further. Had they done so I would have added that the Islamic revolution had sent shockwaves through much of the Muslim world, and that long after Khomeini's departure, his legacy would linger.

But with his death last week at the age of 89, even Iranians will be uncertain about what kind of Iran will now emerge and of Khomeini's position in its history. Though a decade is an insignificant period in

THE SUITS   *Michael Heath*

such an old, sophisticated civilisation, Khomeini successfully set about rebuilding Iran in his own image.

His authority was backed up partly by ruthlessness – no one knows how many thousands went to the firing squads at the dead of night – but also partly by the peculiar hold he had over the poorer sections of the population. On one occasion, in February 1981, I witnessed the strangely comforting influence he exercised over a woman whose husband had just been killed in the war with Iraq. Clutching her baby and a large photograph of her husband, she emerged from an audience with the Ayatollah at his home in Jamaran, in northern Teheran. What had he said? 'Oh, nothing very much,' she replied, 'but I feel better.'

Altogether, perhaps one million Iranians were killed or injured in the conflict against Iraq, but there was never any political backlash against Khomeini, the principal proponent of the 'war, war till victory' philosophy. Most of the schoolchildren who rushed headlong into war – and, in their terms, martyrdom – were genuinely keen to follow their Imam.

That February morning, when I was ushered in to see the Ayatollah, commemorated the second anniversary of an historic occasion. With me were a group of air force officers, some of whom had come straight from flying sorties at the front. Two years previously it was the defection of the air force to Khomeini's side which had sealed the fate of the revolution. Khomeini now entered the mosque which adjoined his home in Jamaran, preceded by his son, Ahmad. The Ayatollah, unsmiling as always, held up his hand in silent greeting but it was the effect of his presence on the air force officers that was the most unexpected. Overcome by emotion, they wept hysterically.

A few months previously, I had met the Ayatollah in the holy but dusty city of Qom, before a mild heart attack made Ahmad move his father to the cleaner, cooler air in the mountains in northern Teheran. It was an occasion which provided a glimpse of his unforgiving nature. His supporters and those of another senior religious figure, Ayatollah Shariat-Madari, had been involved in a violent street clash. Khomeini looked positively Old Testament, his pale, angry face contrasting sharply with his black gown, as he swept in to see Shariat-Madari who was giving me an interview.

The two ayatollahs talked for an hour and made peace but Khomeini never forgave Shariat-Madari, who later died a broken man under house arrest. Ironically, it had been Shariat-Madari who had saved

Khomeini's life in 1964 when the Shah wanted to execute him for fomenting riots in Qom. This lack of sentiment was also evident in his treatment of Sadegh Ghotbzadeh, Khomeini's former foreign minister. The man who had once dressed in dapper suits was unshaven and unkempt, when I saw him for the last time in Teheran. 'It is not the fault of Imam,' insisted Ghotbzadeh, who was planning a revolt against the régime, 'it is those around him.' Shortly afterward, Ghotbzadeh was arrested, made to 'confess' on television and executed particularly hideously (by slow shooting from the feet upwards). He had once loved the Ayatollah and regarded himself as his 'spiritual son'.

There are far too many personal scores to be settled to expect a trouble-free transition to a post-Khomeini régime. Yet it would be foolish to predict a collapse of the theocratic state. The fact is that Khomeini was neither prime minister nor president nor even head of state. He intervened only when disputes between the important figures in the régime got out of hand, but otherwise the machinery for the day-to-day running of the state was efficiently put in place.

Khomeini's legacy will also be protected by the new generation which has grown up over the past decade when Iran's population has registered a huge jump from 33 million to 50 million. He had the curricula in schools and universities restructured to ensure the young emerged as 'true Muslims' — that is, ardent Khomeini supporters. Some 400,000 of them have gone into the revolutionary guards, effectively the armed wing of the theocratic government.

Since Khomeini was the product of unique historical circumstances, when all sections of Iranian society were seeking a unifying symbol of opposition to the Shah, it is safe to assume no one can replace him. Khomeini imposed an Islamic régime on his people, but he was unable to force through a cultural revolution and change the basic nature of his people.

Iranians — even the ayatollahs — remain extremely money-minded, with a marked weakness for the good things of life. Their country was once very rich, producing six million barrels of high-grade oil daily, and will be prosperous again. This is why Iran will make it up, sooner or later, with the United States and the West.

As has happened in countries once ruled by the likes of Lenin, Gandhi and Mao, successive generations of Iranian leaders, while paying lip service to Khomeini, will probably distance themselves from his teaching.

Khomeini would have preferred, one suspects, not to have died of old age in hospital but to have been martyred by agents of the United States — 'the Great Satan'. In 1979, when he returned from 15 years in exile, he made his first speech at Teheran's Behesht-e-Zahra cemetery where this week, amid chaotic scenes, he was buried. This cemetery, which is also the resting place of thousands killed during the revolution and subsequently in the Gulf War, automatically becomes Islam's newest shrine.

Khomeini always sought to place Islam on a collision course with the largely Christian West, and managed it in February 1989, by condemning Salman Rushdie, author of the allegedly blasphemous *The Satanic Verses*, to death. This sentence now loses its force, but equally it can never be removed. Much of the West saw Khomeini as the apostle of evil. It is precisely because of this that his position in the pantheon of Islamic prophets seems assured.

10 June 1989

AFORE YE GO

Over the past few months, I have found cause to emphasise the need for a sense of humour. If one cannot laugh at oneself, one is almost bound to 'take a tumble'. I have many foibles and failings which I am only too happy to chortle at. I am thinking now of my reckless generosity, my too rigorous adherence to a strict code of personal morality, my genuine love of people. 'Oh Wallace!' I sometimes say to myself as the night draws in. 'You really are the most lovable scamp!' And it is this ability to laugh at myself that has, I believe, seen me through thick and thin.

My thoughts returned to the subject when I heard of the death this weekend past of the Ayatollah Khomeini of that parish. He may have been a remarkable old gent in many ways (it took some nerve, I would imagine, to wear such a flamboyant beret, especially at his ripe old age) but I rather suspect that he had little or no sense of humour. Hence that famous down-in-the-mouth expression he chose to employ, even in prime-time news programmes, and hence his extraordinary propensity for getting in an awful flap about nothing. Though a sworn teetotaller, he would have done well to sup the tonic of humour.

Prickly character

I knew him only a little when he was exiled to London in the late 1960s (loathsome decade!). Bill Davies had taken something of a shine to Khomeini, having met him at the launch of *Funny Old World: a Century of British Humour*, and had immediately offered him the plum job of Cartoon Editor on *Punch* magazine. Alas, few cartoons inspired even the mildest of smirks on that grizzled visage, though I seem to remember him chuckling at the priceless antics of the Gambols in Barry Appleby's strip cartoon of the same name. By and large, he felt that no cartoon that failed to reflect his own devout belief in Islam should pass muster, and consequently *Punch* fell into a circulation spiral from which it is still struggling to recover. *The Punch Book of Praise to Allah*, published at the end of that year, suffered from poor sales, alas.

I suspect that I have inadequately stressed the poor sense of humour that formed such a dominant part of his somewhat prickly character. I well remember him popping his head around the door to bid his old messmates ta-ra at the *Punch* offices, just prior to his return to Iran in 1979. 'It'll be awfully dry over there,' I quipped, 'now that the Shower of Rain has departed! No need for wellies, eh?!!' He shot me one of his grimmest looks, and, as I sat there explaining the delicious pun (Shah/Shower − Iran/Rain), he stomped off in a bate.

He never looked very happy out there, to my mind, poor chap. Perhaps it was the climate, perhaps the responsibility. But I rather think that, with a sense of humour, he would have learnt to enjoy himself. May his example be a lesson to us all. There's no medicine like laughter, methinks.

10 June 1989

'Now, along with your eight records, which
book — apart of course from Shakespeare and
the Bible — would you like banned on your
desert island?'

CREDIT WHERE IT'S DUE

Jeffrey Bernard

Three years ago, when I had nowhere to live, I began to use the Coach and Horses as an office of sorts and a poste restante. The place has had many uses. Everybody knows that 29 Greek Street, Soho, is the boozer. Not the nutters who run Barclaycard, however. This is the letter I got from them this week.

> MR BERNARD [printed, not typewritten, to make you feel important] Welcome To Your New Home at 29 Greek Street.
>
> Dear Mr Bernard, Welcome to your new home! Now that you've completed your move to 29 Greek Street you've probably started to think about all the things your new home needs . . . and you may be wondering how you're going to afford it all! Well, Mr Bernard, as an established Barclaycard holder with a good credit history . . . there is no better way for you to finance purchases for your new home than Masterloan. As you may know, Masterloan is a credit programme designed specifically to help Barclaycard holders, such as yourself, make major purchases. Borrow Up To £7,500. . . . No Money Down.

And so on, and so on. They go on to list some items that have nothing to do with my new home, such as school fees (should I send Norman to Eton?), sports gear (some dice and a craps table?) or a car (and a manslaughter charge?).

Well, there are some things my new home needs. The lavatory in the Gents could do with a chain and the staff could be sent to a language school to learn English and to New York or Dublin to learn how to serve a drink. A cleaner could be hired to clean up the disgusting bits of chewing gum adhering to the underneath of the bar rail and the new

French barman could be treated to a shampoo. How strange it is that having paid a few piddling bills promptly they think I am worth £7,500. What the hell do I want to borrow £7,500 for? It has to be paid back with interest and it is a loan I would only apply for if my doctor told me I had just one month to live. Sadly, he can't tell me much because he too can barely speak English. This new policy of Norman's of employing linguistic incompetents and virgin barmen is an unconscious display of contempt for his customers that only a teetotal publican could harbour. What I should do is give him £7,500 to open a tea shop in Clacton.

Anyway, the good news is that after the South African government refused me a visa I am off to Barbados next week. Touch wood. It is still my favourite place, just edging out Thailand by a short head. It is not a suitable resort for intellectuals but excellent for lounge lizards. What is there to do there? Absolutely nothing and who could want for more? The heat of the West Indies melts my bones and lying on the beach or by the side of a pool and listening to the clink of ice against glass which heralds the approach of the waiter I want to jump up and telex Norman as to what he can do with the Coach and Horses.

I used to sit in a beach bar called Kisses in St James and it was run by a black Cyd Charisse. She wore practically nothing and a bead of perspiration on her looked like a diamond. I could spend an entire

'I've often thought, if only I'd settled in Soho, I could have been a really famous drunk.'

afternoon watching her glide between the tables like a panther. You don't see many people gliding like panthers behind the bar in the Coach and Horses I can tell you. Stumbling like deranged sheep more like. So it looks to be a fourth trip to Barbados. I may miss Royal Ascot but not a lot. All these silly people and their silly clothes. They get in the way of the horses.

17 June 1989

'TEACH THE FREE MAN HOW TO PRAISE'

A. N. Wilson

Thomas Cranmer was born 500 years ago, on 2 July 1489. As the first great Protestant Archbishop of Canterbury, as the supervisor and chief architect of the Book of Common Prayer and as a martyr for his beliefs, we should expect the anniversary to be marked with full solemnity by the Church of England. I doubt, however, whether this will happen with any great enthusiasm on a wide scale. For many Anglicans, the date will pass unnoticed. For others, Cranmer represents a religious viewpoint so different from their own that they, who do not use his Prayer Book or revere his character, will find little to celebrate.

Certainly, the anniversary cannot be viewed purely or innocently. It is not like the Salvation Army rejoicing in the existence of William Booth, or the Royal Society revering the memory of its founders. For Cranmer was a flawed man, and he left a flawed Church which was quite largely shaped by him, by his imperfections as well as by his excellencies. He was for much of the time a confused man, and he ensured that the English religious legacy would be uncertain. Ever since his death, people have been wondering where Anglicans stand on one issue or another, and receiving very different answers, depending on which Anglican they ask. But he was also a martyr, and we only discover the reasons for celebrating his birth when we have meditated upon the meaning of his martyr's death. It is a meaning which sheds shafts of light on his lasting memorial, the liturgy of the English church.

His *Recantacyons*, and indeed his vacillations of behaviour and opinion from the moment of Edward VI's death, were viewed with dismay by his doughtier Protestant allies and contemporaries; just as since, it has been easy for detractors to see him as the archetypal Anglican, dithering where he should have been steadfast, or worse, being prepared to use sacred truth as a bargaining counter in order to save his skin and keep in favour with the Tudor despotism of which he had been so adept a servant and instrument. As a serious Erastian, and a believer in the right of monarchs to determine national religion, he had every reason to accept the authority of Queen Mary, even though he knew that she was intent on undoing the work of the Reformation to which he had given his life. And yet he had been bold enough, when Mary acceded to the throne, to defend his Prayer Book against the old mass, the mass which, as he claimed in that controversial statement of September 1553, Satan himself had invented. In the following year, when he had been imprisoned and taken to Oxford, he was subjected to a rigorous cross-examination in St Mary's Church, admitting that he had once held to the 'Papists' doctrine', and explaining why he had changed his mind. His examiner was Thomas Martin.

> *Martin.* Now sir, as touching the last part of your oration, you denied that the Pope's holiness was Supreme Head of the Church of Christ.
> *Cranmer.* I did so.
> *Martin.* Who say you then is Supreme Head?
> *Cranmer.* Christ.
> *Martin.* But whom hath Christ left here in earth His vicar and head of His church?
> *Cranmer.* Nobody.

That 'Nobody' is one of his boldest, and clearest declarations. Its implications are enormous, and they are not always ones with which Anglicans feel happy. Where is the seat of Christ's authority on earth? Who exercises it? Nobody! Some Anglicans, particularly those shaped by the traditions of the Tractarian revival, have always edged away from this stark view, dreaming of the day when Christ's Vicar in Rome would one day welcome back the erring children whom Cranmer rescued from his sway. For, without some such idea of revelation and authority, we are left alone: alone with the Bible, perhaps, and alone with God, but alone, and the Church is no more than a gathering together of alone people, flawed and fallen like Cranmer himself. Much of the Anglican dilemma is contained in this position, and Cranmer was wise and honest enough to say that this was the true state of human beings. His rejection of the Pope is every bit as heroic and absolute as that of the figure who stands before the Grand Inquisitor in Dostoievsky's legend. Mystery, miracle and authority are rejected. Cranmer, himself a man of his age, himself capable of burning heretics — one of his victims was a poor demented woman called Jane Bocher who did not believe in the humanity of Christ — is discernible here as one of the first modern men, discarding make-believe in favour of the risk of being alone, the risk of making up our own minds about how life should be followed, the risk of being wrong; without such a risk, Cranmer's death says, true religion is impossible.

His rejection of the doctrine of Transubstantiation derives from the same doggedly honest attempt to tell the truth before God. It is a rejection of magic in favour of religion. If the substance of the bread had changed, as he argued at his examination, it must have changed forever: and then, what of its fate as, like other foods, it passed through the body? The presence of Christ in the Sacrament was to be understood in less chemical, less crudely materialist, terms. So, too, was the presence of God in the world. And this, again, shows Cranmer to be truly modern, anticipating, in his eucharistic views, a whole view of God and man with which the human race would one day have to come to terms. God is not our ultimate magic. 'The world is that which is the case', and it cannot be changed by the formulas of a liturgy or the incantations of a hierophant. We must accept the unchanging, and cruel, and indifferent world of Nature in which we live, and we cannot change it by words or wishes or even by prayers. God, if He is found or seen, can only be true if He remains God, and not a creature, to be made, or summoned to the altar of the church by an arcane rite. There is doggedness, realism, and risk here: the risk of deciding that, after all, there is no God or that He is unapproachable. Cranmer laid the foundations for such thoughts.

Not that he had them himself. His six *Recantacyons* make sad reading. During the last year of his life he appeared to be willing to commit the ultimate act of intellectual cowardice, to say that he believed other than he did. It would be unfair, though, to say that he did so merely as an act of political expediency. He spent hours and weeks debating these questions in private conversations with the students of Christ Church, Oxford. There is every evidence that, knowing how momentous such ideas were, he had genuine doubts and misgivings. He and his generation were setting themselves up against the received wisdom of the Western Church, and he was not arrogant enough to be certain, all of the time, that he was right. He had a keen piety. It was the fire of Hell which he dreaded, and not the fires of his persecutors. Indeed, after the hideous deaths of Ridley and Latimer, which Cranmer was compelled to witness, his heart was hardened against Catholicism. It was only in later months that he vacillated.

The vacillations ceased when it became clear that, contrary to all precedent, the authorities were to continue with his burning even though he had forsworn his supposed heresy. In normal circumstances, if a heretic recanted his errors, he was regarded as redeemed, and did not need the purgation of fire. Cranmer was burnt out of spite, and not for reasons of religious zeal. It was a brave death. His captors had read and approved his grovelling speech of apology, to be declaimed before they set light to the faggots. They did not know that he had concealed in his breast an alternative version, which he had sat up to write on the last night of his life.

> And now I come to the great thing which so much troubleth my conscience, more than any thing that ever I did or said in my whole life. And that is the setting abroad of a writing contrary to the truth; which now here I renounce and refuse as things written with my hand contrary to the truth which I thought in my heart, and to save my life if it might be. ... And forasmuch as my hand offended, writing contrary to my heart, my hand shall first be punished therefor; for, may I come to the fire, it shall be first burned. ...

The image of this man, old by the standards of that period (67 years), standing with his hand in the flame and not uttering a cry is one of the most potent in the whole intellectual history of Western Europe, and it is all the more powerful in that Cranmer was not a dogged unchanging man, but a thoughtful vacillating character who was intelligent enough to know the difficulties of arriving at the truth. His last words, which scandalised those Catholics who killed him, were, 'I see Heaven open and Jesus on the right hand of God.'

The hand which was to perish in the flames had written the Prayer Books of 1549 and 1552 – or been chiefly responsible for their compilation. Those who have written about Cranmer have sometimes done so in the spirit of W. H. Auden, in his poem of elegy for Yeats, as one whom Time will pardon for writing well. The defenders of the beleaguered 1662 book (so largely based on Cranmer's books) lay understandable stress upon its beauty. Cranmer would not thank us for a purely aesthetic appreciation of his work. True, he had the gift, so sadly denied the authors of more recent liturgies, the genius for writing prose which could bear endless public repetition; a genius for the phrase which can enter the bloodstream, remaining part of the imaginative life of the hearer for ever. 'We are not worthy so much as to gather up the crumbs under Thy table.' . . . 'Create and make in us new and contrite hearts.' . . . 'To pass our time in rest and quietness' . . . 'that so among the sundry and manifold changes of the world, our hearts may surely there be fixed where true joys are to be found'. Those who know Cranmer's book by heart have an incomparable storehouse which shapes and patterns life. But it is not just 'poetry'. Cranmer's liturgies, and occasional services and collects, have had such an extraordinary staying power because they do represent the human experience. His book enshrines a religion which is deeply rooted in life as it is actually experienced by men and women with 'unruly wills and affections', who have left undone the things they ought to have done, and have done the things they ought not to have done, and who reach out to God in the knowledge that there is no magic formula which will change human sinfulness or the relentless march of death. No Christian liturgy is less babyish, or less florid. The funeral service, for example, only consoles by truthfulness, by confronting death head on, and thanking God for delivering 'this our brother out of the miseries of this sinful world'. The fate of the soul, for which requiem masses pleaded, is left to the wisdom of God. Similarly, the preface to the marriage ceremony, and the phrases within it to which modern puritans have taken exception – they are excised from the new books – are written for real human beings, tempted to fornication, but who can distinguish between satisfying lust 'like brute beasts' and wanting to say to someone, 'with my body I thee worship'.

The sinfulness of the human race is something which Cranmer took for granted, and no one has ever held him up as a model of sanctity. He knew about unruly wills and affections. His early academic career was ruined by a precipitate and youthful marriage. His second marriage, after he had taken orders, would appear to have been both a love match and a meeting of minds, since Margaret Cranmer was a German, and Cranmer, by tortuous and circuitous steps, genuinely came to believe in the central tenets of Continental Protestantism. Central to this teaching is the doctrine of justification by faith only, and a certainty that the human race cannot redeem itself, nor partake in the work of redemption. When, in the Communion Service, it states that the burden of human sin is intolerable, a central view of nature itself is being expounded. Modern egotism might make the unthinking reader of the phrase suppose that Cranmer was encouraging a guilt-ridden neurosis. When, however, we state that the burden of our sins is intolerable, we are not saying that we cannot bear a particular feeling. We are stating a theological belief. Sin itself cannot be borne, or paid off, or cancelled, by human desire or by religious observance. For those who found their own sins 'intolerable' in the modern sense, Cranmer left the provision of auricular confession by a penitent, that 'he may receive the benefit of absolution, together with ghostly counsel and advice to the quieting of his conscience'. So much for sins. But sin itself was, for Cranmer, the great and unalterable fact of human life, which had been borne by one means only, the 'full, perfect and sufficient sacrifice, oblation and satisfaction' of Calvary.

This is the core of the Prayer Book faith, Cranmer's faith, for which he died. No such uncompromising view survives in the confession of sin in the newer liturgy of the Alternative Service Book. There is no statement there that the burden of sin is intolerable, and no vast or cosmic hope that our muttered imperfections, committed, we concede, 'through negligence, through weakness, through our own deliberate fault', have received or needed the pardon of sacrificial love.

It was inevitable that Cranmer's Prayer Book would be superseded in the 20th century, not merely because so many Anglicans had become quasi-Roman Catholics, but because the world which the book represents had changed so utterly. It presupposes a renaissance world of 'Christian kings, princes and governors'. Much of the language of the Visitation for the Sick or the Churching of Women could not be uttered by 20th-century human beings without an element of play-acting. The collects for Fair Weather, and Plenty, and Thanksgivings for Restoring Publick Peace at Home seem merely quaint, and in the present intellectual climate which applauds inter-faith dialogue, imams and rabbis sitting down with bishops to thrash out their supposed common ground, liberal Christians could not say the third collect for Good Friday without a blush. But though it would be surprising if a book had not dated in 440 years, it is surprising how much of it remains fresh and contemporary, and how much of it is a serious source of religious nourishment. And this is not just because it is full of 'lovely phrases'. It is because it grows out of the attempts by the reformers to arrive at the truth and to live by it. That mellifluous ex-Anglican, Newman, defined a gentleman as 'one who never inflicts pain'. It is hard to spell out Cranmer's achievement, and his glory, without giving pain to Newman's co-religionists. Better than anyone, Cranmer the politician and servant of Henry VIII knew that the Church of England had very shady origins. But the Reformation itself was not forged solely by politicians. It grew out of intellectual sincerity, hard thinking, deep reading, and it was ultimately baptised by Blood and Fire. Auden's elegy on Yeats, to which I alluded earlier, provides the perfect epitaph for Cranmer, whose struggling, honest and uncertain mind genuinely believed that the human race should not be in the thrall of a spiritual dictatorship of human origins. For more than 400 years, English-speaking people have repeated the offices and services which Cranmer originally compiled. We should revere him.

> In the deserts of the heart
> Let the healing fountain start,
> In the prison of his days
> Teach the free man how to praise.

That is precisely what Cranmer did in his life, in his death, and in his book.

24 June 1989

brian bagnall

DIARY

Peregrine Worsthorne

Andrew Knight told me of his intention to merge the *Sunday Tele-graph*, of which I was then editor, into the *Daily Telegraph* over breakfast at Claridges. I remember well the exact moment when this thunderbolt, coming out of a blue sky, hit me. It was when the waiter had just served two perfectly poached eggs on buttered toast — a dish of which I am inordinately and insatiably fond. In my mind I knew that the information just imparted was a paralysingly painful blow: pretty well a professional death sentence. But for some reason this sense of acute shock did not get through to my taste buds or palate or whatever part of the nervous system or anatomy controls the appetite, and I continued eating the eggs with as much pleasure as usual; and also, a bit later, the rolls and marmalade as well. Even while doing so I was surprised and even shocked at my quite indecent insouciance. Surely an editor, on hearing that his beloved paper is about to be killed, should not calmly continue to eat a hearty breakfast. 'How can you?' I thought to myself. Would not anyone with the slightest sensitivity have his appetite cut clean away, choke on his food, on hearing such unwelcome news? Only later did I recall all those wartime testimonies of how, on being shot, men can feel no pain for quite a while and even carry on as if nothing had happened. Could it be that deeply wounding words have the same delayed impact, temporarily anaesthetising the victim? I don't know the answer. All I do know is that, at the time, I enjoyed that Claridges breakfast and only began to feel sick with indignation and shame some hours later.

At breakfast, of course, one is always pretty slow on the uptake at the best of times. Certainly I am and I think this is true of most English people. One is not on one's guard at breakfast. It is a domestic, non-business meal and if the hostile outside world does intrude it is only indirectly, by post. The Americans are different. They have working breakfasts which must include, I suppose, sacking breakfasts.

These are not a good idea and I do hope other chief executives won't follow Mr Knight's example. For the manner of delivering professional blows can be very important. A friend of mine at Collins, who occupied a senior editorial post and is himself a distinguished author, was outraged recently to be sacked by the chairman over a ham sandwich in a pub. Would it have made any difference, I asked, if the chairman had done the dirty deed over dinner at the Gavroche? 'Certainly it would,' he replied. 'A ham sandwich in a pub really is to add insult to injury.' Another friend, the late Donald Tyerman, was also incensed by the manner in which he was told that he would not get the succession to the editorship of the *Times*, to which he had every right, having, in effect, done the job excellently for several years. Over the spinach soup at dinner in his Carlton House Terrace mansion, the then *Times* chairman, Colonel Astor, casually asked Tyerman what he thought of Sir William Haley, who at the time was director-general of the BBC. 'First-class man,' replied Tyerman, to which the shattering reply came: 'So relieved to hear you think well of Haley, since we have decided to make him the next editor of the *Times*.'

While self-indulgently reminiscing about the recent *Sunday Telegraph* débâcle, perhaps I can use the opportunity of being *Spectator* diarist to put a small matter right. A headline at the time in the *Evening Standard* diary went as follows: 'Perry weeps as Max builds empire.' In a way that was true. That is to say, I did shed a few tears. But not because of being demoted. It is never the big things that make adults cry, and in fact I had got through the painful business of listening to Andrew Knight explaining his decision to the staff without excessive or uncontrollable emotion. What set me off happened a few minutes after the meeting was over when a relatively junior colleague, whose copy I had sometimes spiked and who had no reason to thank me for anything, came in to offer me his sympathy. Most people can cope, at any rate in public, with personal disasters without breaking down. For we are all steeled not to give way to self-pity. Much more difficult to cope with, however, are those unexpected small gestures of human solidarity which succeed in penetrating the thickest emotional armour plating. So the truth is this: Perry did not weep out of hurt at the nastiness of the world but out of wonder at its niceness.

8 July 1989

'Yes, Billy, but Mr Phillips pushes *legal* *drugs.*'

INTIMATIONS OF MORTALITY

Jock Bruce-Gardyne

An obsession with the avoidance of death is the 20th-century heresy. Our forebears were taught by the Church that the sooner they could contrive to shuffle off this mortal coil and get on into the next world, the better for them it would be. I don't suppose that made them any the less apprehensive when the time came. But at least they were not encouraged by their pastors and masters to devote the best part of their time and energy to a forlorn attempt to outwit the Reaper.

How different today. The Church itself is the proud standard-bearer of the Sanctity of Human Life movement. Politicians with even a modest interest in their public images must be seen to be active on behalf of life-prolonging (or at any rate allegedly life-prolonging) campaigns. The claims they make for these worthy causes, apparently without any sense of self-parody, are often remarkable. I once heard a Labour Minister of Health inform the House of Commons that 'heavy smokers will die'. I could not forbear to ask him what would happen to the rest of us. It was an intervention regarded — on all sides — as being in the worst of taste.

All this is by way of introduction to the description of a personal experience. I set it forth in order to explain that I myself have always taken a pretty fatalistic view of death, only inclining strongly to the hope that I might be able to avoid a long and debilitating illness on the way out.

Yet I have always been interested in how people actually react to a sentence of death, or the next best thing. Reading the biography of the great Montrose or of Pierre Laval — or the letters of a young infantry officer at the Western Front in the First World War — I am inclined to turn to the last few pages first. Did he send farewell messages to the family? How did he take it all?

I imagine that if you are condemned to be shot or hanged, a major preoccupation must be with how you will behave when the moment comes. Fortunately very few of us are called upon to die in public. But some of us do receive a pretty specific time-chit. Much to my astonishment, I suddenly find myself in that category. It occurred to me that a description of my own reactions (so far!) might be of interest.

Much though I disapprove of health I have always, in practice, been almost absurdly healthy: and in my late fifties I think the most censorious of the medical profession would have been prepared to concede that I did not look like making their fortunes for them. So when I got my visiting card it arrived completely without warning.

For the past 30 years and more I have been accustomed to working at a clockwork typewriter. I use about five fingers in all: I have never learned to touch-type, and I stare at the keys. But I can get the words down (OK, untidily, and with many corrections) at least as fast as I can think – my critics would no doubt say a good deal faster. Appropriately, therefore, it was my trusty typewriter that tipped me off.

I can fix it to the day. It was the day of Mr Lawson's 1988 Autumn Statement to Parliament. I had undertaken to deliver a routine on-the-spot comment to one of my indulgent organs. Inevitably it was a rush job. But that presented no problem; as I say, I have always been a speedy worker.

'Don't look now, Marjorie, but Mr Barraclough is streaking again.'

Not that night I wasn't. To my dismay — to my horror — I suddenly found I could not get the letters in order. Not the words: I knew what I wanted to write. But the letters. I wanted to write 'year'. Concentrating hard I knew that 'y' came first. But what came next? And I should perhaps add that I was stone cold sober.

I was appalled. I then recalled that there had been another small incident a week or so before, to which I had paid scant attention at the time. I had fallen off my bicycle and I did not know why I had done so.

Armed with this scanty evidence I dropped in on my doctor. He was cosily reassuring. He knew at once what my trouble was. He gave it a fancy name: but what it amounted to was that I had reached a time in life when my blood corpuscles were becoming furred up. They were therefore prone to get stuck in the tubes, from whence they would sometimes emerge with some violence. They might shoot off into my lung, where they would dissolve, and I would know nothing about it. But they might shoot up into the head: and then I *would* know about it. I suggested that it sounded rather like a stroke. Not at all, I was assured: just an 'incident' — no lasting effects. And it is true that on the same evening when Nigel Lawson's Autumn Statement had tripped me up I had composed a totally different article without trouble.

The GP drafted me a note to a gentleman in Harley Street, and told me to dose myself with aspirin meantime. The gentleman in Harley Street sent me round the corner to an ancillary establishment where they stripped me to the waist and rubbed a contraption like a telephone handset over my chest for what seemed like hours. I went to sleep, and had to be aroused by the attendant because my snores were disturbing his computer. Then I was sent off to another nearby basement, where they shoved a tube up my arm and into my heart, all wired up to a computer. Off-putting, but perfectly harmless.

In due course my GP informed me that they could find nothing wrong. But by now three more weeks had moved on, and I could. I still couldn't compose the words at my faithful clockwork. I wasn't all that hot at reading the time off my watch either. And I was unable to look people up in the telephone directory because I couldn't remember the order of the alphabet. I couldn't go on like that. Yet I did not see much point in returning to the GP, who had drawn a blank. I fell into conversation with an old pal — a socialist, as it happens. That allegiance is of no relevance except that in my experience socialists very often go to private medicine-men in Harley Street. This one was no exception. 'I know just the bloke for you,' he replied. 'Cost you a bit – but if anyone can sort you out he will.' Since I was getting the least bit desperate, I decided to give it a whirl.

My friend's medicine-man stripped me down and punched and pummelled me, taking careful note of my odd experiences the while. Finished, he looked up. 'I'm going to send you for a brain scan.'

It was a little like the dread summons faintly remembered from my schooldays: 'Bodkin wants to see you in his study at nine o'clock. You won't need a dressing-gown.' Yet I can't pretend I was surprised. I had been increasingly convinced that a brain scan was what I would end up with.

From then on events proceeded with a sense of smooth inevitability. On the evening of the scan the medicine-man rang up. 'Yes,' he said, 'there is a shadow, and we're going to have to have a look at it.'

They did, and duly told me that a gremlin had attached itself to the inside of my skull at the back, where it was making its presence felt. A sawbones had already been lined up to get to grips with it. If I was lucky he would be able to chip it off more or less like that, and I would be back in circulation as if nothing had happened in a matter of days. If I wasn't lucky . . . but we'd take that hurdle when we came to it.

I was introduced to the sawbones, who turned out much to my relief to be a seemingly straight-talking Ulsterman. I made just two stipulations: I wished to be told the truth, the whole truth and nothing but the truth; and above all I did not wish to be kept going as a vegetable.

The op apparently took about two hours. When I came round I was relieved to find that everything seemed to be entirely back to normal, apart from a rather sore head (the sawbones had pointed out that my little spot of bother was quite near where the brain processes eyesight – but there was no sign of trouble there). The op, the surgeon told me, had gone off 'perfectly'. But I think he added 'so far'. At any rate I had a gut feeling that he did not like what he had found.

Next day he brought the verdict. He was admirably factual and to the point. He'd successfully extracted 80 per cent of my gremlin. But what was left was 'not benign'. The prospect was as follows. As soon as my head wound had been stitched up I could resume my normal day-to-day existence. In a week or two's time they could offer me some radium bombardment. It was entirely up to me. That might prolong my life expectancy for up to a year. Otherwise anything from six months to 18 months was just about my book.

It was a very odd experience. The day after my op I was battering away at my clockwork typewriter at midnight. My spelling was completely restored. Indeed – no doubt because they were stuffing me with steroids – I was on a 'high'. I was eating like a horse, and typing round the clock. Friends rang up asking when they could visit, and were a little shocked to be answered with, 'What d'you have in mind? Lunch at the Garrick?'

Four months later I have, reluctantly, undergone the 'treatment'. They assured me that, because of the location of my gremlin, I would suffer no side-effects except that my full head of hair would probably fall out. I did not believe them, and I was right. For the three weeks of bombardment I found it hard to eat at all, since the scent of food gave me nausea. I also suffered a lot of exhaustion, and my hair did indeed fall out, most of it in a single evening. I have learned that what they tell you about losing body heat through the head is all too true. I was even reduced during the cold spell in May to wearing a woolly balaclava in the House of Lords ('just so long as you don't wear it in the chamber, dear boy').

I have been around the world, as the doctors told me it was the moment to do so, and I have grown a beard in compensation (and very odd colours it has turned out to be). The Prime Minister told me that she thought it made me look 'benign' – which was almost enough to make me shave it off again. No one recognises me. I have lost a stone, and all my trousers show an embarrassing inclination to drop around my ankles.

Otherwise I have resumed my normal life of crime. I no longer pedal my way to the *Telegraph*'s establishment on the Isle of Dogs, but I still turn up on my shabby machine at Their Lordships' House, where I continue at least to make rude interventions at Question Time (like suggesting how wise we are to be importers rather than exporters). I bang away at the dear old trusty clockwork.

Much to my vexation, all this seems to be regarded as awfully brave. (The *Evening Standard* diary column even thought it worthy of a paragraph, complete with photo. They were very short of copy.) It is, of course, nothing of the kind. For bravery, surely, requires both a certainty of consequences and a choice of actions. Those infantry officers in the First World War *were* brave. They knew the odds-on chance that they would be killed (if they were lucky), and they had the choice to run away. Yet over the top they went. I, by contrast, have always been a bit of a workaholic, and to me what *might*, I suppose, be 'bravery' would be if I withdrew into a monastery.

I shall never presumably meet my grandchildren, which I regret — although it is a family tradition. But in other respects I reckon my timing isn't too bad. I always knew 'retirement' would give me the miseries. As it is I've had quite a lot of fun — if the truth be told, something of an ego trip. I've paid the school bills and watched my children grow up. Let's face it, I was on the threshold of the stage of life when one is conscious of being a 'back number'. I would not have enjoyed that. And thank God, at least nowadays the taboos are relaxed. I remember when my father was carted into hospital, where he spent the last 12 months of his life. We all knew he had cancer. But the word never crossed our lips. I realise others may not agree, but personally I incline to telling people (not, I hope, obsessively) that I am a ticket-of-leave man. I just hope and pray they do not feel it necessary to respond with a sombre expression. At least they will no more dare to look censorious when I light up a gasper, or demand that second dram.

So what about the down-side? Well that, I reckon, is obvious. It's the family. The unselfish way to die is — is it not? — to fall under the proverbial bus. No doubt the shock for the family is traumatic. But it is swiftly over. The prospect for my family, by contrast, is one of witnessing and trying to cope with an irreversible and presumably steadily accelerating decline. But then I was never one to choose the unselfish way if others offered.

And what 'lies beyond'? I have not the least idea. As an addictive angler I suppose I just hope I do not suffer the mythical fate of the great chalk stream fisherman who, on arrival at the pearly gates, was

'And if they are aphrodisiacs, how come there's so few of us left?'

immediately packed off to the perfect chalk stream, complete with perfect rod and perfect ghillie. He cast the perfect line, and a magnificent fighting three-pounder took the fly at the first cast. No sooner had he landed it than he was amazed to see another large fish rising at exactly the same spot. That one also took the fly at once. And another. And another. After half an hour our hero reckoned a rest and a smoke were in order. But the ghillie warned that 'the proprietor' would not like it if he rested on his laurels when the fish were rising. So he was forced to return to the bankside. And so he continued, for many a weary hour. Finally to the ghillie he exclaimed, 'But this is hell!'

Came the answer, 'And were you expecting something else, Sir?'

8 July 1989

LOGIC IN HIGH GEAR

Anthony Quinton

In 1948 articles appeared in the *New Statesman* by 'Oxonian' (whoever he may have been) and C. E. M. Joad, which claimed that the doctrines of logical positivism taught at Oxford and elsewhere prepared the minds of the young for fascism. The human incarnation of this dangerous intellectual tendency was Freddie Ayer. In Joad's subsequent *Critique of Logical Positivism* that is made clear by the fact that beside Ayer's name in the index appears the word *passim*. In reality the prophet of moral disintegration was in most respects a highly moral

man, in the standard and conventional sense of the term.

To start with he had a very strong sense of duty. He took endless trouble with his pupils, reading, discussing and amending their work and then, when it had secured a degree, energetically seeking academic posts for them. Unlike some people, he did not trot out the same old lectures, year after year, from an ever yellower bundle of notes, but constantly prepared new ones in his appalling handwriting.

In his younger days the philosophy professors at Oxford had given weekly 'informal instructions', to which anyone could come. By 1960, when he came back to Oxford, they had fallen into disuse. He revived them and they proved to be oases of spiritual refreshment for graduate students who found the Oxford philosophical scene rather insipid in the light of the reputation for excitement it had gained in the preceding 15 years.

His chief instrument for invigorating the teachers of philosophy was the 'group', meeting in his rooms on Tuesdays in the two hours before dinner. A paper would be read and lively discussion would follow. At about 6 p.m. the host (this was a rotating office) would produce whisky and, as the dinner hour drew near, the exchanges would steadily become more sibilant and colourful. In his 13 years as professor at University College, London, he transformed a completely moribund department into what was probably the liveliest centre for philosophy in the country.

The sense of duty on its own is an austere piece of moral equipment. In Freddie's case it was tempered or alleviated by unwavering geniality and good nature. One of the more unacademic traits of his personality was his remarkable freedom from malice, a characteristic which gave him a quality of almost childlike innocence by comparison with contemporaries of similar gifts and interests.

He was a generous and immensely welcoming host. His parties took place in different houses of identical structure, all being many-storeyed edifices with lots of small rooms. All of these and the stairs joining them would be filled with interesting or attractive people (the 'or' is not exclusive, to be logically explicit). Little could be heard through the noise, but the presumption was that everyone present was clever enough to work out what was being said from the few audible fragments.

By and large he was a practising utilitarian, concerned to augment the greatest happiness of the greatest number. With Bentham as its

'Folk i' t' North are generally friendlier than folk down South.'

secular patron saint, University College, London, was an appropriate
setting for him. He was not, perhaps, a champagne socialist but rather
a Margaux one, for his egalitarian sentiments were associated with a
discriminatingly comfortable mode of life, not a luxurious one.

Disagreement in opinion was no obstacle to close friendship. We
used to mock each other's political convictions, but that generated
laughter, not heat. Even opposition to his philosophy, which was more
important to him than his politics, did not stop him making good
friends of A. C. Ewing, who, I think, believed the precise opposite of
everything Freddie believed, and of his occasional sparring partner, the
distinguished historian of philosophy, Father Frederick Copleston.
Ewing was an engagingly unworldly man. Freddie, in *More of My Life*,
reports him as being keen on immortality because it would enable him
to find out once and for all whether there are or are not synthetic a
priori propositions. When in a philosophical discussion someone said
that the most intense of human pleasures had an element of pain in
them, Ewing said in his high, piping voice, 'I cannot imagine what they
can be.'

Freddie's socialism had taken on a largely symbolic or incantatory
form by the time I got to know him well. But he was essentially a man
of the Thirties and he remained loyal to ideological attachments hard

for a thoughtful person not to form in that decade. What is more, in its early days his politics had received a gruelling practical expression. He was for a time chairman of the minute Soho branch of the Westminster Abbey division of the Labour party and there is a memorable account in *A Part of My Life* of his regular harangues to the unheeding citizens of Westminster from a step-ladder in the vicinity of the Berwick Street market.

It is a sad fact that in ordinary conversation when someone is described as highly immoral what is meant is not that they are cruel or dishonest but that they are sexually promiscuous. In this field of human interest Freddie was active and at times at fault, even in terms of a liberal view of the relations of the sexes. There were unkept promises and unkind partings. On the other hand, numerous girl friends remained on excellent terms with him. It is characteristic that those he goes on about at greatest length in his memoirs are dead.

Freddie was a metropolitan man and realised early in life that London was the best place for him to flourish in. Some of the games he was good at were rural − cricket, for instance; but his excellence as a chess player, full of bold stratagems, seems more appropriate. He *looked* metropolitan; suits, not tweed jackets, were his natural attire. He always pulsated with energy, releasing some of it by twiddling his key chain. He was wonderfully, often disconcertingly, rapid in argument. I have often thought that just as there is a revealing ambiguity in the fact that Sartre's mother was an Alsatian, there is also one in the fact that Freddie's mother was a Citroën. His highly-geared mind got away from a standing start much faster than the slow-moving Morris engines of us, his fellow-philosophers.

In the spirit of A. C. Ewing I declare an interest in the immortality of the soul. Were it to be the case, it would be enjoyable to witness Freddie's good-natured indignation at the fact.

8 July 1989

'*O not so rare Ben Johnson.*'

REFLECTIONS ON THE FRENCH REVOLUTION

A. J. Ayer

A. J. Ayer wrote his first article for The Spectator *in 1936. This is the last article he wrote before he died.*

'Bliss was it in that dawn to be alive; but to be young was very heaven!' The young Wordsworth gave expression to a favourable view of the French Revolution which was strongly held by quite a formidable minority of his English contemporaries. He himself changed his opinion of it in later life. Others did not. Charles James Fox's enthusiasm for it extended to an admiration for Napoleon Bonaparte. Byron and Shelley spoke for many English radicals, then and thereafter, in taking sides with revolutionary and imperial France against the younger Pitt and the stern unbending Tories who followed him in England. There is no doubt that the Tory governments of that time were extremely repressive. Nor did the Whig oligarchy, which super-seded them, care much for levelling, either socially or economically, in spite of its engagement in parliamentary reform. Both parties, the Tories, and Edmund Burke, from the start, and most other Whigs subsequently, saw the French Revolution as a threat to English liberties. Were they not right?

Unfulfilled conditionals set a problem for philosophers. The histor-ical questions which they are used to posing call for fanciful discus-sions more than serious answers. What would have happened if Nelson had lost the battle of Trafalgar? Would the victorious French fleet have enabled Napoleon to land his troops in England? Let us assume that it would and that the French would have been victorious. What would have happened then? I suppose that the consequent change in the form of government from an imperfectly constitutional monarchy to a republic would not have been unwelcome: the institution of monarchy at that time was far from enjoying the popularity that, with Edward VIII omitted, it can be said to have acquired in England in the last three reigns. On the other hand, the spirit of patriotism among the British people surely outweighed their grievances. They would not have been grateful for a better order which was imposed on them by a foreign and, above all, a French invader.

I am prepared to argue that it would have been a better order. To this day, in my view, we suffer from the lack of a written constitution and a comprehensive bill of rights. The inquisitional system of justice which was instituted in France and in other European countries has its defects, but I think it preferable to the adversarial systems, developed in Britain and the United States, which unduly favour those who can afford to hire the ablest lawyers to plead their case. In politics, we should most probably now be accustomed to some form of proportional representation, which would yield a better reflection of popular sentiment, at the cost of having weaker governments, which anyhow I think desirable. For what it is worth, we would have adopted the metric system of measurement a century and a half before we did.

Before I succumb even further to the lure of such speculations, let me repeat that they are idle. Even as speculations, they are not securely based. It is more persuasive to argue that the conquest of England would not have satisfied Napoleon. He would still have embarked on his Russian campaign with the same result. Even if he had won the battle of Waterloo, as he very nearly did ('a damn close-run thing,' as Wellington admitted, 'the closest-run thing you ever saw in your life'), he would not have reconquered England, and the recovery of power by the English oligarchy would have made their governments even more repressive than they actually were.

Let us, then, return to the French Revolution and try to assess it on the basis of fact. Or rather, let us try to give an accurate account of the facts in sustaining a judgement of value. In this case, it is convenient to adopt a utilitarian approach. Did the Revolution do more good than harm?

In France, hardly anyone would hesitate over the answer to this question. It is generally agreed that the Revolution did much more good. But that is very largely because the French have allowed their Revolution to acquire the status of a myth. Its first centenary endowed Paris with the Eiffel Tower. The second centenary will pass without having produced anything so spectacular, but it will have recorded an even larger payment of verbal tributes. Just as the bellicose second verse of the National Anthem is almost unknown in England, so when Frenchmen sing the 'Marseillaise' they pay little or no attention to the bloodthirsty fashion in which it ends. When they speak about the Revolution, they do not dwell upon the Terror.

In England, it is just the other way round. Thanks to Carlyle's *History of the French Revolution* with its marvellous image of Robespierre as 'the sea-green incorruptible', and even more to Dickens's *The Tale of Two Cities*, and Baroness Orczy's *The Scarlet Pimpernel*, and the films made from these novels, the whole Revolution, apart from the capture of the Bastille, is almost condensed to the Terror in most people's minds. Historians, who see further, tend to regard the Revolution as a failure because it saddled France with Napoleon as its first Emperor: and, indeed, the emergence of Napoleon would vindicate Plato's dictum in the *Republic* that thoroughgoing democracy leads directly to dictatorship, were it not that it was only in theory, and not in practice, that the régime which the Revolution instituted was a thoroughgoing democracy.

In the light of the condition of France between the First and Second Empires and the establishment of the Third Republic after the Franco-Prussian war and the defeat of the Parisian *commune*, Marxists are justified in treating the French Revolution as terminating the long process of the replacement of feudalism by bourgeois capitalism. Not that the *ancien régime* which was destroyed by the Revolution was exactly feudal. It was, indeed, a strongly hierarchical society but the political power of the nobility had passed almost entirely to the king. The French Revolution had this much in common with the 'glorious', if bloodless, English 'Revolution' of 1688, that each put an end to absolute monarchy, with the greater tendency in England until the present century for the ghost to come back to life. It is true that the Congress of Vienna replaced the Bourbons on the throne of France, only to prove that the French Revolution had not been a total failure. Having 'learned nothing and forgotten nothing', the two of them reigned for a mere 15 years. But what of the Emperors? The power of the first Napoleon at least might qualify as absolute, but he was not an absolute monarch. There was no question of his ruling by divine right.

The representatives of the Third Estate who brought about the Revolution were predominantly bourgeois and it was the French bourgeoisie that eventually profited by it, but in Paris at least it had the fervent support of the common people. Dickens's nightmarish depiction of the frenzy of the mob has a foundation in fact. Women did knit beside the guillotine in what only later was named the Place de la Concorde. The heads of enemies and 'traitors' were carried about on pikes, with spectators gloating over them. In the provinces also the

Revolution was supported fervently by the people, if they supported it at all. The soldiers in the armies of the Republic, including those commanded by Napoleon Bonaparte, owed their success in part to their belief in their cause.

In the provinces, however, popular support for the Revolution was far from universal. According to the American historian, Robert Darnton, to whose essay 'What Was Revolutionary About the French Revolution?', in the 19 January issue of the *New York Review of Books*, I am very much indebted, the total number of those who fell victim to the guillotine was as small, by modern standards, as 17,000, and three-quarters of that number were rebels captured in arms. So far from its being the case that the Terror was a manifestation of class war against the artistocracy, no more than 15 per cent of its victims could plausibly be described as aristocrats. The most serious popular revolt, celebrated by Balzac in his novel *Les Chouans*, took place in the Vendée, but there were also uprisings in the provincial cities of Lyons, Marseilles and Bordeaux: the uprising in Lyons was put down with particular severity. The horrible massacre of prisoners in September 1792 disposed mainly of commoners from priests to prostitutes. As in the Spanish Civil War of the 1930s, the priests may have suffered from the identification of their Church with the oppressors of the people; the prostitutes may have been casualties of the puritanism which the Revolution engendered. For the most part, however, the massacre was an insane expression of loyalty to the Republic. Its victims were seen, most implausibly, as counter-revolutionaries.

Professor Darnton's statistics are an overdue corrective to the myth of *The Scarlet Pimpernel*. Even so, they should not blind us to the fact that the Revolution was primarily directed against the monarchy and aristocracy: even though 85 per cent of those who succumbed to the Terror were commoners, these commoners were viewed as honorary aristocrats. The repudiation of monarchy and its associates went to extraordinary lengths. Persons whose names were associated with royalty or the Church, like the French equivalents of King or Bishop, changed them for such names as the French equivalents of Law and Liberty. These changes have mostly been reversed. The revolutionary *abeille pondeuse* – the laying bee – has reverted to being a queen. An exception, not noticed by Professor Darnton, though he draws attention to the revolutionary changes, is to be found in the naming of chess pieces and court cards. Kings have returned in both cases, but queens are still no better than ladies in French; the French jacks are not young princes but servants, *valets*. In chess, the French still have towers in place of castles and their equivalents of knights and bishops remain horses and madmen. The rank and file have always been pawns in all social systems, though in the French naming of chessmen they have moved up slightly. *Pion* has become a slang term for an assistant schoolmaster.

I rather regret that the revolutionary revision of the calendar, with its renaming of the 12 months according to the weather, did not last beyond 1805. The division of the month into three weeks of ten days each left at least five days over in the year. They were to be national holidays. Perhaps some lack of a sense of humour was shown in their being respectively dedicated to Virtue, Genius, Labour, Opinion and Reward, but then a sense of humour would probably be a handicap to anyone who was engaged in obliterating every feature of a former régime in the interests of social progress. The English Revolution that best deserves the name was carried out by Cromwell's Puritans, and Puritans are not conspicuous for their sense of humour: neither were the manufacturers who participated in the Industrial Revolution: their workforce had little enough to laugh at. How far does the fact that the average Englishman prides himself upon his sense of humour account for his lack of revolutionary fervour?

I have remarked that Napoleon profited by the spirit of nationalism which the French Republic breathed into its armies. Though he sacrificed his soldiers in his pursuit of military glory, he did not just negate the Revolution. There was never any prospect of the revival of the Bastille: France still enjoys the benefits of the *Code Napoléon*. It can even be said that he spread the Revolution in his conquests. He initiated the liberation of the north of Italy from Austrian rule, a stepping-stone to Italy's becoming a nation state. By overthrowing their rulers, and presenting them with the French example, he brought, admittedly with no such purpose, the spirit of nationalism into the states of Germany. Nationalism now predominates as a source of evil but 200 years ago it was a liberating force. I wonder how long it will take all the governments of Western Europe to realise that its day has passed.

So, did the French Revolution do more good than harm? My judgement that it did more good is strongly influenced by the superiority of all of the successive French Republics to the injustices of the *ancien régime.* The frequenters of Parisian salons in the late 18th century might claim that they alone had experienced *la douceur de vivre,* but they were a small minority and their happiness was precarious. Voltaire was exiled to England and after a spell in Prussia at the court of Frederick the Great found it prudent to live on the border of Geneva. It was only in extreme old age that he made his triumphal return to Paris, where the Church denied him burial at his death.

Voltaire believed in liberty; not so much in equality or fraternity; and indeed the Revolutionary ideal of *Liberté, Egalité, Fraternité* has never yet been realised. One may doubt whether its three parts are mutually consistent. There is certainly at least a tension between liberty and equality. The concept of equality is, indeed, the most contentious. In theory equality and fraternity are Christian concepts; we are all equally the children of God. But the theory has never been put into practice except perhaps at the outset among the Christians themselves and subsequently in small communities. Otherwise equality and fraternity have been kept in heaven: until quite recently most members of the human race have been consigned to a literal hell. The ideal of fraternity has made a showing in America, though barely yet extended to Indians, Hispanics or blacks. Its prevalence among white Americans has resulted in a conformism which is destructive of liberty. It is also at the expense of liberty that communist countries have pursued nominal equality. The present British government is at least not hypocritical: it openly pursues inequality at the expense of liberty. It is only in time of war that the British people are much addicted to fraternity.

I am content to let Charles Dickens have the last word on the French Revolution. I would only reverse the order of the two clauses in the sentence with which *The Tale of Two Cities* begins. It was the worst of times, it was the best.

8 July 1989

'You spoil that suitcase.'

WHEN SHE WAS BAD SHE WAS HORRID

Anne Chisholm

AMBITION
by Julie Burchill
Bodley Head

Once upon a time there was a naughty little girl called Julie. Julie discovered, when she was only just grown up, that she could be quite rich and quite famous by writing rude, aggressive things in newspapers and magazines, shocking all the boring middle-aged middle-class readers by showing them what a rough, tough little girl she was, and how she didn't care at all about being polite, or having acceptable views about poor people or old people or black people, and how she knew a lot more than they did about sex and drugs and popular music. The owners and editors of the papers and magazines she worked for, like Mr Rupert Murdoch and Sir David English and Mr Si Newhouse, mostly boring middle-aged middle-class men, seemed very pleased with naughty Julie, who amused them and the readers by using rude words and having rude views which made them all feel younger and tougher and a bit rude too, like her.

One day little Julie thought she would like to write a book. She decided to write a really rude, really naughty book, not just a bit naughty like lots of books these days. She decided to write about a rude little girl journalist, rather like herself, who was really really successful and really really tough and ambitious. This little girl, whose name was Susan, had a lot of adventures, just like the little girls in children's books who are captured by a wicked king and made to do awful things before they are allowed to get what they want and live happily ever after. The wicked king in Susan's life is her boss Tobias.

The rude things are all to do with you know what, and lots of boys and girls do you know what to Susan and with Susan while Tobias watches, and hopes he can make her cry. If he can make her cry, all her magic will be gone, she will never be editor of his newspaper and he will be able to do whatever he wants with her. He gives everybody lots of magic drinks and magic powders so that they never feel tired. But Susan is such a brave little girl that she really doesn't mind all the nasty dirty things Tobias makes her do, in fact she really rather likes it, in a funny sort of way, so her magic is really stronger than his magic. In fact her magic is so strong that two nasty men, including Tobias, actually *die* while doing you know what with Susan, which Julie seems to think is really funny and serves them right.

Little Julie had fun writing her book, especially because a boring middle-aged middle-class publishing house paid a lot of money for Julie's dirty book because they thought that if they published it they wouldn't seem boring and middle-aged and middle-class any more and lots of people would buy the book and everyone would be even more rich and famous. Some of the people who worked for the publisher were a bit worried about Julie's dirty book because it was not the sort of book they had published before, but a nice new friend of Julie's called Caroline persuaded everybody, including Mr Si Newhouse, who had recently bought the boring old publishers, that it was a really good idea.

Once upon a time there was a boring middle-aged middle-class book reviewer. When she read Julie's dirty book she felt really sad. She was sad because Julie is a clever little girl, and it is always sad when clever people write silly, dirty books to try to make a lot of money. She was also sad because Julie's book makes magic powders and everyone doing you know what to everyone else all over the place seem such fun, whereas in real life, not in fairy stories or dirty books, these things often end in tears. She was saddest of all because she realised that the more she tried to tell people how really disgusting and contemptible Julie's dirty book is, the more likely they are to want to read it. While she was thinking about all this she read in the newspaper that Mr Si Newhouse had decided that the boring old-fashioned publishing house was no good anyway and had waved his magic wand and made it disappear. Alas, he did not make Julie's dirty book disappear at the same time.

8 July 1989

MY FRIEND THE PRIME MINISTER

Patrick Leigh Fermor

Mani

It is always a surprise when a friend is suddenly propelled into the limelight. It has just happened to one of mine in Greece.

About 20 years ago, in the middle of the Colonels' régime, an acquaintance had told me about a Greek captain — one of the best in the Navy, it seemed — who, with a number of others, had resigned his commission the day after the Colonels had seized power. He was promptly arrested, locked up for a time in Attica with like-minded fellow-prisoners and eventually packed off to island-arrest on Kythera, between Crete and the south-east cape of the Peloponnese. His family

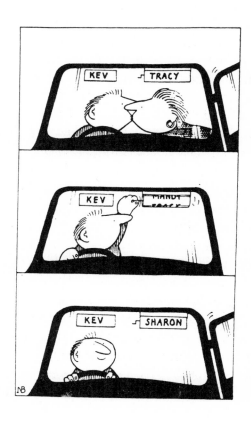

came from the Mani; he was devoted to the region and its spartan inhabitants, and the occasional Maniot fishing-caiques that dropped anchor there would remind him of that mountainous and sea-girt peninsula. His exile lasted three years and half-way through somebody had sent him a book I had written about his wild and unusual homeland.

In the late 18th century, the Mani had become a sort of elective principality under shadowy Ottoman suzerainty but, in reality, so close to total freedom that the bey, as its ruler was called, had reduced the yearly tribute to a single sequin, which, they say, would be tossed to the sultan's messenger from the tip of his scimitar; but, in the late 18th century, the reigning bey was the exiled captain's great-great-grandfather. Tzanni Bey reigned for 14 years, led fierce attacks on Turkish garrisons, and mounted raids on their fleets, and, 30 years before the War of Independence, during the Campagne d'Italie, he exchanged emissaries with Napoleon, in the hopes of combining against the Turks and setting Greece free. He remains a great name in song and story. The book was much concerned with similar figures, the towers they lived in, their customs and their history, and the exiled captain suddenly decided to lighten the tedium of banishment by translating it, which he brilliantly did. After many vicissitudes, he was allowed back in circulation, we met and became friends.

Tzanni Tzannetakis was in his early forties, tall, good-looking, charming and quiet in manner, half naval officer and half scholar. Everything about him was stamped with kindness, intelligence, civilisation and humour. His house among the pinewoods of Kiphisia, where I stayed for days while we checked and revised, was full of books on philosophy, history, poetry and art; he had already published an excellent translation of the Upanishads. He missed his life at sea, where he had been a specialist in submarines; he had studied new techniques and new vessels for a year or two in the United States, and then sailed them back to Greece. The book, when it finally appeared, struck lucky; there were gratifying pats on the back for translator and author; and when the Colonels fell and Karamanlis came to power, he was elected to Parliament and eventually became a very successful minister, first of tourism, then of public works. Now and then he and his wife Maria and their children come to stay in the Mani (where this is being written) and they are sojourns of great delight.

When his New Democracy party won the elections a week ago, the majority over the losing Pasok was too small for a government to be formed and the third runner, the small communist coalition, held the balance. Tzannetakis's leader, Costa Mitsotakis (well-known to British SOE hands in German-occupied Crete for his work in the Resistance), was too old an adversary to be an acceptable team-mate of the Communists in a caretaker government till fresh elections in October; and Andreas Papandreou, because of the scandals which had lost him the election, was equally rejected. Deadlock loomed. It was then that my old friend whom I hadn't seen for a year or so suddenly dominated the scene. Transparently honest, endowed with calm, authority and the gift of inspiring trust, and too young for the fierce post-war conflicts, he was chosen in an inspired moment, and only a few hours after his name was put forward, there he was on every television screen in all the thronged cafés in Greece, surrounded by his rapidly assembled cabinet, being sworn in as Prime Minister with all the candles and incense and ceremony of the Orthodox Church. It was an extraordinary moment, and a hopeful one.

15 July 1989

BRINGING OLIVIER TO BOOK

Mark Amory

'Of course Larry's a gangster,' said a distinguished actress, 'which is why he was so good as Macbeth.' That was all the first-hand information I had on Laurence Olivier when I agreed to help in some unspecified way with his autobiography. With most actors it is necessary to make a conscious effort to banish the effect they have created while speaking other people's lines. In Olivier's case there was no temptation to think I knew him from his roles; they were too various, and it was often said that he was less than the sum of his parts, a blank on which bold colours looked their best. Often too he had agreed.

So it was fitting that when he made his entrance at the exact time and place arranged I failed to recognise the most famous actor in the world – he was shorter, older and more ordinary than I had expected – and he had to introduce himself. We never became completely efficient about meetings or addresses. He called me 'darling' almost immediately to cover the fact that he could not remember my name, which is, I suppose, why theatre people in general use it so much. I could never manage 'Larry', no one said 'Lord Olivier', so under pressure I resorted to 'Sir Laurence', which was simply wrong. The next year I flew to Los Angeles to work with him while he was making one of the big bad films of these years, *The Jazz Singer* this time. He was under no illusion about their merits but he was proud of being the only British actor among his contemporaries whose name still came above the title. When I rang up, he said, 'How delightful to hear your voice, dear boy, you must come and have lunch.' Lunch was pleasant but no work was done. If he really had forgotten, however, the incident was uncharacteristic. Even in an area about which he knew nothing, his approach was rigorously professional. It was just that at that moment he was being a professional actor, not a professional writer.

At the dinner at which Lady Hartwell and Lord Weidenfeld had persuaded him to write a book there had apparently been a suggestion that it would somehow resemble Kenneth Clark's *Civilisation*. I pondered but could see no parallel. There was some preliminary talk about great actors of the past, Garrick, Kean, Irving, etc and I became restive. When I shared my worries with a close friend of his, she said, 'You mean you think you will have trouble getting Larry to talk about himself? I don't think *that* will be your main problem.' Nor was it. We worked sometimes in his Chelsea house, more often in his cottage near Brighton, occasionally in a hotel in Somerset. When I stayed with him I would accompany this frail and scarred man of over 70, who had undergone cancer, thrombosis and muscular dystrophy, on his early morning, naked swim. It was not tact but exhaustion that made me reach for the towel after ten lengths or so and watch while he went on to 25 or even 50. He took lots of pills with some expertise: 'I shall be rather deaf today because I have taken two green ones as my cramp was hurting.' When we were alone he insisted on cooking me breakfast, boiled eggs started in cold water, occasionally forgotten by both of us. The garden and the gardener delighted him. He would learn names in order to reel them off, or so he said. Similarly he had planted a bed with the flowers mentioned in Shakespeare so that he could say

'I know a bank whereon the wild thyme blows,
Where oxlips and the nodding violet grows

it's just round the corner on the right, actually.'

We talked of his life and career all day, whether officially working or not. He enjoyed quoting, acting really, Shakespeare, particularly *Hamlet*. He could be disconcerting, as when he demonstrated what a row with the National Theatre board had been like, his eyes blazing with fury straight into mine, his fist pounding the table. It was hard to know how to react, rather like catching the eye of someone who is laughing at what they hear on the telephone. It was, incidentally, disappointing to hear how little he had enjoyed even the triumphs of the National — it seems to have been a burden from the beginning. He revelled in accents. In *Inchon* (never released for contractual reasons) he played MacArthur and worried that he would be accused of hamming it up though he had in fact acquired rare records that showed that the voice had varied a great deal at different times in MacArthur's life and imitated them exactly. Also in that film, though I think it had been cut, was his rendition of the Lord's Prayer, which he saw as an immense technical problem: how to hold an audience who knew literally word for word what you were going to say next. After gossip, revelation and swear words had gone by unheeded he suddenly gestured at the tape-recorder and said, 'Turn that machine off for a moment.' I did so and leant forward for something sensational. 'For God's sake never repeat this,' he said, 'but [a friend] is simply no good at accents.'

Then he went on holiday, to stay with Sir William Walton in Ischia, and took his typewriter. When he came back he was determined to write every word himself and duly did so. It did not come easily to him and at times he really hated it; typing actually made his fingers bleed. I put nothing in, though I made suggestions and tried to get some things out. There was a particular tussle over his description of someone as a 'preciously valuable' friend. I put forward the view that the words meant much the same and that one, either, would be better than both. He just read the passage again with a hint more bravura and said he liked it as it was. My only success was when I got him to change, 'I peeped open a door,' to, 'I peeped through a door'. A friend said, 'Of course his is much better,' and on reflection I agreed. Some things I left because I could not understand them. Does he mean that he slept with

Noël Coward? I think not, but nearly.

The resulting book is extraordinary and far more interesting, important even, than the anodyne version I could have produced. The faults are glaring but a fascinatingly complicated man is half-revealed, perhaps more than he knew, but there is much in that 'perhaps'. Ronald Bryden writing brilliantly in the *London Review of Books* (September 1988) is the only person to struggle through the prose and the code to the revelations. He decided that guilt was Olivier's chief emotion (Olivier insisted without hesitation on the title, *The Confessions of an Actor*) and Oedipus the part in which he most found himself:

> By knowing greater suffering than any man alive, enacting it publicly for the purgation of the city, the outcast king finally achieves an unearthly peace, his sins forgiven his white hairs by the Gods, in the company of his children.

Unearthly peace may be a bit strong but that was what I saw, whom I met . . . I think.

22 July 1989

HIGH LIFE

ELEGY FOR MY FATHER

Taki

Athens

The only person I lied to when I got busted back in 1984 was my father. He first heard of it through the Greek newspapers and rang me at once. But I told him the stuff had been planted on me. I was too ashamed to tell him otherwise. Not afraid, mind you, but ashamed. He believed me without reservation. Ironically, someone had planted dope on him during the German occupation and then given him away to the

Gestapo, but that had been an obvious plant and he had been released almost immediately.

My father had a terrific Resistance record. He first fought in Albania with courage as an officer in the machine gun corps and then financed and published the chief Resistance underground newspaper throughout the Nazi occupation. He had closed down his textile factories despite German threats, and he was the man who smuggled George Papandreou out of Athens and on to a waiting British submarine so he could head a Greek government-in-exile.

When the constant Anglo-American bombing would terrify me to tears, I still recall him looking disapprovingly at a six-year-old's fear. I vividly remember his coolness under fire, especially during the civil war. When the Reds blew up his factories, he never once complained. It was the bleak winter of 1944 and Athens was one great cemetery. Still, he foraged around and managed to get watches for my brother and me.

After I was thrown out of school in America for being violent, I spent a harrowing three days waiting for him to come and get me. I had seen his temper before and was not looking forward to it. But when he heard the reason for my dismissal, he smiled at me and said, 'I thought you had done something unmanly.' Throughout the next 30 years he complained constantly about my way of life, but continued to support me in style.

Last Friday morning, at 9.30, my mother rang to tell me my father had dropped dead getting out of bed. The news didn't register right away because I was still drunk from the night before. When it did, I broke down for probably the first time in more than 40 years. I was not ashamed to do so, although he would have hated it.

My father had received the two highest decorations the Greek nation has to offer, one for bravery, the other for achievement. He never wore them, just as he never used a broken-down Venetian title his family was given long ago. He left home at 14 because of a dispute with my grandfather. He was self-made and a gentleman of the old school. He took care of my wife as if she was his daughter, and he was a businessman who created jobs, not junk bonds. He had 5,000 workers in the Sudan, hundreds of sailors on his ships and hundreds employed in his hotels.

Ironically, it took me five years to write my prison book because I didn't want to hurt him with the truth. Just as I decided finally to come clean, he passed away. I had been extremely close to him the last ten years, in fact always, and can't remember a day that went by without me thinking of him and being proud. Two days before his death I watched *Voyage Round My Father*, and John Mortimer's words still ring in my ears: about how lonely one feels without a father, and in my case, how unprotected for the first time in my life.

On Monday morning, the Athens heat wave subsided and a cooling breeze helped my aged mother through the funeral ordeal. Once again, I was proud to be his son. The high and mighty all came, including the head of the government and most of parliament. But so did all the men and women who had once worked for him, including those of the fairer sex who frequent the night. There were many speeches. Then he was lowered into the family crypt, next to his German and Italian ancestors, and was gone forever.

22 July 1989

TRYING TO GET THE MAD, BROODY CHICKEN OFF HER ADDLED EGGS

Auberon Waugh

A friend who is not normally receptive to left-wing or republican ideas suddenly exclaimed at dinner in my house the other day that he was bored, sickened and disgusted by the Queen and all the royal family, and thought it was high time they were removed. In the mood of the moment, nobody seemed disposed to disagree, although compassionate noises were made from some quarters about the Queen Mother and the Waleses. In the ensuing discussion, everyone observed that they were not aware of having felt this way before, but agreed that they felt it now – that is to say, at about 9.45 p.m. on Saturday 12 August 1989. There had been nothing to annoy us about the royal family in the news. It traditionally keeps a low profile at this time of year.

There was no reason to attach the slightest importance to this sudden feeling in the company. Apart from the young, whose opinions on most subjects are worthless and two of whom, on this occasion, were in any case French, the company consisted of industrious, successful people in their forties, none of them within twitching distance of the levers of power. Nor did any of the company attach much importance to their change of heart.

Goodness knows how my friend Wallace Arnold would have reacted, had he been present (he is not the sort of person one has ever yet actually asked to dinner), but my own reaction was to enquire why this change of heart had come about. There seemed to be a general feeling that the royal family had been around long enough; there were too many of them; there was too much about them in the newspapers and magazines; they exercised a generally stultifying influence on the country. More particularly, there seemed to be a feeling among the successful, industrious people in their forties that they had achieved what they had achieved in life without the slightest help from royal quarters, which had never acknowledged their existence by so much as a nod or a wink, let alone a medal for industry or general respectability and taxpaying. Those who did qualify for some mark of royal approval were enjoying an unfair advantage. The whole circus was a faintly hostile irrelevance.

I wonder if similar feelings go any way to explain the almost universal loathing in which Mrs Thatcher is now held in her own party and throughout the upper reaches of the country. It is certainly not that the country has rejected Thatcherism, or thinks that more should be done for the poor, the ill, the mad in our midst. Most aspects of Thatcherism are now firmly rooted in the national consensus. Liverpool and all who live in it are now the great laughing stock of the country. For all of which we should be grateful. But even as the country has accepted the major tenets of Thatcherism, it repudiates Thatcher with increasing vehemence.

If there is an element of personal disappointment among the motives for this, we must admit it as unworthy and extremely ridiculous, but nobody should be frightened of looking ridiculous in the search for Truth. It is true that in ten years of power and unfettered discretion in these matters Mrs Thatcher has never asked me to lunch. She has never offered St Peregrine de Worsthorne the knighthood he so richly deserves. She has never even let it be known that she quite enjoyed my last joke but eight about Roy Hattersley, let alone asked us both to help save the nation from modern poetry, universal illiteracy and the Green Death. After ten years it is plain she is never going to do any of these things. It is time for a change. Step forward Sir Geoffrey Howe.

But however much one may convince oneself by scrupulous examination of conscience that one's own motives are less than totally pure, nobody can seriously suppose that many people outside the tiny circle of her own backbenchers share these lunatic fantasies and subsequent disappointments. Disgust with Thatcher is, as I say, almost universal in the upper reaches of British society, and I refuse to believe that it can be explained by anxiety about the effects of poll tax on the poorer classes, or privatisation of water. At times, it seems to boil down to little more than personal dislike. But she has always been disliked and it has never before persuaded anyone that she was not the best person to lead the Conservative Party into the next election.

I think that the reason this dislike has now crystallised into permanent loathing is that people have begun to see her obstinate determination to lead her party to defeat as the greatest obstacle to their future serenity. Poll tax may be the prime cause, and it seems extraordinary that nobody in the Conservative Party realised how unpopular it would prove among their own supporters. But poll tax could be dropped even now at this late stage, and the feeling would remain in the upper reaches of the country that Thatcher has lost her touch: she no longer communicates, like mastodon calling to mastodon across the primaeval swamp, with our typical *Sun* reader in all his endearingly greedy, halfwitted and revolting tastes and prejudices. She quite simply gets it wrong every time.

Perhaps the last time she got it right was when she sent in an assassination squad to gun down suspected terrorists in Gibraltar. How we all cheered! Good old Maggie, that's the way to deal with them! The only way to meet terrorism is with terrorism. It is all they understood. That incident may have been the one that convinced me she was not a fit person to run the country, but everyone has had a different sticking point, and everyone has been confirmed in it on numerous occasions since. Perhaps the miscalculation which is most potent of all, and will become more evident as 1992 approaches, is over Europe.

No doubt a majority of the *Sun* readership, if asked, would declare a preference for being bossed by the British Government over being bossed by a bureaucracy based in Brussels, but the truth is that practically nobody gives a fig for British sovereignty. It is something which has no application to their lives or aspirations. The EEC is seen as a great opportunity; the prospect of open frontiers and cheaper booze is all that is left in our spiritually inert age of the prospect of heaven. Nobody but Mrs Thatcher and her cronies cares about the easier movement of drugs and terrorists across frontiers within the Common Market. Those who take an intelligent interest in current affairs would welcome the adoption of a French legal system, based on the inquisitorial rather than the adversarial approach. People are fed up with such of our ancient institutions as are incompetent, unjust, hideously expensive and ultimately cruel, like the law. For every criminal sent to prison for far too long in revolting conditions, two or three get off scot free. The year 1992 offers adventure, change and renewal. Mrs Thatcher threatens to sit on it like a mad, broody hen on addled eggs. The terror is that by behaving like the cat in the adage, Howe will leave it too late to get rid of her before the next general election. Early may fly the Babylonian woe!

19 August 1989

'It's the future of modern architecture — all the amenities on the outside of the building.'

THE BEGGING-BOWL

C. H. Sisson

It cannot matter much how I grew up,
Housed in this body which is now so thin
A parapet for me to lean upon.
Fall I must: and with me will go down
The entire empire of my former days.
Look, sun, upon my last, and so you be
The Light which made the world, I have my part.
It is a public country that I want
And so indeed it was, the world I had,
Growing from nothing to the edge of doom.
But what was in between?
The hope and love I had in fields and moors,
In hills, in waters lashing on the coast.
The coast of where? And where but you,
  O England,
Which name has gathered all my hopes and loves.
Changed like a dream, the land which never was
And yet to which I gave my dearest wish
Which contained all the wishes that I had,
The contents of my begging-bowl, perhaps,
Into which time had thrown so many things,
So many persons, a few held most dear,
A many who had helped to make them so,
Whether as tributary to the stream of time
Or as companions as I swam along,
Given rather than chosen: it is as a gift
We love those whom we love, and not by choice,
For choice is but our own, and what we love
Is other, other which we inly crave,
Not to be what we are and who we are
Which is the nothing which we brought with us,
The nothing that we take out of the world.

19 August 1989

RESTAURANT

STICKY FINGERS

Nigella Lawson

Your modern pop singer is essentially a businessman. Any cash left over after the accountants and the cocaine dealers have been paid off goes into unit trusts, pension funds and water shares. Bill Wyman, the Rolling Stone more recently famous as sagging groom to a leggy child-bride, Mandy Smith, is of a gentler, Aquarian age, when it was the duty of a conscientious rocker to give something back to his people. What Bill has now given us is a café restaurant in Kensington.

Like others of its kind Sticky Fingers is what the marketing men are pleased to call a theme restaurant. Except that the only theme here is the owner himself, and so, as if this were the bedroom of some Stones-fanatical teenager, we eat against walls decked with the signs of Jaggerophilia. Here is a collection of Stones posters, circa 1972, there a newspaper clipping showing Wyman at his Sixties toothiest. In the middle of the longest wall is, encased in glass, the *very guitar* that Bill inadvertently forgot to smash during that unforgettable concert in Hyde Park — or at Shea Stadium or the Marquee or somewhere.

Wyman is justly proud of his achievements as a musician: not only do the walls serve to remind us of almost three decades of raunchily revamped 12-bar blues, but the menu is there to follow the memory through. Bill is no longer a young man, but he can still remember quite a bit of many of the numbers he helped make famous. You toked along to *Goat's Head Soup*? Well here's Goat's Head Gumbo, a fishy, chickeny, prawny stew and, writes Bill, 'almost a meal in itself' which is probably true if your idea of a balanced diet is a pre-gig bottle of Scotch and a couple of joints. You got on down with 'Jumpin' Jack Flash'? Now eat to the beat with Jumpin' Jack Flesh: 'Cajun popcorn ... crispy peppery crayfish bits with a hot mustard dip' and with, mmmmm, that unforgettable Student Union taste of left-over fish cakes. You get the idea.

But for all that the Wyman motif is emblazoned over everything motif-able, the restaurant itself could be the product of, let us say, a used car trader with fond memories of a patchouli-scented night in 1969 and some liquid dosh to invest in a burger bar. The floor is from the stripped-pine catalogue: the overabundance of tables, pattern-book, mahogany-stained, semi-rustic. Change the posters on the walls and rejig the menu and the place could equally convincingly be La Bamba ('Capture That Tex-Mex Mood of Richie Valens with Good-Time Guacamole') or even Henry Hall's ('the English Eaterie where we *always* say, "Here's to The Next Time" ').

The youngsters seemed to like it, though, or, as Bill had it (and if Bill didn't have it it just wasn't haveable), 'The Kids are Alright'. Not that any of the customers seemed old enough to remember Bill at his peak. Indeed, I doubt if many of them were up to much more than gurgling when 'Brown Sugar' came out; and the party of pre-teens noisily

wolfing birthday hamburgers at a long table were strictly of the Kylie Minogue generation. The canned music didn't help to rekindle what dormant Stone-age memories any of us had: it was solid Tamla all night long.

Regular readers will by now have noticed that I have not undertaken my usual encomium on the subject of the food. This is simply because there's not much to say. In his years with the Stones, Bill has travelled the world: Japan, Europe, Australia, the States. If his interest in food has led him to collect exotic recipes on his travels, then it doesn't show here: translated, the menu reads: burgers, steaks, chicken, chilli, salad and sticky puddings. I had the spare ribs, which in all honesty made up half the ribby complement of a single baby pig and lay glutinously across my plate like something from *The Flintstones*. When I had eaten my fill there were still some dozen ribs spare.

Why do I bring you this intelligence? Partly it's because the theme restaurant is where much of the high street catering business is going nowadays, and I feel some of you need to know what you're missing. The main reason, though, is that I recently received a note from a young reader whose name I would give you if I hadn't thrown his letter away. 'Why is it', he wrote (as far as I remember), 'that *The Spectator* offers a special student discount on its cover price, but never mentions restaurants to which a student would want to go?' Sticky Fingers, gentle reader, is why. And anyway, at £32 for two – including a couple of cocktails but no wine – you should be spending your grant cheque more productively.

19 August 1989

'The waterhole at sunset, then? A few drinks, a few laughs?'

NEW LIFE

BINGO GETS IT RIGHT

Zenga Longmore

'It's definitely a boy because your belly hangs downwards and goes into a point.'

Now be honest. How many times have you been stopped in the street to hear that one? Just three weeks ago, it seemed that someone was waylaying me at least once every five minutes to divine the sex of my unborn child in many and varied ways. There seems to be something about pregnancy that encourages people to become prophets, just as newborn babies spur people's memories to generations back. What baby doesn't have its great-great-uncle's chin, and the hairline of an aunt from a bygone era?

Old men in bus queues would tap me on the shoulder to whisper that they knew it was a boy by the way I was leaning on my right leg; the left, presumably, meant a girl. Women pushing prams used to call me over to the other side of the road. Thinking they were in urgent need of help with the baby or shopping, I'd waddle across, only to hear a great long speech about their friends and relations whose tummy stuck out at the side or the front in exactly the same way mine did, and that meant a boy. Because my nieces have reached the tantrum age and would hurl themselves around in fits of rage whenever I approached them, my relatives would nod to one another, muttering that little girls never take too kindly to women who are carrying boys.

Only Mrs Wright, the wise old woman from the ninth floor, pooh-poohed all the nonsense about right legs, and tummies going up, down and sideways. 'The only way to tell', she insisted, 'is to hold a needle over your head, and if it spins clockwise [or anti-clockwise, I can't remember] then mark my words, a boy 't will be. This must only be done on a Friday at nine o'clock, when the moon is full and bright.'

I told her I'd heard that it only worked when the father of the child was spinning the needle.

'No, no,' she grumbled, 'that's just superstition.'

The needle spun clockwise (or anti-clockwise).

Even Olumba, dear trusted Olumba, predicted a boy, 'because you have become so much more masculine of late. All your femininity has been swallowed up by the male presence within you.' I told Olumba at the time that there was no need for that sort of talk. You see, I knew it was going to be a boy. All the old wives' tales in the world and even new-fangled technology have nothing on the deep, primaeval instinct of a mother. I could feel the boyishness of the baby's movements. I could even picture the boy vividly in my mind's eye. He was very dark and burly, a cross between a mini-Frank Bruno and a Greek fisherman.

Clawhammer Jones Bingo was the only one to be contrary. Clawhammer, who sells bush tea in the local market, takes a special interest in childbirth. He has seven children and so thinks of himself as somewhat of an expert. 'It a girl pickney for true,' he pronounced. 'Only girl pickney dem give the mother such a long sour face.' Everyone, of course, just laughed at him.

Imagine my amazement when a delicate, doe-eyed little girl was held up for my inspection. The nurses, who had all predicted a boy by my staunch attitude during labour, practically dropped her with the shock — maybe that's what's known as a midwife crisis.

It only goes to show that nature does not give away tell-tale signs regarding the sex of the child. It's meant to come as a surprise, and what better surprise could I have than seeing my little Omalara for the first time.

9 September 1989

HOW TO SPEND MONEY LIKE
WATER AND MAKE US DISLIKE
WATER

Christopher Fildes

Eggs used to come with little lions stamped on them and shopkeepers would be prosecuted for scrubbing them off. The lion was the badge of the British Egg Marketing Board, which placed large advertisements intended to endear it. 'There's a lion on your egg!' Customers, though, concluded that an egg with a lion on it had been sitting in a warehouse, but a lionless egg might be fresh. So out came the Brillo pads, off came the lions, and in marched the inspectors to enforce the Egg Control Order or whatever. Rare indeed is the promotion campaign which, like the eggmen's, contrives a positive aversion from the product – though Watneys came close with Red Barrel – and rarer the campaign enforced by prosecution. The water campaign may be one. Torquay's local water board, or, as it would now call itself, the water and sewage business, took an elderly paying customer to court the other day for watering his tree. That sits a little awkwardly with the watermen's campaign, on which they seem to be spending some £22 million, to show us that (a) they exist (b) they are splendid fellows (c) water costs money. I can't see what else it is for, since the watermen tell us it is nothing to do with the Government's privatisation campaign, which by coincidence is coming shortly. For that, I hear, one of the slogans proposed is 'Water floats'. Water, by definition, does not float. A better slogan for share-pushing would be 'Water bubbles'. No doubt the water-sellers are in a hurry, for already their successors are treading on their heels, as a group of power stations takes prime time on television to play a souped-up version of 'I vow to thee, my country'. I suppose we shall soon be told that this has nothing to do with privatisation, either. Over these campaigns hangs a weary air of selling by rote – the identity campaign, the soft sell, the blockbuster, the hard sell, the clip-out coupon – the sequence is routine now and can be used to sell anything from water to atomic weaponry. Just add money, as the watermen do not quite say. They should try adding respect. As for their product, I suspect there is a lion on it.

2 September 1989

DON'T DROWN IT

Christopher Fildes

The water-sellers, whose saturation campaign now drips all around us, should call up the spirit of Mr Macquiston, KC. He could show them where they have gone wrong. My father tells me that this eminent lawyer, who was standing counsel to the distillery industry, found himself on some public occasion called upon to speak in praise of water. He did so with an eloquence which puts today's cheapjack slogans to shame, conjuring up the images of water in its myriad guises. 'I have seen tears', said Mr Macquiston, 'glistening on the slumbering lid of infancy. I have seen tears flowing down the blushing cheek of youth. I have seen tears coursing the rugged face of age. I have seen the raging torrent, crashing like a mass of silver upon a bed of diamonds. I have seen the mighty ocean, bearing upon its bosom the commerce of continents and the natives of the world.' He paused. 'But, gentlemen,' he continued, 'having said all this, in my opinion, water, as a beverage, is a bloody failure.'

9 September 1989

HESELTINE'S LEAN AND HUNGRY LOOK

Dominic Lawson

A plush new car had – to my surprise – met me at the station when I came to have lunch with Michael Heseltine. It was in fact one of the better sort of minicabs, spotless and with a cordless telephone. But when, as it deposited me at the door of Mr Heseltine's 17th century Palladian mansion, Thenford House, I took out my wallet, the driver waved it aside, saying, 'I'm sure it will all be taken care of, Sir.'

As the car had half-completed the winding return journey down the

Heseltine drive, it rounded my benefactor. I suppose it is some sort of a tribute to Michael Heseltine that he must still be the only British politician, even after three and a half years of exile, who is recognisable to the naked eye at a distance of two hundred yards. Then the unmistakable figure began shouting: 'Dominic! Dominic! Come here! Come on!' I thought this behaviour to a complete stranger overfamiliar, even rude, so I stood my ground.

'Hello,' said Mr Heseltine when he eventually arrived at his front door – 'I'm Michael Heseltine, and this' – he indicated a long-haired dachshund panting behind him – 'this is Dominic. Dominic, say hello to Dominic.' I think he was talking to the dog. Either way, Mr Heseltine had elegantly demonstrated the Art of Taking The Initiative in a Meeting by Disconcerting The Other Side at The Outset.

Once inside, Mr Heseltine disappeared to remove his Wellington boots. Later I realised that they could have been carefully chosen to match the nature of the occasion: on my way to the lavatory I wandered through a large room which seemed to contain nothing but about fifty pairs of Wellington boots, a collection of which Imelda Marcos would have been proud.

Heseltine re-emerged shod in black velvet shoes with gold buckles. I am told this is the way all wealthy publishers dress. Whether they, too, wear figure-hugging jeans is more doubtful. This was clearly Mr Heseltine in relaxed holiday mood. Even so, our lunch was in the main dining room, served by a white-jacketed flunkey. Mr Heseltine sat at the head of a vast dining table, more suitable for a full assembly of cabinet ministers than for one ex-minister and a journalist.

We looked out at a lake, on which I complimented the owner. 'Good,' said Heseltine. 'I built that.' So I complimented him on the far horizon as well. 'I don't own the view,' Heseltine owned up. 'But I get on well with the farmer who does, so that's OK.'

As we munched through our steaks (good meat, overcooked) I pointed out to Heseltine that in his days as a property developer in the 1960s he would have covered such a vista with rows of bright new houses. Surprisingly, he took the ribbing seriously. 'I think you will find,' he chewed thoughtfully, 'if you look at my time as a property man, that I never built on green-field sites. Never. I may have bought and sold them, but that is another matter.' (How careful must the future politician be, to do nothing in his business career, however rational, which might subsequently look bad in an election manifesto!)

The dining room was covered with rare and gaudy paintings, some of which pulled away to reveal themselves as parts of doors painted on both sides. But nothing which graced the table was as odd as the silver salt and pepper grinders, the one cast in the image of Gladstone, the other as Disraeli.

We took coffee in the drawing room, ablaze with gilt and matching everything, right down to MH footstools. Before I began to point my tape recorder at him, Heseltine suddenly said, 'You know, I never get cross. Never.' At this point Dominic sent a careful array of fire pieces crashing noisily to the floor. That, it is true, did not disturb Mr Heseltine's good humour. But it was an odd remark to make, unprovoked. I suppose Mr Heseltine is only too aware that the famous 'Mace' affair, and his sudden storming out of the Cabinet, have given people the idea that he is a man who is too uncontrollable to be trusted with the job of, say, Prime Minister. 'I can't believe you are never cross,' I replied. 'Perhaps you mean that you are just very skilled at controlling your temper.' This was a proposition which Mr Heseltine readily endorsed.

How badly does Mr Heseltine want to be Prime Minister? It is a Critchleyism – a fact about Michael Heseltine to which Mr Julian Critchley has given currency and which is both plausible and unsubstantiated – that as an undergraduate he had worked out a life's career which was to be consummated with the prime ministership at the age of 55. The first part of that programme – the attainment of sufficient wealth to live in both politics and comfort simultaneously – had, if anything, been overfulfilled. But Mr Heseltine has seen his 56th birthday come and go. . . .

'It does at least appear', I said to Mr Critchley's golden goose, 'that you are single-mindedly running an American presidential primary style campaign for the leadership, speaking at every constituency in the land, to endless small meetings. . . .'

'Big meetings, *if* you don't mind.'

'Sorry . . . endless big meetings, boosting the funds and the morale of the local constituency parties so that, one day, you can call in the IOUs, and collect the votes of the grateful MPs in a leadership election.'

'Neither they nor I see it in those terms. The day I left the Government – within a matter of hours – I made my plan for the future. I decided to respond to whatever the Conservative Party had in mind for me. What did they have in mind for me? A very large number of invitations. After that . . . who knows what else? At the moment it is like being in opposition: you have no power, so you try to influence people, to argue a case which others come round to accept, or not, as the case may be.'

I told Mr Heseltine that nothing he had said had convinced me that he was not running an expensive American-style, long-drawn-out run for office. He tried again: 'I reject your analysis. It's true Reagan did something like this after he was defeated by Ford in his 1976 Presidential campaign. But he was only doing what Churchill did in the 1930s. There's nothing American about it. It's what politicians do if they find themselves outside the mainstream of their party at a particular time. Then they have to rely on the grass roots of the party for continued support and recognition. I can see no other way in which one could remain a national politician.'

A less ambitious politician would probably have contented himself with waging a campaign for change through the agency of a disaffected member of the Cabinet. Surely, I asked Mr Heseltine, there are one or two remaining members of the Government he admired? 'It wouldn't be fair to them to single them out for praise,' said Heseltine, roaring with laughter at the thought of what such a pronouncement would do to the victim's chances of promotion.

Clearly Mr Heseltine is a great frustration to those who would enjoy a rematch between him and Mrs Thatcher, on the scale of their Westland set-to. He is just careful enough to bide his time, and wait for the optimum moment to strike.

For example he studiously made no criticism of Mrs Thatcher's apparent anti-Europeanism during the European elections, even though he is as passionate a supporter of the European ideal as Ted Heath, who showed no such reluctance. 'I could have made big headlines then,' admitted Mr Heseltine, 'but the biggest headline is always the last headline. I don't want the last headline. You don't if you want a future in politics. Which I suppose I have.'

So for the time being the only headlines which Mr Heseltine is generating are those making up the chapter headings in his books. First there was *Where There's a Will* and then a book on the importance of European unity, curiously subtitled *Can Britain win?* Given the known fact of Mr Heseltine's mild dyslexia, I asked him whether or not it would be true to say of his books that it would be unfair to criticise them, because one doesn't know who wrote them. 'Well, not even my best friends would call me bookish − I had a lot of help,' Mr Heseltine conceded.

Having read the books, I was stunned by the extent of Mr Heseltine's corporatist and interventionist views, although I would not go as far as one ex-Cabinet colleague who described him to me as 'Bennite'. Chapters 4 and 5 of *Where There's a Will* − 'Who's for Laissez-faire?' and 'Industry: a Strategy' − are particularly eye-opening. In the latter, Mr Heseltine gives as concise a summary of the corporatist's manifesto as could be imagined: 'The capitalist system works best when owners, managers, employees and government understand a common interest and work as a team to that end.' This follows shortly after the insight that 'it is not intervention that is wrong ... What was wrong (with intervention) before was the subsidising of losses and the cosiness and lack of professionalism associated with that. Intervention and feather-bedding are not the same. The trick is to distinguish between them.'

So who is the industrial genius who will know in advance when Government aid would result only in the subsidy of a loss-making enterprise (such as Inmos, the ill-fated Callaghan Government plan for a state-funded microchip manufacturer), and which would be crowned with success (I couldn't think of an example here)? Would it be Prime Minister Heseltine? Ex-Cabinet Minister Heseltine waved aside my question: 'Such decisions are made by civil servants every day.' A case of the man in Whitehall knowing best? Not if that means the man in the Treasury apparently: 'The country is dominated by the Treasury and there are malign effects which flow from that. We need a much stronger Department of Trade and Industry,' Heseltine told me.

I pointed out that we have heard all of this before from Mr Wilson in the 1960s, right down to the creation of the Department of Economic Affairs, with which George Brown was charged to counter the 'malign effect' of the Treasury.

'Yes, you have heard language like this before. There aren't that many new ideas − it's a question of whether you can carry them out effectively.'

'So, you want to resurrect old ideas, but just implement them more skilfully?'

'Wilson and Brown came up with these ideas, but made a mess of them, because they weren't tough with industry. But don't throw the baby out with the bathwater.'

But what does it mean to be tough with industry, in the Heseltine style? I think I know. Earlier, while we were slurping through our home-made chocolate mousse, Heseltine reminisced about his days as a Parliamentary Secretary at the Department of Transport. The electronic signals on the motorways were not working well. GEC, then in its heyday as bespoke supplier of electrical services to the nation, was the manufacturer of the offending items. So, to his civil servants' apparent amazement, young Heseltine summoned the great Weinstock to his office, to tell him that something had to be done about the flickering signals. Weinstock duly arrived with all the responsible line management in tow, and, as I understood the story, the result was that in future the lights on the motorways shone clear and bright. So perhaps this is the difference between the Harold Wilson brand of interventionism, and its new improved version with Michael Heseltine in charge: under Wilson the trade union leaders were constantly being summoned for beer and sandwiches at Number Ten. Under PM

'*Brian threw out the remote control gadget to encourage a more active retirement.*'

Heseltine the nation's *industrialists* would constantly be having working lunches in Downing Street.

Just as Wilson's and Brown's fetish for planning was inspired by admiration of foreign experiences, notably the French, so Heseltine is inspired, as his book *The Challenge of Europe* makes clear, by the greater industrial cohesiveness, as he sees it, of our European rivals. But, I asked Heseltine, did the British voters' small turnout at the recent European elections suggest that the public shares his intense interest and support for Europeanism? His answer was both odd and characteristic:

'You explain otherwise why there's not a newspaper left on the street which isn't pro-Europe or moving that way. That's because their market research *shows* that the public won't buy anti-Europeanism any more. That's what they tell me. I had lunch the other day with Nick Lloyd, the Editor of the *Daily Express*, who said, "I've just come from my marketing people who say we just can't do this any more." '

'Does that represent the popular endorsement you are looking for?'

'It's as hard-headed an endorsement as I can produce. If every newspaper in Fleet Street is pro-Europe, or moving that way, it represents very big commercial interests.'

I could not help feeling that Mr Heseltine was applying his commercial publisher's mind to the rather wider issue of the national will. But then the independence of his political outlook is directly attributable to his success in publishing. Having control of a company – Haymarket Publishing – worth an estimated £100m has given Mr Heseltine the courage of his convictions in a way peculiar in modern British politics, though commonplace a century ago.

'It must have been relatively easy for you to resign, knowing that the chauffeur-driven ministerial limousine could simply be replaced by one out of your own pocket.'

'Absolutely.'

I suggested that Mr Heseltine's personal wealth was fundamental to his ability to sustain his political influence, financing, for example, the use of a helicopter during the European elections.

'Exactly. What chance otherwise do you have in a monopoly party after you have resigned? It's the little star up there looking after me. I have all the options in the world.'

But is there a different star looking over Mr Heseltine? I just had to ask him: 'Do you think you would have had a less successful political career if you had been a brunette?'

Mr Heseltine looked appalled, though whether it was at the thought of what it must be like without a mane of blond hair, or at the impertinence of the question, I was not sure.

'I've no idea . . . really.'

'But would you have had such a hold over the ladies at the Tory conferences if you had been five foot four with a pot belly and mousy hair?'

'You're talking about Iain MacLeod. Look, there is a lot of nonsense about me being the darling of the blue rinse brigade. There is greater admiration for me among men than women.'

'How do you know?'

'It's always been clear to me from the attendances at my meetings.'

Whatever one makes of that as an analysis of the sexual breakdown of Heseltinian support, there is no doubt that with one woman in particular Mr Heseltine has no chance of gaining preferment.

I was sorry that I could not persuade even such an experienced subject of the political interview to come up with a ringing – or even a faintly tinkling – denunciation of the Prime Minister. But a treat was in store for me after we had finished talking. Before I left Thenford House I went to the lavatory. Actually it was – typical Heseltine – a commode, with a wonderful view of the gardens. But it was not that which drew my attention. It was the hardboard black and white cut-out of Mrs Thatcher's face, from whose open mouth streamed the lavatory paper.

16 September 1989

THE SUITS   *Michael Heath*

DIARY

Alan Rusbridger

Mr Kelvin MacKenzie, the editor of the *Sun*, is, contrary to many expectations, a rather private man who, to my knowledge, has only given two interviews in the whole of his editorial career. So it was unusual, at the least, for him to invite four journalists to lunch this week and engage in free discussion about his paper. He had seen the error of his ways, he told them over the meal. *Sun* journalists now double, double, double checked their stories. 'Whereas we might have been happy with two people's word, now we need 22 people.' The lunch was ostensibly to celebrate the impending 20th anniversary of Rupert Murdoch's buying the paper (who remembers the time when its staff included Dennis Potter, Nancy Banks Smith, Posy Simmonds and Frank Johnson? Not, I should say, me) and the impending book in celebration, *Sunsation*. His lunch guests suspected it might have more to do with his desire to get a mea culpa on the record in the year of the million pound libel settlement and various parliamentary attempts to muzzle the MacKenzie style of bonk journalism. The *Guardian*'s media correspondent, Georgina Henry, said after the lunch that she had found MacKenzie to be extremely funny and that she had laughed a lot, which she supposed was vaguely reprehensible. I know the feeling. I buy the *Sun* every day and am constantly catching myself smiling at the contents or reading bits out to my wife over breakfast. That, of course, is part of the paper's brilliance – why something like half the adult population are *Sun* readers. Once you laugh, they've got you.

One of Mrs Thatcher's most acute realisations, back in the mid-Seventies, was that the *Sun*, and not the *Times* or the *Telegraph*, was the most important paper in the country. If the *Sun* must take much of the blame for creating the lager lout, it must also take much of the credit or blame for creating Mrs Thatcher. Theirs is a symbiotic relationship built on simplicity, bluntness, and pretty ruthless Little Englishness.

My favourite MacKenzie story concerns the reporter who approached him with a plan for a trifle unlikely *Sun* campaign to get rid of Sir Nicholas Goodison as Chairman of the Stock Exchange. MacKenzie, ever the doughty guardian of the people, demanded to know on what grounds. The reporter considered the complexities of the matter for a while and decided to tell the boss in terms he would immediately comprehend: 'Basically, Kelvin . . . the man's a c—.' MacKenzie immediately grasped the point. 'Oh well, if he's a c—, let's get 'im.' Sir Nicholas resigned shortly thereafter.

This week's edition of *The War Cry*, the Salvation Army paper, examines Neil Kinnock's remark after escaping from a fatal road accident in Ireland that 'Somebody up there likes me.' The writer, Molly Blythe, wonders (a) why Mr Kinnock, a non-believer, should think such a thing and (b) whether this implies that Somebody up there didn't like his driver, Mr Tom Conlon, who, you may recall, died. These seem reasonable questions. But Miss Blythe concludes: 'But I do believe that God has a place for Neil Kinnock in his plans . . . I am sure that it is God's will that he should be saved.' So where *does* that leave Mr Conlon?

Ever since falling victim to a somewhat hostile book review by her some time ago, I have taken a mild interest in the career of Miss Julie Burchill. I have watched her progress from mid-market Glenda Slag through mid-market Jackie Collins to − last week − writer of concerned letters to the *Independent*. The subject of Julie's concern was an article by the paper's esteemed columnist, Peter Jenkins, whom Julie described as 'hopelessly ignorant'. Jenkins has apparently exercised his hopeless ignorance on Enoch Powell and his views about race. It was perfectly clear, said Julie, that Enoch had been right all those years ago when he warned of foaming rivers. Most *Independent* readers will not, I suspect, have known that Julie has long taken a concerned and knowledgeable interest in race. Myself, I treasure an interview she gave to *New Musical Express* back in May 1986 in which she was asked to defend her description of Arabs as, how should one put it, people who take an unusual carnal interest in camels. Julie said she just didn't like Arabs, that was all there was to it. But would she not disapprove of people who were racist about blacks or Jews? 'People who hate blacks and Jews tend to be very stupid people,' she purred. 'Very intelligent people hate Arabs.'

23 September 1989

GARDENS

GLITTERING PRIZES

Ursula Buchan

After more than 15 years, I can still recall the shame and disappointment of being the only girl to leave school without a prize — not even the Low Tackle Shield or that poisoned chalice, the Effort Cup. Yet last year it was my children who felt shame and disappointment when I lost the Mothers' Race by slowing down, when well in front, for fear of seeming too eager to win.

I decided then it was time to hone my competitive edge, worn blunt in the intervening years. It is a bit late for me to become a bond dealer, which is why I found myself in early August sitting in the front passenger seat of the car, clutching a decapitated plastic lemonade bottle full of water and sweet pea stems, on the way to enter the 'Four Vases of Three Stems' class at a local show.

All the long, hot, dry summer I had toiled over the sweet pea plants, grown specially for exhibition by the 'cordon' method, that is, tied individually to eight-foot bamboo canes. My evenings were taken up pinching out sideshoots, second leaves and tendrils, to keep the plants as single stems, and watering, endlessly watering. It was a bad summer to grow show sweet peas and an even worse one to take the decision not to use insecticides in the garden. The rest of my spare time was therefore spent squeezing the fat bodies of greenfly in the (forlorn, as it turned out) hope of halting the spread of debilitating virus.

By mid-July I had taken to scanning the plants for sturdy long shoots holding well-placed flowers, but lack of water at the roots meant that the stems were pitifully short and, despite much time spent tying likely candidates loosely to their canes, they were also rather bent. I consoled myself, as exhibitors have since the world began, with the thought that my rivals would be in much the same boat, although I suspected that the man who always won (and who, this year, took the sweet pea cups at Peterborough and Oundle as well) buried dead donkeys in his sweet pea trench in winter. Invited to see his flowers some days before the show, I almost regretted that my entry card was already in the post.

On discovering that I possessed no proper, green, wasp-waisted show vases in which to put my flowers, my rival generously lent me four of his and even went to the lengths of filling them with 'Oasis', leaving two holes into which sweet pea leaves could be inserted to set off the flowers.

The evening before the show, I took a bucket of water up to the cordons and picked the best of what seemed, to my jaundiced eye, a depressingly short, virus-flecked, sun-scorched collection of stems, many of which had three rather than four flowers. I put them in the bucket up to their necks and set it in a cool shed near a window so that, I hoped, the pollen beetle would decamp overnight. Some hope.

Arriving at the village hall in early morning, I prepared the vases outside in the warm sunshine. Although I had brought plenty of 'spares', there were only just enough good 'blooms'. They had been cut too late, when they were already fully out, and it was hard to find ones which were not going past their best. I selected three each of the four varieties and carefully pushed their stems into the Oasis, in the shape of a fan: 'Terry Wogan', 'Red Arrow', 'Hunters Moon' and 'Black Prince'. The vases were placed on the green hessian staging, under the stare of long-dead football teams, between 'Floral Art' and gladioli.

It was three o'clock in the afternoon before the show opened after the judging. Propped up against one of my vases was a blue card — second prize. Later, at the end of the show, I went to give my amiable and victorious friend his vases back. He refused them, saying that if I kept them, he would have some competition next year. Did he mean enough to spur him on, but not quite enough to win? He may not have realised that, in the period of waiting, I discovered that I minded. The edge is back — razor sharp.

23 September 1989

GOODBYE TO BERLIN

Michael Freedland

Two songs written by Irving Berlin seem to sum up the man better than all the other 3,000 he produced in the 101 years that ended last week: 'I Love a Piano' and 'All Alone — by the Telephone'.

By chance, on the day he and I spoke, those two songs seemed to come together perfectly. We had a mammoth telephone conversation, Irving — then in his mid-eighties — telling me how that very day he had given the Smithsonian Institute, in Washington, the piano on which he had 'written' most of his colossal output. I put 'written' in quotation marks, because writing was the one thing he could never do; writing music, that is. He couldn't play the piano either — except on the black notes in the key of F-Sharp. But the old upright had loyally seen him through. He called it his 'Buick' and he took it with him everywhere he went, a much-abused cigarette-stained instrument that was fitted with a lever with which he changed key, much as a driver shifts gear on a car. He thumped out his songs on the Buick's keyboard and a secretary took down the notes, like a stenographer taking a letter.

'I'm very proud of that piano,' he told me. 'I couldn't have written anything without it.' Occasionally, he felt guilty about that, but not for long. 'I've never bothered very much with the science of music. One time, I decided to take lessons. Then I thought that, heck, I could have written a couple of songs in the two days I was wasting there.'

He knew I was writing a book about him — I had sent him a letter asking for an interview both for it and a BBC Radio Two programme I was doing at the same time. I told him I appreciated his kindness in agreeing to talk to me. 'How could I refuse when you wrote me such a nice letter?' he asked. I told him I meant it. 'I'm sure you do,' he replied, 'but I don't want a book ... I bet you don't know how I started?'

I asked for confirmation. Surely, he wasn't really born in Siberia? 'Certainly, I was,' he replied. 'We weren't all convicts there, you know.' Then, once more, 'No books please. I'll see that you get all my papers, after I die, but not now. ... Incidentally, did you know that London went crazy for "Alexander's Ragtime Band" ... ?'

And that was how our conversation went on. He didn't want it recorded, and the engineers at the BBC's New York studios at Rockefeller Center dutifully turned off all the machines – much, I am ashamed to say, to my frequent subsequent regret. He had promised me ten minutes. He spoke for more than an hour, perhaps an hour and a half. He liked the telephone. It was his way of keeping in touch. 'Who have you seen?' he asked me.

I said that Bing Crosby had been with me the day before. 'Ah', he answered. 'You know, I don't want a book. But . . . have you seen Fred Astaire? You must see Fred. He's my best friend. I'll ring him for you.' And he did – the very next day. 'I'd rather have Fred sing my songs than anyone else,' he said. 'You know, his phrasing is perfect.' Astaire was equally pleased with Berlin. 'If he likes the way I sing the songs, it's only because I think they're the best ever written.' He meant it.

I made Berlin laugh when I told him of Crosby's recollections of first hearing 'White Christmas'. Berlin had played the piece, looking as anxious as if he had just been wheeled out of the intensive care ward. 'I don't think you need worry about that one,' said Bing. What Berlin worried about was that someone else could be making money that should have been his. Crosby told me that the director of the film *Holiday Inn*, Mark Sandrich, planned to fade out a scene on one long note. 'One of my notes . . . ?' Berlin asked. It is not a surprising question from the man who always had a prohibition against parody on printed copies of his music and could read a balance sheet better than a song sheet.

Occasionally, in our conversations, he feigned modesty. 'Let me tell you something about songwriters and their figures,' he said. 'A song becomes a hit and sells perhaps 7,500 copies. To the songwriter, that's always two million. But the figures for "White Christmas" are really very impressive.' The latest 'White Christmas' figures are impressive to the tune of 300 million.

As a five-year-old, I had been taken to see his all-soldier show *This is the Army* at the London Palladium. From the balcony I saw him in his ill-fitting First World War uniform, complete with the Boy Scout-type hat on his head, singing 'Oh, How I Hate to Get up in the Morning'. I knew then what it was like to put real emotion into a song.

'Oh, yeh,' he said, 'I know what you mean. But that's just what I do. I wrote "Oh How I Hate to Get up in the Morning" because I really do like to sleep late.'

'You're not writing a book, are you? . . . But I bet you didn't know that it was Lady Edwina Mountbatten who got that show going for me in London. She persuaded Churchill to lift paper rationing so that we could print copies of my song, "My British Buddy".'

We talked about songs of the day. The big hit then was called 'Little Green Apples', which contained the line, 'God didn't make little green apples, and it don't snow in Minneapolis.' He liked that tune. 'But,' he told me, 'I'd never have written it that way. I'd have said, "God didn't make little green apples and we don't pray in churches and chapels. . . ." '

What was safe to discuss was his then new occupation − painting pictures that he had sent to Fred Astaire of birds wearing top hats, signing them 'Izzy' or sometimes 'Vincent'. He never painted them with feet. 'I can't paint feet,' he said. 'As a painter, I'm a pretty good songwriter.' As a songwriter, he was a pretty good songwriter, too. I told him I was going to write that − and for once he didn't pretend he wanted to stop me.

30 September 1989

BUMPING AND BORING

Christopher Fildes

My flight to Washington was heavily overbooked, and the distinguished economic commentator William Keegan was offered £150 to get off the aircraft. Sound principles saw him through. 'Make it a thousand', he said, 'and I'll think about it.' When I called in to confirm my return flight, I was urged to get to the airport exceptionally early, because the same thing was likely to happen again. It seems bizarre to me, and it must be bad marketing and bad management, that passengers who have paid full fares or even premium fares should, as on my Washington flight, find themselves bumped from class to class or off the flight altogether. It is the natural consequence of a system which allows aircraft seats to be booked without cost and cancelled without penalty. If customers are free to overbook, of course they will. I know of a public body which, when its chief has to cross the Atlantic, habitually books a first-class seat for him on every flight of the day. The airlines then have to apply actuarial principles and guess how many of those who have booked will turn up. If they are to guess wrong, they would, no doubt, rather err in favour of filling the aircraft. Hence all the bumping and boring at Heathrow, and the cash offers. The time for incentives is earlier, when the bookings are made. A booking fee paid in advance ought to guarantee a particular seat. While the airlines persist with their present way of doing things, they should at least give the customers the option to convert their tickets into firm contracts for the flights and seats of their choice, with no refunds. The passenger would be sure of his place, and the airline of its revenue. It is no more than the deal now struck for holders of Apex and other cut-price tickets. Mr Keegan and I would be ready to advise − or, if suitably approached, to think about it.

7 October 1989

THE DAY I NEARLY KISSED AN UNKNOWN YOUNG WOMAN ON THE TUBE

Auberon Waugh

Last Tuesday, on 3 October 1989, I woke up feeling unusually pleased with myself. I cannot explain why this should have been the case. It just happened. Others must experience the same sort of thing. Sometimes one is irrationally elated to the point of insane conceit, at other times dejected and self-recriminating. On this occasion I was the former. Having no one else on whom to inflict my happiness, I tripped down the road from my flat in Brook Green to the underground station at Hammersmith Broadway, bought myself a ticket to Piccadilly Circus, smiling inanely at the machine which produced it, and climbed into a train in the absent-minded automaton-like haze which all daily commuters will recognise.

The carriage was crowded and I had to stand. Seated below me, her

nose perhaps on the level of my navel, was a young woman of no
particular beauty, although perfectly pleasant-looking. I should guess
she was about 25 years old. From her slightly brown face and pointed
chin – possibly, also, from some arrangement of her light brown hair –
I decided she might easily be French, but had no means of knowing.
Having glanced at her, I put her out of my mind and resumed my
complacent meditation.

Two or three stations later, possibly between Gloucester Road and
South Kensington, she raised her head to stare at the roof of the train.
She was totally absorbed in what she saw. Looking down at her
uplifted face, but still preoccupied by my own thoughts, I suddenly saw
her as a vision of the purest beauty, innocence, sweetness and grace.
With less than a quarter of my mind on what I was doing in that
crowded train I found myself bending down to kiss her . . .

I will never know whether I intended to kiss her on the lips, as I
rather fear, because by great good fortune some guardian angel woke
me out of my trance when my face was still 18 inches from hers. She
was never aware of the intended assault, and probably decided I was
suffering from stomach cramps. For the rest of the journey, I found
myself sweating and shivering with fright as I brooded on the narrow
escape I had had.

For the first half-hour, I fear my reflections were entirely selfish. I
had no thought for the unhappy young woman, suddenly finding
herself kissed on the lips by a plump, bald, middle-aged stranger in a
crowded train. The very least I could have hoped to get away with was
a slapped face and evasive action. If she decided to get off at the next
station, as she probably would, I could not have got off with her, and
would have had to remain in the same carriage, red-faced and smarting,
being stared at by my fellow-travellers.

But that was the softest option. Far more likely, she would have
screamed and denounced me in a torrent of outrage, using whatever
language came easiest to her. What on earth could one say? 'Excusez-
moi, mademoiselle. Je regrette infiniment, je ne pensais pas ce que je
faisais.' No doubt some public-spirited passenger would put me under
arrest and take me to a policeman, even if I was not manhandled by a
crowd of them.

At the police station, they would ask me why I had done it. I could
not possibly tell the truth, that I was thinking of something else and it
just seemed the most natural, the most obvious thing to do. No doubt I

would tell some more plausible lie — that I had mistaken her for a friend, cousin, niece, daughter, wife. . . .

'Perhaps you would give us the name and address of this person you claim to have mistaken her for?'

'Oh, ah, I have forgotten the exact name and address. . . .'

On the charge sheet, a stolen kiss becomes indecent assault, which sounds much worse and might indeed cover something close to attempted rape. In the same way, old gentlemen who find themselves caught short in a public place are liable to be charged with indecent exposure, which always strikes me as most unfair, since everybody supposes they have been flashing. Indecent assault covers groping and the equally objectionable habit of pinching, but its name suggests something even more violent and perverted.

One could be sure that no sooner had my name been written on the charge sheet than it would be circulated to the *Standard*, and *Sun* and sold 'exclusively' to Murdoch's stinking *News of the World*, Maxwell's filthy *Sunday People*. . . . Every journalistic enemy I had made in 30 years of hard application to the task would move in for the kill. I might be able to laugh off appearing as the Beast of Beak Street or the Taunton Terror for a month or two, but nobody would ever let it drop. How could I expect my dire warnings about junk money to be taken seriously by readers of the *Sunday Telegraph* if everybody knew they were coming from the Somerset Sex Fiend?

Press interest might even have persuaded the court to send me to prison, as it undoubtedly did with Rosie Johnston, imprisoned by the wretched judge for 'supplying' drugs when she had merely fetched some for a friend. So far as one could make out, this was because the gutter press had inaccurately labelled her 'privileged'. Reading Johnston's book of her prison experiences (*Inside Out*, Michael Joseph) you meet many victims of even more capricious injustice: the gentle 18-year-old who received six years for grievous bodily harm because she had illegally bought alcohol for a delinquent, 14-year-old sister who proceeded to terrorise the neighbourhood; another woman serving nine months for stealing a bottle of vodka. . . .

It can reasonably be pointed out that I did *not* kiss the young woman, I was not arrested, I do not face imprisonment, public humiliation or loss of my livelihood. Anybody who calls me the Beast of Beak Street risks an instant writ. Why, then, am I boring on with conditional self-pity? The reason is that having just read Johnston's book, I feel I have looked into the jaws of hell. Prison is a vile place, and I feel ashamed that I have even for a moment smiled that anyone — Lord Kagan, for instance, or Jeremy Thorpe — should be sent there.

I was saved by my guardian angel but it was a narrow squeak. Others may not be so lucky. If anybody finds himself hauled off by the Filth, sold to the gutter press and threatened with a spell in Wormwood Scrubs because of something they have done in a genuine fit of absentmindedness, I hope they will point to this article as disinterested testimony that such things can happen. Of course I am not sure quite how far down the criminal scale this plea in mitigation can extend. Do sane people ever flash absentmindedly? What about the elderly clergymen arrested every year for rubbing themselves against schoolgirls at Wimbledon? I am almost sure that nobody was ever raped absentmindedly. But it is quite possible to kiss someone absentmindedly just because it seems the most natural and obvious thing to do.

14 October 1989

KISSING AND TELLING

Charles Glass

When I read Auberon Waugh's account last week of 'The day I nearly kissed an unknown young woman on the Tube', I rather wished he had kissed the girl. Perhaps they would have fallen in love, gone for the weekend to the Côte d'Azur and conceived a child. It is out of such encounters, when the opportunity is seized, that life takes on meaning and moves forward. Instead, he admitted, 'by great good fortune some guardian angel woke me out of my trance when my face was still 18 inches from hers'. How sad for both of them that the angel intervened. By greater good fortune, my guardian angel is of a more compassionate nature.

On a warm morning in Jerusalem many years ago, I awakened like Auberon Waugh 'feeling unusually pleased with myself'. If there had been any justice in the world, I would have been suffering a hangover of epic proportions, having spent the entire night drinking and dancing with friends, including a troupe of Israeli actors and actresses who had joined us after a performance of their play. As it was, I felt wonderful. The sun was rising over the Judaean hills, when someone awakened me to say it was time to go. The driver who was taking me to Tel Aviv was shouting in my ear, 'Get up! You have an appointment at the Ministry of Defence in an hour.'

I had been asleep for all of 20 minutes, but I jumped into the shower and dressed still feeling all the joy and bonhomie of the night before. Nothing was going to spoil that day for me, not the long drive through the hills and the traffic in Tel Aviv, not the carping of the Ministry of Defence officials who wanted to complain to me about articles I had written and news reports I had broadcast concerning Israeli plain-clothes security agents in south Lebanon, whose job was assassination. I was well disposed toward the world, and I had within me a kind of optimism that the land the Israelis and Palestinians each gave a different name might soon provide peaceful homes for them both.

A girl soldier came down to the gates of the Defence Ministry to escort me upstairs to my appointment. She was young, and her long, dark hair was tied back lest it interfere with her military duties. She was pretty and correct in every way, neither flirtatious nor familiar. I followed her into the building and to the doors of a lift. We went inside the lift, and she pushed the button for one of the upper floors. The doors rattled shut, and the old carriage ascended slowly. Then I looked carefully at the girl.

She was a soldier in an army that was occupying part of the country in which I then lived. That army had demolished houses of people I knew. It had bombed the city in which I had my apartment. It had expelled thousands of Palestinians and occupied the West Bank and Gaza, denying its inhabitants even the simplest civil rights. To many of her own people, she was a disciplined fighter in a force that had saved the country from annihilation. Yet, she was a girl of astonishing allure, and I was feeling unusually happy and hopeful, nearly on the verge of song. I did not think, I acted.

Without a word, I leaned to my side and kissed her on the cheek. I returned to my previous position, facing the doors. Perhaps I was expecting her to slap me or to laugh, I do not remember. I did not mind. The lift passed another floor, and she looked at me. Then she stood on tiptoe. She kissed me. When she finished, she too resumed standing quietly. The doors opened, and neither of us spoke as she led me to the office of her commander.

During the course of a meeting in which the commander and I harangued each other about my coverage of south Lebanon and his troops' behaviour there, the girl brought us coffee. As she set the cups on the desk, she gave me a knowing smile. Later, she escorted me out of the building and, as I left, gave me a kiss goodbye. It was the only day in my life I had ever kissed a soldier, and I do not regret it.

I must confess to an impulsive nature that often confronts me with the choice of whether or not to act on my impulses. At times, it would be a denial of life itself to resist, whatever the consequences. If more Palestinians and Israelis surrendered to similar impulses, the armaments manufacturers who supply them both would lose one of their most lucrative export markets. If men and women demanded less and gave more to one another (for an impulsive kiss is a gift rather than a theft), their time on this planet would be more bearable. And if guardian angels became less censorious, some lonely young woman on a train bound for Somerset or on the dismal London underground might win the favour of a kiss from the well-intentioned Mr Waugh.

21 October 1989

LETTERS

KISSING

Sir: Auberon Waugh's and Charles Glass's reflections on the kissing of strangers (14 and 21 October) reminded me of a productive encounter one midsummer evening in 1960. Out of the then Partisan Café in Carlisle Street off Soho Square, wafted a young woman whose grace and beauty surpassed even that of the bestower of flowers in Botticelli's *Primavera*. Transformed by this vision, I found myself hugging her — and being hugged back with more tenderness than I'd hitherto imagined possible. For the following 20 years we lived together deeply in love and for the most part in great happiness.

This is not to suggest, three decades on, with the shadows of overpopulation, AIDS, rape and other sex abuses apparently still spreading day by day, that everyone possessed of such spontaneous impulses act on them without question. Since Auberon Waugh is by his own admission so happily married to his wife, wine cellar, magazine and club, it would probably have been disastrous for him to have done so on the tube even if, as Charles Glass hypothesises, he and the unknown traveller had proceeded to fall in love.

Nevertheless, Glass's militantly human experience in the lift of the Tel Aviv Defence Ministry does reaffirm my conviction that making love is better than making war, and that the large majority of people across the globe agree on this. If all

'Pull yourself together, bud! Everybody gets the blues from time to time.'

decision-makers, researchers and workers on defence and attack, munitions and wars, could be commissioned to kiss and hug all alleged enemies instead of abusing and killing them, wars of the future would surely end much more quickly. If it were efficiently implemented, they would be unable to start. As Dick Gregory said regarding the Vietnam War in 1966: 'When Christmas rolls along, you have a truce which proves that man can stop fighting. If he can stop fighting for Christmas, he ought to be able to stop for life.'

Michael Horovitz
Piedmont,
Bisley,
Stroud, Gloucestershire

4 November 1989

LETTERS

MORE KISSING

Sir: No doubt your 'Kissing and Telling' piece and that of Mr Waugh (14 and 21 October) have produced numbers of romantic reminiscences. May I add mine?

Long ago I was in a taxi inching down Bond Street in a severe traffic jam. A man hailed my taxi, seeming to be unaware it was occupied. When he realised it was, he continued walking beside the taxi, staring through the window in the strangest way. Suddenly he opened the door and hurled himself onto the seat beside me. When he began kissing me ardently, I was quite unable to utter. This impulsive creature was clearly not English, but a *beau ténébreux* in type, and I found myself returning his kisses. I never saw him again. But I have never forgotten that chance encounter, from which I draw no conclusions, moral or immoral.

Lesley Blanch
9 Chemin Vallaya,
Garavan,
Menton 06500

25 November 1989

DIARY

Nicholas Coleridge

Since last I wrote this diary I have got married, and ten weeks into it my only domestic problem is having a house too small to store the many wedding presents we have been given. So, until we move, we are camping between piles of cardboard boxes containing tumblers, casserole dishes, bath mats and wooden towel rails. In the Fifties, I gather, the most popular wedding present was the toast-rack, until this was overtaken by the pop-up toaster. Nobody gave us a single toast-rack or pop-up toaster but we did receive four splendid asparagus steamers: tall, thin saucepans made of stainless steel with special narrow baskets

'He was trying to bring me the Sunday papers.'

inside to hold the stalks. I mentioned to a friend, also recently married, that four asparagus steamers seemed almost too much of a good thing, but she told us we had got off lightly. When she married last December she and her husband were given 57 photograph frames and 34 cache-pots. I assumed she was exaggerating, but she insisted not. They had 400 to the wedding, and people who give photograph frames tend to give a pair of them, so it only took about one in 15 guests to have that particular brainwave to add up to 57 frames. 'Where have you put them all?' I asked. 'Oh, we were incredibly lucky,' she replied, perhaps a trifle unsentimentally, 'while we were away on honeymoon we were robbed. They must have had a van, because they got away with almost all our presents.'

My wife, as I am getting used to describing her, recently went to a Friday night 'hen party' for a childhood friend who was getting married. The evening began with dinner for 20 at Monkeys restaurant in Chelsea, then moved on to Tramp nightclub. This was her first visit to Tramp and she was interested to see in the queue outside not only a host of quite famous pop stars and footballers but the Editor of the *Sunday Times*, Mr Andrew Neil, with a brace of beautiful Asian girls on his arm. Last week we went to a party at George Weidenfeld's flat to mark the publication of Nigel Dempster's new biography of Christina Onassis. Here also was Andrew Neil who, on being introduced to Georgia, said 'Haven't we met somewhere before?' 'Not really,' she

'Yes, I think I'll have the "fish in a bucket"
as well'.

replied brightly, 'but I did happen to be next to you in the queue at Tramp recently.' 'Which night was that?' asked Neil, bringing his full expertise into play. 'Friday? That's a very bad night at Tramp. So are Thursdays and Saturdays. You should always go on Monday, Tuesday and Wednesday for a good time at Tramp.' Some months ago Peregrine Worsthorne wrote a classic leading article about the editor's place being, not in a nightclub, but at the Athenaeum having dinner with an octogenarian Nobel prizewinner. But I can only marvel at Mr Neil's energy, though six nights at Tramp is the one fate that sounds worse to me than a lonely dinner with a nuclear physicist at the Athenaeum.

Some friends in Wiltshire were recently burgled while they were out having lunch with neighbours. The burglar had shinned up a drainpipe, entered through a bathroom window, and spent an hour or so taking his pick. His pick included clearing the entire contents of their safe, the key to which he had come across in a desk drawer marked 'Safe' along with another smaller key marked 'Mower'. The Warminster police arrived swiftly, reckoned they had a fair idea who'd done it (there being only a handful of cat burglars in the area) and promptly arrested the prime suspect who, sure enough, had all the stolen bits and pieces hidden in his house. Our friends' troubles were not over, however. None of the stolen property can be returned to them until the trial which is not scheduled for another six months, in case the burglar changes his plea from guilty to not guilty and the jury need to be shown the booty as evidence. Might they, they asked, be allowed their two large suitcases back, which the burglar had used to carry their stuff away, since they were going on holiday to France the next week and wanted to use them? Sorry, said the police, it can't be done. What, then, about the little key to their lawnmower? Surely that wasn't substantive evidence, and the old mower can't be started without it. Again the police are playing it by the book. Perhaps they are getting their own back on our friends for an embarrassing moment during the identification of the stolen goods. Virtually everything, of course, they could recognise at once. But a large case of silver fish knives and a massive silver salver meant nothing to them. Indeed, they mildly objected to the fish knives being thought theirs, on Mitfordish grounds. 'And we've certainly never seen that awful ornate silver plate before,' they declared. 'Well, that's odd, sir,' replied the policeman, 'since your name is written on it.' The salver was a leaving-present on his departure as British ambassador to Venezuela, engraved with the grateful thanks of the entire Venezuelan foreign office; so ugly, they had never fully unwrapped it in the intervening 15 years. Insult was recently further added to injury by the news that the burglar had been given special dispensation by a local magistrate to have his BMW back. The car was impounded by the police after his arrest, since it was used as the getaway vehicle in the burglary, but since he has pleaded guilty there are no grounds for hanging on to it.

Still on the subject of wedding presents, we needed to send something to a couple who got married in the spring and live on a farm in Devon. At the time we couldn't decide what to buy for them, so bought them nothing, an easy solution. But hearing that they have a duck pond and no ducks, we decided that a pair of Aylesburys would fit the bill. Our part of the Cotswolds is a convenient place to buy ducks, since the whole area has lately sprouted with duck farms and rare breed centres selling every imaginable variation of Indian runner ducks and Lantau geese, elegant, blousy and inbred. The owner was delighted to sell us two Aylesburys and offered to Red Star them right away in a cardboard box to Okehampton railway station. The price for the ducks was £70. It seemed a lot, but I didn't click quite how much until later when we wandered into a local hotel and saw roasted Aylesbury duck, on the blackboard for £7.95 including vegetables, orange salad and VAT. Were

the £70 ones a particularly rare kind of Aylesbury duck, I asked a neighbour, more countryish than I? 'God, no,' he laughed. 'These duck farms are a great joke round here. They rely on people not having a clue, so invent their own prices. Just so long as you didn't buy any!'

21 October 1989

A FOUNDLING FATHER TO OUR CHILDREN

Alexandra Artley

On the north side of Brunswick Square there is a bronze statue of a rather genial man seated on a robust Queen Anne chair, his flared coat thrown back and the royal charter of the Foundling Hospital, Blooms-bury, in his hand. On a marble plinth beneath are incised the simple words: 'Thomas Coram 1668-1751. Pioneer in the cause of child welfare'. The statue sits between the two independent charities which continue Coram's work today. To his right is the Thomas Coram Foundation and to his left Coram's Fields — seven acres of mature parkland set between Holborn and Kings Cross and once described as 'the best children's playground in Britain'.

This Tuesday, after the Archbishop of Canterbury had preached in the Wren church of St Andrew's, Holborn, at a service of thanksgiving for Coram's life, a boy and a girl dressed in the original brown and white Foundling uniform walked to bright Handelian trumpets carrying a wreath of flowers to place on Coram's tomb at the west end of the church. In Dr Runcie's words, 'A rough, hot-tempered, rather uncouth seaman had turned the moral climate of Britain in favour of child welfare . . . when God distributes his gifts of character, he knows what he is about.'

Thomas Coram was born in Lyme Regis in 1668 and went to sea before he was 12. In 1694 he led a company of craftsmen to establish a shipyard in Massachusetts and he married a Bostonian. Coram became a Trustee of the Colony of Georgia before being driven from America in 1720 by Puritan pastors who (hostile to a staunch Queen Anne

Anglican) encouraged the sacking of his shipyard at Taunton, Massachusetts.

Half Americanised at the age of 52, Captain Coram saw early Georgian London with fresh eyes. In the short winter days as he walked early to the City and returned late, he was shocked to discover babies and young children, some dead and others dying, put out on dung heaps at the side of the roads. Then followed the moral panic which faces all men and women of conscience when daily faced with social need greater than their own hearths can relieve: 'I could take one of these children home . . . perhaps six. . . .' For Coram ('a man whose head was fertile with expedients') it was the start of the Foundling Hospital, his 'Darling Project'.

On the Continent foundling hospitals were commonplace, supported by Church and state – the Church wanted souls and the state, often criss-crossed by invading armies, wanted soldiers. At Lisbon's House of the Wheel, for example, a wretched mother put her infant on a device which whisked it inside the institution walls, no questions asked. In Britain, outside the charmed sphere of the aristocracy (in which bastardy was tolerated), illegitimate children and their mothers were treated with puritan savagery.

The vast social problem Thomas Coram faced had already been studied by the early Georgian journalist, Jonas Hanway. He exposed, for example, the 'killing nurses' employed by local Poor Law officials, 'because no child can ever come out of their hands alive'. In one Georgian London workhouse only 11 out of 174 babies reached the age of six months during the period Hanway investigated it. Personally pleading with a parish officer in Holborn to allow a young woman 2/6 a week to nurse her own child, Hanway recorded this reason for refusal: 'But . . . after a month or six weeks with a parish nurse we hear no more of the child, whereas your young woman will probably preserve hers.' Joseph Addison also urged the case for a foundling hospital.

Although styled 'Thomas Coram, Gentleman', Captain Coram had 'great simplicity of manners'. Lacking both social graces and connections, he failed in his first attempt to petition the King for a foundling hospital charter. The saltiness of the angry seaman springs from this letter to a friend in Boston:

> I could no more prevail on any Arch Bishop or Bishop or
> Nobleman . . . to speak to the late King or his present

Majesty on this affair than I could have prevailed with
any of them to put down their Breeches and present
their Backsides to the King and Queen.

Next, Coram decided to 'petition the ladies'. Beginning with the
Countess of Somerset, who first signed the petition at Petworth, it
took Coram 17 years of waiting, asking and dancing attendance ('Lady
Isabella Finch gave me rough words and bid me be gone') to establish
the petitions he needed to secure a royal charter. His friend Dr
Brocklesby describes Thomas Coram's 'ardour and anxiety' as if every
deserted child had been his own; 'even people of rank began to be
ashamed to see a man's hair become grey in the course of a solicitation
by which he could get nothing'. The charter was at last granted in 1739
when Coram was 71. To decorate the massive red wax seal which
dangles from the rolled-up charter in Hogarth's portrait of Captain
Coram, he chose Moses in the bullrushes, 'the first foundling we hear
of'.

The site for the Foundling Hospital was bought from the Earl of
Salisbury in 1740 — four fields in an outlying area called Bloomsbury.
Theodore Jacobson, a City merchant turned architect, was chosen to
design it and his scheme was a simple classical building arranged on
three sides of a square (a wing for boys and a wing for girls separated by
a chapel). While building began, the Foundling first opened its doors in
March 1741 in a house temporarily rented in Hatton Garden. The first
two children were baptised as Thomas and Eunice Coram and Captain
Coram stood as godfather to 20 more. Although the Foundling Hospital
was demolished in 1926 (the conservation *cause célèbre* of its day) the
unique dignity and warmth of this great institution can still be sensed
at its newer premises, the Thomas Coram Foundation in Brunswick
Square.

On Tuesday, after the service in St Andrew's, Holborn, the Governors of the Thomas Coram Foundation invited 400 people to a party
in the Court Room. Beneath an exuberant plasterwork ceiling by
William Wilton, the rich apricot-coloured walls glowed with paintings
by Hogarth, Francis Hayman, Gainsborough and James Wills. Apart
from the Foundling Hospital, Captain Coram was also the father of the
Royal Academy. By encouraging his friend Hogarth to show his works
at the Foundling to attract donations from the fashionable public,
Coram spurred Hogarth's friends (in a painters' colony in St Martin's

Lane) to found the Royal Academy.

The bar was set up under Hogarth's red-coated portrait of Coram. To its right was Roubilliac's bust of Handel (another benefactor) and a scroll bearing words from the 27th Psalm. 'When my father and my mother forsake me, the Lord taketh me up.' Chattering happily beneath the art, the guests were former Foundling children grown to adulthood, present-day foster and adoptive parents (whom the Governors seek out for particularly 'hard-to-place' children), teachers past and present, clergy, fund-raisers, and the mayors of Camden, Islington and Lyme Regis. 'We won this in a raffle,' said the present Director, Colin Masters, pointing to Hogarth's 'March of the Guards to Finchley'. (Hogarth had indeed raffled it to raise money for Coram, and his wife, Jane, was one of Coram's early foster-mothers.)

The windows of the Court Room look out over a haze of trees in Coram's Fields. Beneath them on quieter days stand three or four dignified wooden cases lined with dark blue velvet and filled with the pathetic tags and tokens attached by sorrowing mothers to the babies they were about to leave.

What would you choose to leave with a child you will never see again? Tokens left between 1741 and 1760 include a frayed pink silk purse with 'ND' embroidered in black beads; a mother-of-pearl heart with the letters 'EL'; fragments of coral necklaces; some glass buttons; an ivory fish with a gentle eye drawn on it; a flat piece of shell scratched with the words, 'James, son of James Concannon, Late or Now of Jamaica'; a silver thimble perhaps deliberately crushed; a small dark red heart made of a heavy ribbed silk called lute-string; a piece of cloth hastily ripped from a dress or jacket; a scrap of paper edged with brown silk bearing the words, 'in remembrance of E.B. November 2nd 1756' and a yellowing lawn baby's cap edged with lace. On a small bronze disc is inscribed, 'Nov. 10th, half an hour after 12 o'clock' — perhaps the exact time of a birth engraved for ever on the mother's heart. The conflicting emotions of relief and pain which swept over applicants to the Foundling Hospital were recorded by an eye-witness at its gates:

> The Expressions of Grief of the Women whose Children could not be admitted were Scarcely more observable than those of some of the women who had parted with their children, so that a more moving Scene can't well be imagined.

Among the nine tons of documents which the Foundling has accumulated in the course of dealing with 27,000 children are notes by mothers who could write or whose friends could write for them.

> No. 6575: It is Earnestly intreated that the Child may be taken Care of as the Disconsolate parents Hope soon to be in a situation to own it. . . . Cruel Separation. Wednesday December 7th, 1757.

> No. 12719: Joseph, Born in London April 28, 1759. *Va! mon Enfant prend la Fortune.*

> No. 734: 'Who Breathes must suffer. And who thinks must Mourn. And He Alone is Blest Who ne'er was born.'

The details of one baby were taken down very briefly by the recording clerk: 'A paper on the breast – Clout [cloth] on the head.'

Besides these manuscripts lies another with which we are instantly familiar – the Foundling Hospital version of *Messiah* copied by Handel's amanuensis, John Christopher Smith. Handel was another great artist-benefactor of the Foundling and his fashionable concerts given in the hospital chapel raised £7,000 (a stupendous sum in those days).

From March 1741 when the Foundling Hospital first opened its doors to March 1756 when, for four years, Parliament made a grant towards the admission of children on demand, 1,384 children were received (a figure much lower than similar institutions in Europe). 'Alas,' wrote Jonas Hanway, 'what were 1,384 infants to the thousands that were still drooping and dying at the hands of parish nurses?' The Governors, who through limited resources had been forced to restrict admission by a ballot using red, black and white balls, were themselves appalled at the enormous numbers of children they had to turn away. Aged 74, Thomas Coram began to petition (in vain) for a second Foundling Hospital in Westminster. At this stage in his life Captain Coram had impoverished himself and it was a subscription raised by the kindly Jewish financier Sampson Gideon that kept him in his last years. It is recorded that at this time he liked to sit in the Foundling Hospital's colonnades distributing gingerbread and watching the children with tears in his eyes. He died on 29 March 1751 in lodgings in Spur Street (now Panton Street) near Leicester Square and had asked to be buried under the Foundling chapel then nearing completion. As his body was carried through the gates in Guilford Street, his plain elm coffin disappointed the crowd.

In the 18th century, the Governors of the Foundling Hospital pioneered the best social case-work of today. Young apprentices, for example, were often at risk from brutal treatment, and the Governors usually attempted to prosecute on their behalf. Some cases were utterly barbarous. William Butterworth, a weaver of Manchester, regularly kicked his apprentice Jemima Dixon so hard in the stomach that she became incontinent; he forced her to eat her own excrement. Job Wyatt, a wood-screw maker of Tatehill, raped his 11-year-old apprentice Sarah Drew and beat her if she refused him. Mary Jones, apprenticed to Mrs Brownrigg of Fetter Lane, escaped back to the Foundling with an eye so badly injured it was feared she would lose it (Mrs Brownrigg, a notorious sadist, was later hanged at Tyburn for the torture and murder of innumerable parish apprentices who had no one to turn to). To many people in the outside world Coram's children were foundlings – illegitimate and therefore almost subhuman. In legally pursuing bad masters, medically attending to the children and offering them support and counselling in later life, the Governors of the Foundling Hospital set a precedent for protecting young people 'leaving care'. The Thomas Coram Foundation now runs sheltered accommodation for young people leaving care and settling into the adult world of work.

Long-established charities have an almost Darwinian response to 'adapt or die'. On a bright autumn morning I arrived at the Coram Homeless Children's Project to see just one example of the way an old foundation has adapted its work to meet contemporary needs. One of the many tragedies of 'hotel homelessness' is that children cooped up in squalid hotel rooms lack not only space (even to learn to walk) but play materials appropriate to their age. In child development, 'play', said the great child psychologist, Jean Piaget, 'is the child's work.'

The Coram Homeless Children's Project is run by Lonica Vanclay, who first showed me the Coram toy store. In a small classical building (which housed a swimming pool in the latter days of the Foundling Hospital) were racks of very clean playthings, ranging from soft furry toys for babies to first books, crayons, paints and mechanical 'play-centres'. Chess and draughts were available for older children. Heaped about, because a toy firm in Yorkshire happened to donate £800 worth of them, were several dozen big red and yellow plastic mechanical diggers for toddlers to drive. Lonica Vanclay explained that on Mondays one Coram team made a monthly 'toy library' trip to bed-and-breakfast hotels in West Hampstead. First the names, ages and addresses of children were checked on a card index file. Then playthings were loaded into orange and blue plastic crates.

In front of Gregory House, beneath mature rustling trees, Dominic Fox and Hasina Khan loaded the crates into a royal-blue mini-bus which had the words, 'Thomas Coram; Caring for children since 1739' scripted in a copper-plate style on the side. Driving purposefully out of Mecklenburgh Square, Dominic explained that the West Hampstead area alone encompassed 50 homeless families (placed there by Camden and Westminster) who have approximately 100–150 children between them.

Half an hour later we reached a shabby north London neighbourhood.

The first hotel call was on Room 3, occupied by an Irish nurse, her unemployed husband and their 16-month-old son. Hotel homelessness is a timeless zone. At 11.15 in the morning, the curtains were drawn, the television glowed quietly on top of a fridge next to the double bed and the mother greeted us warily in a dressing-gown. The purpose of these 'toy visits' is also to lend adults a sympathetic ear. While the nurse talked about her idea of 'going back on night duty' if her husband could look after the boy, the child stumbled forward to the plastic crate for toys.

'What would you like, little one?' said Hasina Khan, as he finally settled on a pack of three bright fabric 'bricks', one with a bell inside.

Fifteen minutes later, in the same hotel, Dominic Fox negotiated his crate of toys through a rabbit warren of heavy fire doors, dog-leg bends in the stairs and converted landings to reach Room 8, occupied by a Bengali couple with four children. Three of the children were at school. As there were no chairs (and no table) in the room, the father lay on a bed covered with a brown candlewick bedspread. Above him was suspended a plastic carrier-bag containing several bars of Cadbury's fudge.

Hasina Khan interpreted lightly and comfortably in Sylheti (now the second language in inner London). Soon the worn Bengali mother brought a child from a second room. Shelim turned out to be a mentally handicapped boy of 12 who is partially deaf and whose left ear was bound up from a recent operation. Dominic Fox offered him things from the toy crate. There was a packet of crayons, a small painting set, a good wad of scrap paper to draw on, a bottle of non-toxic children's glue and a Puffin large-format copy of Raymond Briggs' famous children's story, *The Snowman*. Shelim was delighted by the bottle of children's glue.

'For me?' he asked.

'Yes. For you.'

His father explained, via Hasina, that he could not offer us a seat or, indeed, anything else. Instead, he insisted that I take a cigarette. Later, as we strangers left the room, Shelim, still seated on his parents' bed, clumsily seized *The Snowman* with joy.

On the plight of thousands of British children growing up in bleak hotel rooms, the Governors of the Thomas Coram Foundation recently remarked that it 'should be as horrific to sensitive people as the children cast aside on dung heaps were to Thomas Coram 250 years ago'. To try to help the growing number of needy children and young people in London the Foundation is, in the words of its director, Colin Masters, 'seriously fund-raising for the first time in a hundred years'. Thinking of the artists and musicians who had provided the 'Live Aid' of the 18th century, he added, 'And this time we have not got Handel.'

Donations would be separately welcomed by: The Thomas Coram Foundation, 40 Brunswick Square, London WC1N 1AZ and by: Coram's Fields, 93 Guilford Street, London WC1N 1DN.

21 October 1989

LOW LIFE

STAGE FRIGHT

Jeffrey Bernard

Monday was hectic. First, I went to Broadcasting House for Melvyn Bragg's *Start the Week*. Then I went to the Groucho Club to be interviewed by a woman from the *Sunday Times Magazine* for 'A Life In The Day Of', and after that I climbed two floors for a book launch party for *More Low Life*. After that, Keith Waterhouse took us downstairs again for lunch. After that, your guess is as good as mine. These are stirring times. There was even a tin of pea and ham soup on my desk this morning. Unopened, thank God. I have enough trouble already with toast crumbs and dog-ends.

I enjoyed *Start the Week*. Melvyn's easy professionalism calmed the ragged nerves, as did a large shot of vodka concealed in my companion's handbag. The other guests were Sir Hardy Amies, Denis Healey and Carl Davis. I took an immediate shine to Mr Healey. He was very, very friendly and not at all pretentious, as I thought an ex-minister might be. Neither is he daft as a politician might be.

Before we went on the air I asked Sir Hardy did he appreciate the fact that his showroom in Savile Row is the house in which that great man Sheridan died. He did. Those premises with the ghosts of bailiffs thronging the hall would be wasted on the likes of Zandra Rhodes. He wouldn't tell us anything about the Queen and said he wasn't allowed to. I asked him whether or not she ever gave him a tip for a horse. He nodded me a no. In deference to his dislike of smoking I refrained from lighting up for 50 minutes, which is the longest I have been without a cigarette since I was last in a coma.

Denis — Yes, I am allowed to call him Denis now — and I had a word about George Brown after the show and he confirmed my suspicion that Brown didn't drink too much, he just couldn't take it. Some years ago I got chatting to Brown in a buffet car of a train going to Manchester. He was going there for a book-signing and I was going there to examine the ladies' knickers that are stuck on the ceiling of a pub called Tommy Ducks. After only two gins and tonics he was almost legless. Nice man but a trifle irascible. Anyway, Denis surprised me when he told me that he reads this column from time to time. I gave him a copy of *More Low Life* and now wonder what he'll do with it.

Then to the Groucho and the *Sunday Times* woman. I think she had a hard time. How on earth do you write a Life in the Day of somebody who doesn't do anything? When I told her I spend four hours every morning in bed chain-smoking, drinking and staring at the framed photographs on the wall she was kind enough at least to ask me whether I was *thinking* all that time. Oh yes indeed. We mouth silent cries for help here from 4 a.m. until 8 a.m. Occasionally the thought process is interrupted by a scream from the genito-urinary hospital behind me, but otherwise the photographs trigger off a relentless speculation ending in remorse. (There are three ex-wives staring at me at this very moment.)

And now for Wednesday and the opening night of the play. I suppose it is the day of my life. I have cold feet and I haven't even been able to feel them for five years. My heart is in my mouth, my hands are shaking and other parts of my anatomy defy description. But it isn't just me. I desperately want it to go well for Keith Waterhouse and Ned Sherrin. They worked so well and hard while I have just been staring at the photographs on the wall.

21 October 1989

THEATRE

LAUGHTER FROM THE DEPTHS

Christopher Edwards

JEFFREY BERNARD IS UNWELL
(Apollo)

Readers of *The Spectator* will need no explanation about the contents of this production, based as it is upon the weekly column of our own

Low life correspondent. When I recently tried to arrange an interview with Jeffrey Bernard for *Drama* magazine, I was told the best way of reaching him on the telephone was to ring the Coach and Horses pub just after 11 o'clock (in the morning). Sure enough he was there. Apologies were made for disturbing him at the pub. 'This is my office,' he replied. Well, this play is set in his office after a hard day's work. The time is very early in the morning. Bernard (brilliantly played by Peter O'Toole) has passed out in the lavatory and woken up to find that the pub is locked and everyone has gone home. The clever set, by John Gunter, is the interior of the pub but the perspectives are slanted. The design offers a view of the inside of the Coach and Horses as seen by a drunk lying on the floor – which is precisely where we first encounter Peter O'Toole.

After he has picked himself up, tried, unsuccessfully, to open the door and helped himself to a vodka, O'Toole embarks on a series of anecdotes and reminiscences about Soho past and present, childhood, death, women, racing and drink. Many of the characters are brought on to the stage for sharp little vignettes, played with great virtuosity by Timothy Ackroyd, Sarah Berger, Annabel Leventon and, notably, the talented and funny Royce Mills. But it is Peter O'Toole who anchors the production with his great charm and excellent timing. Most of the jokes and stories are good, many of them hilarious. And, with a drink-befuddled voice that manages to be both whimsical and elegiac, he beguiles you into this demi-monde and makes its rules of conduct seem almost normal.

The script, while based upon Bernard's life and writings, is composed by Keith Waterhouse. Much of the credit for the success of the production must go to him. There must have been some danger that material that is touching and amusing in a short weekly column would not stay the distance of an evening. So, by allowing this dramatisation, Jeffrey Bernard ran the great risk of turning himself into the creature he so eloquently abhors, the buttonholing pub bore. Waterhouse deftly avoids this pitfall by mining his subject for its variety, wisdom and wit. Is the production authentic? Is the sage chronicler of Low life this engaging, or has Waterhouse played down Bernard's self-pity and self-censure – the latter being, as Dr Johnson remarked, an invidious form of self-love? You can check up for yourselves each week a few pages on from this column. In the meantime, I can, without any hint of a conflict of interest, recommend this production in the most quotable form possible as 'a triumphant and witty excursion into the Lower Depths of England's foremost pub philosopher; Peter O'Toole is magnificent', safe in the knowledge that it will be a deserved hit without this incestuous, but sincere, endorsement.

21 October 1989

NEW LIFE

MIXED BLESSING

Zenga Longmore

Claudette was most sympathetic when I related the strange, rather terrifying occurrence which took place last week. I was innocently travelling on the Tube, sitting quite happily with Omalara in my arms, when I chanced to glance up at the ceiling of the train. At that moment, a plump, bald, middle-aged man bent forward to *kiss* Omalara or me — it doesn't matter which. Luckily he appeared to change his mind just before the crucial moment. Omalara and I were dumbstruck with terror! At the next stop the transport police were contacted, but they have as yet failed to find a clue. Of course, a description of the man is in their files.

Claudette shivered with emotion when I had finished this gruesome tale.

'Let's change the subject,' she suggested, and this we did. It took a while, mind you, for the conversation to develop any meat, but after her boyfriend had brought in the coffee, we discussed Omalara's blessing.

The blessing took place last Sunday at the Church of God of Prophecy. It was not quite a christening because no water was involved, but it was an extremely solemn occasion. The Pastor's voice sailed above Omalara's roar as he called blessings down upon her. Now two and a half months old, her cry has changed from a raucous squawk to a hearty bellow, and very dramatic it sounded too when blended with the Pastor's rich tones. In fact I was very moved. Christenings and blessings are so much more heart-stirring than weddings, where one always finds oneself feeling sorry either for the bride or for the groom. When have you seen a couple who, in your opinion, were well matched? No wonder so many tears are shed at weddings. With christenings there's no need to feel sorry for anyone, except perhaps the preacher, who has to hold a heavy, occasionally wet, screaming child.

After the blessing we threw a small party at my sister Boko's flat. Omalara, no stranger to parties, acted beautifully in her role as star of the show. The fire-and-brimstone sermon which had unnerved a few of the party revellers left her gurgling with delight. Everybody took turns to dance with her to the accompaniment of loud reggae, whose thumping tones sounded somewhat jarring after the beautiful gospel-singing in the church. In short, the day was an undisputed success, except perhaps for my eldest sister, who appeared to take the preacher's speech a little too personally.

'But I *know* he was looking directly at me', she moaned, rouged lips all a-quiver, 'when he said that bit about brazen women, painted with the devil's paint-brush.'

Luckily, it didn't take long to persuade her that he meant the woman sitting next to her, and after a few Scotches, she was right as rain.

Sadly it will take more than a few Scotches to persuade me to travel on the Tube again for a long, long time.

21 October 1989

DIARY

Nicholas Coleridge

Some Indian friends, who live in Calcutta but fly to Delhi every month for a few days' work, are amused by the cut-throat hotel wars that have erupted there over the last six months. Normally, whenever they are in Delhi, they stay at the Taj hotel, where they invariably take the same small suite. Lately, however, the refurbished Oberoi hotel has adopted a remarkably aggressive sales policy, apparently designed to poach the

Taj's longstanding customers. Their intelligence-gathering is remarkable. A couple of months ago our Calcutta friends were sitting at home when the telephone rang. 'Hello, it is the Oberoi hotel speaking. We hear that you are considering making a visit soon to Delhi. Can we suggest that you stay with us this time and not at the Taj.' Our friends were initially reluctant to change horses, but so persistent was the honey-voiced girl from the Oberoi that they decided to give it a try. No sooner had they unpacked, however, than the telephone rang in their strange suite. 'Hello, it is the Taj hotel here. We think you are making a big, big mistake, and would like to send a car to collect you and your luggage this very minute.' 'No,' replied our friends. 'Now that we're here we'd like to see what the Oberoi is like.' But the next morning the Taj were back on the line. 'You see,' said another honey-voiced public relations person, 'you have tried your experiment but you don't like it very much. Our car has already set off to collect you.' And so it had. And our friends, suddenly homesick for their old suite, meekly got into the Taj's limo and were driven back, where half the hotel's staff of managers and bellhops were lined up to greet the prodigal guests. How did the Taj's people know our friends had checked into the Oberoi? And how, indeed, did the Oberoi know they were planning a jaunt to Delhi? The theory is that both hotels have infiltrated informers into the reception and reservation desks of their competitors, who constantly report for a few rupees a day. How long, I wonder, before similar tactics are adopted by Mr Rocco Forte and Sir Hugh Wontner, and guests unpacking at the Grosvenor House are wooed into defecting by a PR from the Savoy, or vice-versa.

There is consternation in Stow-on-the-Wold, where we do our shopping at weekends, because the car park has been invaded by scores of gypsies and their caravans. The gypsies were certainly expected, since they are permitted to camp in the car park for the annual Stow horse fair, but not until next week; they have arrived early, misled over the correct date of the fair by *Horse and Hound* magazine. *Horse and Hound*, it seems, publishes a calendar of forthcoming horse fairs, and a single slip has led the hordes of gypsies to arrive prematurely from all over the country. Now the local Cotswold District Council is split over what action to take, and exactly how many extra litter sacks and large wheeled dustbins will be needed to cope with the gypsies' elongated stay. What impresses me is that England's gypsies are such keen readers of *Horse and Hound*. If I worked in their advertising department I don't know whether I'd hush this up, or boast about it. What other magazine can prove so dynamically its reader response? It must be comforting for the manufacturers of horse-trailers and polo sticks to know that their big colour advertisements are being so carefully scrutinised by romanies and tinkers. The new, yuppie, *Horse and Hound*-subscribing gypsy has certainly made an impression on Councillor Rex Williams, as reported in the *Cotswold Journal*. 'The true gypsy, with his small caravan and a couple of horses, always parked on the verges and would not use the car park,' he said. 'It is the new travellers with their large posh caravans and Range Rovers who will go there.'

28 October 1989

LETTERS

CAMP FOLLOWING

Sir: As the gypsies sit round the camp fire, stewing something succulent in a pot, they peruse their copies of *Horse and Hound* pausing only to remark: 'I see Ginny Leng won at Burghley Horse Trials again.'

Yes, it is a beguiling picture of our readership conjured up by Nicholas Coleridge in your excellent Diary (28 October). He comments on the huge influx of gypsies into Stow-on-the-Wold because the wrong date for the horse fair was published in *Horse and Hound*.

We were somewhat stunned here to learn that scores of police had been called in to control our traveller readers who were busy trotting horses and ponies up and down in a car park. What happened was that a person who has advertised with us before sent in a small, single-column advertisement for the Fair giving a date which we printed accurately. But our inquiries reveal that there are several factions seeking to hold a Stow fair and thus there was confusion. Another gathering took place the following week.

As your diarist remarked: 'What other magazine can prove so dynamically its reader response?' The horse makes no distinctions in choosing his friends; nor does *Horse and Hound*.

Michael Clayton

Editor, Horse and Hound,

Kings Reach Tower,

Stamford Street,

London SE1

11 November 1989

TRAGICAL-COMICAL-HISTORICAL-PASTORAL

Jaspistos

In Competition No. 1597 you were asked to write a villanelle about a scene which may have been pastoral once but certainly isn't now.

There was such a large and talented entry that I shall make room for the prizewinners only . . . The bonus bottle of Cognac Otard VSOP, kindly presented by the Château de Cognac, goes to Elizabeth Thomson for the neatest contrast between ancient and modern.

> The lights of Oxford shine in gathering dark,
> Watched by a shadow from an ear-marked field
> Where Thyrsis haunts a future Science Park.

An acid rain is trickling down the bark
Of his old oak, a tree not quickly healed.
The lights of Oxford shine in gathering dark.

Long since the Morris car outsang the lark
And now a ring road keeps the city sealed
Where Thyrsis haunts a future Science Park.

(The views of my lord Clarendon were stark
On the brash Centre which his name must
    shield.
The lights of Oxford shine in gathering dark.)

Even the scholars bear the weary mark
Of traffic with the world: for worlds have reeled
Where Thyrsis haunts a future Science Park.

In these days we must cultivate the quark
And, for our masters, calculate a yield.
The lights of Oxford shine in gathering dark
Where Thyrsis haunts a future Science Park.
                                    (Elizabeth Thomson)

Nowhere by motorway is all that far,
Not even driving down to Land's End, where
It's two-pounds-fifty just to park your car.

Where sheep once safely grazed, the cliff walks
    are
An overflowing noisy thoroughfare:
Nowhere by motorway is all that far.

The all-night discos and the hotel bar
Keep you awake with *son* and *lumière:*
It's two-pounds-fifty just to park your car.

And, if you've come to tap the reservoir
Of the Atlantic's once free, fresh, salt air —
Nowhere by motorway is all that far —

Or watch a sunset, or an evening star,
Or feel the west wind blowing through your hair,
It's two-pounds-fifty just to park your car.

Here in this Cornish sort of Shangri-La
You'll find the madding crowd's already there:
Nowhere by motorway is all that far.
It's two-pounds-fifty just to park your car.

(Robert Roberts)

In Mayfair there's no maypole in the streets,
In Brook Street you will find no babbling brook,
In Shepherd Market not a lambkin bleats.

The faded resident of Farm Street greets
The morning after with a jaded look;
In Mayfair there's no maypole in the streets.

In these brick lanes the new fast food defeats
The farmyard chicken and the homely cook;
In Shepherd Market not a lambkin bleats.

In this grey maze where man with woman meets
It's not to dally midst the corn in stook;
In Mayfair there's no maypole in the streets.

From barn to bahn, from town to country seats,
This is the land the landed ones forsook:
In Shepherd Market not a lambkin bleats.

Metropolitan policemen on their beats
May be observed inscribing in their book:
In Mayfair there's no maypole in the streets,
In Shepherd Market not a lambkin bleats.

(Richard Blomfield)

This village that I used to know so well
Is lined with gift shops selling rural kitsch.
(Or have I died? Is this my private hell?)

The village hall — at least its gutted shell —
Is now a 'Crafte Shoppe', run by some old witch.
The village that I used to know so well

Has been betrayed; obscenely keen to sell,
The natives flogged it to the filthy rich.
(Or have I died? Is this my private hell?)

Was that the bakery, whose yeasty smell
Would drift across our makeshift cricket pitch?
This village that I used to know so well

Has changed so much, it's very hard to tell
Which tarted-up old property is which.
(Or have I died? Is this my private hell?)

'I'd like to hire a bulldozer,' I yell,
'And sweep into the nearest bloody ditch
This village that I used to know so well!'
(Or have I died? Is this my private hell?)

(Peter Norman)

The branches wither once the root is killed.
These tall hotels grope vainly at the sky.
We cannot reach as high as we can build.

No matter what their architects have willed,
They look like hospitals where patients die.
The branches wither once the root is killed.

Where fields were torn up and foundations
   drilled
Loud Watney bars and discos testify
We cannot reach as high as we can build.

The port where shoals of fishing vessels milled
Abounds with kitsch that drunken tourists buy.
The branches wither once the root is killed.

The beach is spread with foreign bodies, grilled
Like oily chicken portions, breast and thigh.
We cannot reach as high as we can build.

Here, holidays are work for the unskilled,
Routines for those whose fancy has run dry.
The branches wither once the root is killed;
We cannot reach as high as we can build.

(Basil Ransome-Davies)

Stratford, where Shakespeare spent his
    childhood days,
Nursery of genius beyond compare
(If it was Will, indeed, who wrote those plays)

Now draws the tourists to its dud cafés,
Simply because they are located there:
Stratford, where Shakespeare spent his
    childhood days.

Dreaming of Lear's creator's ghost, they gaze,
See the 'same' sights and breathe the 'selfsame
    air!'
(If it was Will, indeed, who wrote those plays).

'Are these *his* footmarks or Anne Hathaway's?'
'*He* could have stood here, climbed that very
    stair!'
'Stratford! where Shakespeare spent his
    childhood days!'

'Some claim the works are Bacon's.' 'Others
    praise
De Vere.' 'And Marlowe!' 'Shall we ask the
    mayor
If it was Will, indeed, who wrote those plays?'

Watch how the placid Avon's waters laze
Between the Theatre and the striped deck-chair.
Stratford! where Shakespeare spent his
   childhood days
(If it was Will, indeed, who wrote those plays).

(Gerard Benson)

28 October 1989

THE ISOLATING OF MARGARET

Noel Malcolm

There are times when one does not know whether to eat one's words or to serve them up réchauffé. Just two weeks ago I wrote in this column that Mr Nigel Lawson was now more unsackable than he had been for a long time. By this I meant that to sack him would shake confidence in the economy, damage the reputation of the Government and cause serious dissension in the party. All this has been proved true. But I had forgotten the old rule which states that the best time to jump is when no one is able to push you.

Mr Lawson has done well out of it, which is not the same as saying that he has done well. Had he applied for a transfer at the last reshuffle in July, he would have been branded, however unfairly, as a mere fair-weather friend of the economy. Had he resigned, *per impossibile,* on the first day of the Tory Party conference last month, he would have spent the rest of his life with the hysterical headline of that day's *Daily Mail* pinned to his back: 'This Bankrupt Chancellor'. As it is, he is already in the process of being beatified as an upholder of all that is true and sacred about the British constitution − a defender of 'collegiate' government, and an implacable foe of all sinister secret advisers − and it looks as if he may even be canonised, most improbably of all, as a Euro-martyr. For someone who is said to be disdainful towards 'image'-oriented politics, he has not done at all badly for himself this time.

Addressing the House of Commons on Tuesday, Mr Lawson placed his first emphasis on the 'destructive potential' of Sir Alan Walters' glacial charm. This is the explanation with a handy human angle (clash of wills, sinister Rasputin-like figure, etc). But it just won't do. The ex-Chancellor can scarcely pretend that he was driven over the edge by Sir Alan's rambling autobiographical article, published last month but written nearly two years ago, in which the most damaging statement was (in the section on the Exchange Rate Mechanism) 'so far, Mrs Thatcher has concurred'.

Nor can he claim that he is opposed to the very idea of ministers having special advisers (of whom he has had several in his time). The constitutionalist bandwagon on this issue is a rickety vehicle travelling in no particular direction; most of the people on it can be found, at other times, complaining that elected ministers are constantly being thwarted by a conspiratorial, unelected civil service – against which they should therefore arm themselves with advisers of their own choosing. And neither can Mr Lawson really be advancing the dubious constitutional claim that individual ministers have the right to veto the appointment of personal advisers to the Prime Minister.

During her conversation with Mr Brian Walden last Sunday, Mrs Thatcher came within a whisker of explaining the real nature of the disagreement. Asked whether Mr Lawson would have stayed if she had sacked Professor Walters, she replied, 'I don't know'. At this, Mr Walden exclaimed 'You never even thought to ask him that?' and this earned the most revealing reply of the interview:

> I ... That is not ... I don't know. Nigel had determined that he was going to put in his resignation. I did everything possible to stop him.

That second string of dots could be filled out, perhaps, as follows. 'That is not the point that was really at issue. I told Nigel that whether Sir Alan stayed or went, I would continue to argue for the sort of policy which I had argued for, with Sir Alan's support, in the past.' When Mrs Thatcher says she did everything possible to stop him, what she means is that the one thing that would have succeeded in stopping him going was impossible for her, namely a promise that she would no longer oppose his economic policies. This, she felt, would be an abdication of her responsibility – so that in her eyes the real threat Mr Lawson had presented to her was not 'either he goes or I do' but 'either I go or you do'.

Put it like that, and it looks as if the Prime Minister should take some of the blame for not having seen this one coming. It would have been less damaging, for her, to have shuffled him willy-nilly out of the Treasury in July. But her reasoning then was that after more than a year of semi-public wrangling, Mr Lawson had shown he could put up with it; that one contentious issue, entry into the ERM, had been sorted out at Madrid in a compromise which they could both live with; and that since both she and Mr Lawson now wanted high interest rates (albeit for rather different reasons), they were less likely to disagree about tactics in the short term.

But that tactical agreement was already coming unstuck during last week. In Mrs Thatcher's and Sir Alan Walters' view, interest rates of 15 per cent were probably high enough to create the necessary squeeze on credit. For Mr Lawson, however, the rates would have to move higher if and when the defence of the pound required it. Management of the exchange rate had become his primary concern; her first priority was the control of the domestic money supply. This was the fundamental division between them. Even if the ERM had never been invented, this division between Mr Lawson and Mrs Thatcher would still have yawned, sooner or later, into an unbridgeable abyss.

The ERM may be something of a side-show to the real issue, but that has not stopped Mr Lawson from being enlisted already in the growing army of Euro-martyrs put to the sword by Mrs Thatcher. In the words of Mr Paddy Ashdown, 'her lonely hostility to Europe has cost her four Cabinet ministers'. (So Sir Leon Brittan left her Cabinet out of sympathy for Mr Heseltine's policy on Europe. Before long we shall be told that they marched out of the Cabinet room together, arm in arm, singing the European anthem.) Mr Lawson was playing to the ideological gallery a little when he ended his apologia on Tuesday with the argument that 'Britain's destiny lies in Europe'. He qualified this with the phrase, 'a Europe of nation states'; but he must have known that any qualifying clauses would wither away in the popular imagination, which would classify him as 'pro-Europe' and Mrs Thatcher as 'anti'. And this is a pity, because the detailed evidence he gave to the Treasury Select Committee in June showed that he was one of the most robust anti-federalists in Mrs Thatcher's Cabinet.

It has already become a commonplace that Europe is the real issue behind the Thatcher-Lawson split. Part of the explanation for this may be that Europe is a more 'sexy' topic for commentators to write about than the economic theory of exchange-rate management. But a more important reason is that a number of senior Tories *want* the European issue to become the universal solvent into which all rows with Mrs Thatcher are dissolved. For years, their complaints against her amounted to no more than saying that she was going too fast or too far; they would not challenge her sense of direction, only her lack of sensitivity. Now for the first time they have an issue on which they can accuse her of back-sliding, heel-dragging and being generally 'left-behind'. Hence, for example, Sir Geoffrey Howe's speech on Saturday, in which a routine statement of the Government's position was transformed, in the twinkling of a few adverbs, into a brave, visionary exhortation to a reluctant Prime Minister.

If this strategy works in the long term, it may eventually bring about the political eclipse of Mrs Thatcher. It will be a slow process (despite the strengthening of the European lobby's hand in last week's re-shuffle), given that the two ways for a senior Tory to grow in stature in the eyes of the public and the party are a) to disagree with Mrs Thatcher and b) to support her in her time of need. That is why it will be easier for them to demote her ideologically than to pull her down politically. The Howes and the Hurds will try to persuade us that they are the ones with a Great Cause now, the visionaries and the states-men. But the truth is that their attitude to politics remains far more managerial than Mrs Thatcher's, and that the appeal of Europe, to them, is that it represents managerialism writ large. Mrs Thatcher likes to argue straight from principle to immediate action; her princi-ples include the free market on the one hand and free nation-states on the other. Hers is a kind of politics which seeks first to judge the world and then to change it (or, as the case may be, to refuse to change it). The managers prefer just to manage the system as they find it — to respond a little here, yield a little there, and organise a little more thoroughly everywhere. If Mrs Thatcher feels betrayed by Mr Lawson, her deepest sense of betrayal must arise from the fact that he too, in his way, had become a manager.

4 November 1989

BOOKS

SUSPENSION OF DISBELIEF

Ferdinand Mount

COLERIDGE: EARLY VISIONS
by Richard Holmes
Hodder & Stoughton

Coleridge had already walked 40-odd miles through Somerset when he first caught sight of Wordsworth's house, Racedown Lodge, a Georgian box in the valley below him. Instead of going round by the road, he hurdled the gate and burst through a field of corn to greet the startled Dorothy. Neither she nor Wordsworth ever forgot this impetuous vaulting into their lives. One never forgot one's first sight of Coleridge. Hazlitt, a shy 17-year-old minister's son, was bowled over by STC's sermon in the Unitarian chapel at Shrewsbury: 'I could not have been more delighted if I had heard the music of the spheres. Poetry and philosophy had met together.' Two days afterwards, at the Hazlitt breakfast table, Coleridge received a letter from his equally dazzled young friend Tom Wedgwood, offering him £150 a year if he would waive the ministry and devote himself to poetry and philosophy: 'Coleridge seemed to make up his mind to close with this proposal in the act of trying on one of his shoes.'

His energy was at the same time appealing and appalling. Until well into his fifties, he would plunge into the sea without warning, just as precipitately as he enlisted in the 15th Light Dragoons under the alias of Silas Tomkyn Comberbache, to be discharged four months later as insane. Words poured in entrancing torrents in his never-lost Devon accent from his great slobbering ever-open mouth (he could not breathe through his nose).

Tipsiness, he said, had the unpleasant effect of

> making me talk *very* extravagantly; and as when sober,
> I talk extravagantly enough for any *common* tipsiness,

> it becomes a matter of nicety in discrimination to
> know when I am or am not affected – An idea starts up
> in my head – and away I follow it through thick and
> thin, Wood and Marsh, Brake and Briar – with all the
> apparent interest of a man who was defending one of
> his old and long-established Principles.

He would loll incontinently on young ladies' laps, gorging himself
on clotted cream, before slinking behind some door or bed-curtain to
dose himself with brandy or laudanum, dashing out for a quick one to
chemist or inn if supplies ran short. His literary appetites were just as
incontinent. He was a 'library cormorant', in his own famous phrase,
and he scribbled as fast as he read, notebooks being filled deep into the
night.

Even his fecund pen, though, could not keep up with his promises of
great works. Coleridge was, as the later, disillusioned Hazlitt said, the
past master of the Prospectus. He promised Godwin a 500-page printed
octavo, analysing 'all possible modes of true, probable and false
reasoning, arranged philosophically', the first half of which could be
'ready for the printer, at a fortnight's notice'. He promised his brother-
in-law Southey a 'six or eight' volume history of British literature
which would also include a running history of 'metaphysics, theology,
medicine, alchemy . . . medicine, surgery, chemistry, etc, etc, naviga-
tion, travellers, voyagers, etc, etc'. During his early enthusiasm for the
ideal fraternity he and his friends were going to found in Pennsylvania
on the banks of the Susquehanna, he instructed his fellow Pantisocrats
to learn the theory and practice of carpentry and agriculture and to free
their wives from household drudgery by themselves 'washing with a
machine and cleaning the House'.

When he became a full-scale drug-addict, not only were his night-
mares as frightful as any modern junkie's, but he could be just as
tediously importunate, writing to friends with naval connections, such
as Sir Joseph Banks and Wordsworth's brother John, demanding quanti-
ties of Indian hemp or 'Bang'. Some Coleridge-worshippers like to
portray him as a saintly figure inveigled into the agonies of addiction
by neuralgia and silly doctors. There was another, more hedonistic,
side, as shown in his letter to Banks: 'We will have a fair trial of Bang.
Do bring down some of the Hyoscyamine Pills and I will give a fair
Trial of Opium Hensbane, and Nepenthe. Bye the bye, I always

considered Homer's account of the Nepenthe as a Banging lie.' Or to Sir Humphry Davy of the wonderful prospect from Greta Hall: 'My dear fellow, I would that I could wrap up the view from my House in a pillow of Opium, and send it to you.'

It would be impossible to write a dull life of this torrential character. And Holmes's two-decker (he has already written an earlier brief life of STC) is a delightful helter-skelter through the first half of Coleridge's life, up to his departure for Malta at the age of 31, his best poetry already written, his marriage already tattered, his self-confidence as a poet shattered by Wordsworth's rejection of *Christabel*: 'as to Poetry I have altogether abandoned it, being convinced that I never had the essentials of poetic Genius, and that I mistook a strong desire for original power.'

Mr Holmes wants us, above all, to *meet* this extraordinary man, 'to set Coleridge *talking*', to 'unearth his "human story", his living footsteps through the world'. In particular, he wants us to see STC striding over the lakeland fells, over the length and breadth of Wales, over Quantock and Mendip, and up into the Harz mountains of Germany during his intoxicating months at Göttingen. 'I have taken Coleridge into the open air', Mr Holmes tells us, rather in the tones of a therapist who is confident his patient will be quite all right when he gets away from his unhealthy indoor life.

This approach has the great virtue of showing Coleridge at his best — the generous, full-bodied force of nature, with his eyes and his wits so flashingly about him. He was so *quick*, his sketches so exact. After rain on Ullswater, for example:

> a large Slice of calm silver — above this a bright
> ruffledness, or atomic sportiveness — motes in the sun?
> — Vortices of flies? — how shall I express the Banks
> waters all fused Silver, that House too its slates rainwet
> silver in the sun, & its shadows running down in the
> water like a column.

Or making a bonfire on the island on Grasmere lake:

> the wood, & mountains, & lake all trembling, & as it
> were *idealized* thro' the subtle smoke which rose up
> from the clear red embers of the fir-apples which we

had collected. Afterwards, we made a glorious Bonfire
on the Margin, by some alder bushes, whose twigs
heaved & sobbed in the uprushing column of smoke −
& the Image of the Bonfire, & of us that danced round it
− ruddy laughing faces in the twilight −

In this luminous air, that glorious period which produced *The
Ancient Mariner*, *Kubla Khan* and *Frost at Midnight* looks less like a
flash in the pan than a tragically brief glimpse of the real Coleridge, his
imagination concentrated upon its proper task, undistracted by circumstances (the self-imposed distractions were usually the worst).

When Coleridge is on song like this, with his biographer panting
along behind, we cannot help wishing that it could all go on for ever.
Mr Holmes does tell us that other biographers have been less inclined
to take STC's word for it and have found a darker side in him right
from the start. Coleridge has been variously described as a humbug, a
plagiarist, a liar, and a cruel and feckless husband. Mr Holmes merely
records the existence of such alternative verdicts without examining
them too closely: he himself is setting out to recapture Coleridge's
fascination as a man and as a writer. 'If he does not leap out of these
pages − brilliant, animated, endlessly provoking − and invade your
imagination (as he has done mine) then I have failed to do him justice.'

But will this approach quite do? We all know Coleridge is a
wonderful leaper. It is what he leaps over that is the trouble. We are not
judging the national high jump championships. The accusations made
against Coleridge are not merely academic nitpickings, and they
cannot be laughed off as the sort of prosaic questions that the Person
from Porlock would have asked.

Coleridge's oldest friends warned over and over again that his
testimony on any subject was extraordinarily unreliable. Lamb, who
had been a Bluecoat boy with him, wrote that as long as he had known
Coleridge, so long had he 'known him in the daily and hourly habit of
quizzing the world by lies'. Wordsworth said that 'Coleridge is a
subject which no Biographer ought to touch beyond what he himself
was eye witness of.' The indictment set out by Norman Fruman, in
Coleridge, The Damaged Archangel (Lamb's description), is almost
heartbreaking it is so overwhelming. For Coleridge's malpractice adds
up to rather more than occasional cribbing and fibbing. It is, I suppose,
a measure of the breadth if not the depth of his reading that no single

scholar could be sure of measuring how much he stole. When Coleridge copies out large chunks of Schelling, Kant and Schlegel, not merely does he fail to acknowledge his sources, he often mangles their intentions beyond recall. His famous critical distinctions, such as the one between Fancy and Imagination, were, Fruman asserts, for the most part not original but commonplace jargon in the Eng. Lit. debates of his day.

When compared, say, with the driving steadiness of Wordsworth's great preface to the second edition of *Lyrical Ballads*, Coleridge's ruminations often seem rambling and unfocused, suggestive, yes, but somehow fruitlessly suggestive. Mr Holmes appears to imply that, at any rate in this first volume, we need not bother our tiny English minds with the outpourings of German idealist philosophers. But how far Coleridge's prose writings are the product of his own marvellous sensitivity and acuity and how far they are ill-digested borrowings from imperfectly understood philosophers writing in a language he was still learning is surely a question which our insular self-confidence should not entirely excuse us from tackling – especially since Coleridge is one of the patron saints of the Eng. Lit. schools of today.

Worse still, the unacknowledged borrowings in the *poetry* make deeper and deeper inroads into what Fruman calls 'the shrinking canon' of Coleridge's work. For example, while arguing for Coleridge's later poetry as some of his most moving and revealing, Mr Holmes claims that 'it is impossible to understand him without reference to such works as "A Tombless Epitaph" (1811) which re-explores the symbolic caverns of his youth'. Yet Fruman points out that not only is 'A Tombless Epitaph' based on a poem by the 16th-century Italian poet Chiabrera (which Coleridge did acknowledge) but also it bears a remarkable similarity to Wordsworth's earlier translation of the same poem (which he did not).

Most autobiographers – even or perhaps especially those who do not shrink from showing us their own warts – allow themselves a good deal of licence with the truth. It does not really matter whether STC could, as he claims, read a chapter of the Bible by the age of three. Mr Holmes admits to being puzzled by some of the inconsistencies. Sometimes Coleridge describes himself as a spoilt mother's darling, sometimes as being 'hardly used from infancy to Boyhood and from Boyhood to Youth most, MOST cruelly'. Sometimes he claims to have been miserable at Christ's Hospital, sometimes he sounds quite a cheerful or at any rate resigned schoolboy. Both things can be true at once, but at the very least we should be on the look-out and should be wary, for example, of taking at face value Coleridge's picture of his own wife as a commonplace shrew. Another view is forcefully presented in Molly Lefebure's life of Sara, *The Bondage of Love*.

Mr Holmes does not dodge Coleridge's shortcomings entirely, but he lets him down a little lightly. When Coleridge asserts in a letter to Sara that 'in sex, acquirements, and in the quantity and quality of natural endowments whether of feeling, or of Intellect, you are Inferior', Mr Holmes merely comments that 'his lack of marital tact had become quite formidable'. Now of course geniuses often make rotten husbands and tend to believe in and act on the principle — enunciated in the same letter — that 'I can neither retain my Happiness nor my Faculties, unless I move, live and love in perfect Freedom'; in other words, Number One must come first all the time. All the same, there is something peculiarly creepy about Coleridge's persistent but unconsummated pursuit of the other Sara, Mrs Wordsworth's sister, Sara Hutchinson, nicknamed Asra. When Sara was about to have yet another baby, he even tried to persuade her to invite Asra to attend her lying-in, so that she could get to know her better.

Coleridge's in-and-out running is no more unusual among poets (or

'*Porlock Drug Squad. You're busted, Coleridge.*'

non-poets, come to that) than his self-pity — 'No-one on earth has ever LOVED me'. And if he were to be taken simply as a poet who had a few years of greatness, during his association with Wordsworth, and wrote four or five of the most wonderful poems in the language, then Porlock prodnoses ought to be silent. But his greatness as a poet, like his greatness as a human being, is inextricably entangled with his greatness as a philosopher, critic and sage (one reputation, so to speak, supports the other) and the charges against him do have to be met.

Mr Holmes says he hopes 'this book will read like the most traditional form of popular narrative biography'. Well, so it does, and a fresh, high-stepping representative of that stable too. But STC has been entered in an altogether more demanding race and he deserves a more vigorous if less enjoyable examination. Perhaps in Volume Two Mr Holmes will give him more of a going over.

11 November 1989

AFTER THE PARTY

Timothy Garton Ash

Berlin

Once upon a time, and a very bad time it was, there was a famous platform in West Berlin where distinguished visitors would be taken to stare at the Wall. The Queen, Mrs Thatcher, American presidents from Kennedy to Reagan stood on that platform looking out over the no-man's land between two concrete walls. They were told that this, the Potsdamer Platz, had once been Berlin's busiest square, its Piccadilly Circus. Their hosts pointed out a grassy mound in the middle of no-man's land: the remains of Hitler's bunker. Armed guards watched impassively from the other side. It was *the* image of the Cold War.

Last Sunday morning I walked across that no-man's land with a crowd of East Berliners. Bewildered border-guards waved us through the new crossing-point. (As recently as February their colleagues shot dead a man trying to escape.) On the far side, vertical segments of the Wall stood at ease wherever the crane had dumped them, their

multicoloured graffiti facing east for the first time. A crowd of West
Berliners applauded as we came through, and a man handed out free
city plans. Then I turned round and walked back again, past more
bewildered border guards and customs officers. Ahead of me I noticed a
tall man in an unfamiliar green uniform. He was one General Haddock,
the US commandant in Berlin. The US commandant, strolling across
the death strip.

By nightfall, West Berlin workers had dismantled the famous platform, like an unneeded stage-prop. Europe's *Mousetrap* has ended its
28-year run. Clear the stage for another show.

Everyone has seen the pictures of joyful celebration in West Berlin, the
vast crowds stopping the traffic on the Kurfuerstendamm, *Sekt* corks
popping, perfect strangers tearfully embracing — the greatest street-
party in the history of the world. Yes, it was like that. But it was not
only like that, nor was that, for me, the most moving part. Most of the
estimated two million East Germans who flooded into West Berlin
over the weekend just walked the streets in quiet family groups, often
with toddlers in pushchairs. They queued up at a bank to collect their
DM 100 (about £34) 'greeting money' and then they went, very
cautiously, shopping. Generally they bought one or two small items,
perhaps some fresh fruit, a Western newspaper and toys for the
children. Then, clasping their carrier bags, they walked quietly back
through the wall, through the grey, deserted streets of East Berlin,
home.

It is very difficult to describe the quality of this experience because
what they actually did was so stunningly ordinary. In effect, they just
took a bus from Hackney or Dagenham to Piccadilly Circus, and went
shopping in the West End. Berliners walked the streets of Berlin. What
could be more normal? And yet, what could be more fantastic — '28
years and 91 days,' says one man in his late thirties walking back up
Friedrichstrasse: 28 years and 91 days since the building of the Wall.
On that day, in August 1961, his parents had wanted to go to a
late-night Western in a West Berlin cinema. But their 11-year-old son
had been too tired. In the early hours they woke to the sound of tanks.
He had never been to West Berlin from that day to this. A taxi-driver
asks me, with a sly smile: 'How much is the ferry to England?' The day
before yesterday the question would have been unthinkable.

The people on the streets of East Berlin look the same as they make their way home – except for the tell-tale Western carrier bag. But everyone is inwardly changed, changed utterly. 'Now people are standing up straight,' says a hotel porter. 'They are speaking their minds. Even work is more fun. I think the sick will get up from their hospital beds.' And it is in East rather than West Berlin that this weekend has the magic, pentecostal quality which I last experienced in Poland in autumn 1980. Ordinary men and women find their voice and their courage – *Lebensmut*, as the porter puts it. These are moments when you feel that, as in the Jewish legend, somewhere above you an angel has opened his wings.

Ordinary people doing very ordinary things (shopping!), the Berliners nonetheless immediately grasped the historical dimensions of this event. 'Of course the real villain was Hitler,' said one. And the man who counted the 28 years and 91 days told me he had been most moved by an improvised poster saying 'Only today is the war really over.'

Bild newspaper – West Germany's *Sun* – carried, on its front page, an effusive thank-you letter from the editors to Mikhail Gorbachev.

The East Germans also feel grateful to Gorbachev. But more important, they feel they have won this opening for themselves. For it was
only the pressure of their massive, peaceful demonstrations that
compelled the Party leadership to take this step. 'You see, it shows
Lenin was wrong,' observed one worker. 'Lenin said a revolution could
only succeed with violence. But this was a peaceful revolution.' And
even the Communist Party's Central Committee acknowledges at the
beginning of its hastily drafted Action Programme that 'a revolutionary people's movement has set in motion a process of profound
upheavals'.

If the Party leaders thought that by opening the frontiers they could
reduce the pressure from below, they may soon have to think again.
For the sentiment of everyone I talked to was: 'This is only the
beginning.' Having cast aside their gags and crutches they have no
intention of taking them up again. In Leipzig the by now traditional
Monday evening demo was reportedly slightly smaller after the opening of the frontiers. But the demands were clearer and louder than ever:
free elections and an end to the leading role of the Socialist Unity
Party.

'Good story,' remarked the American television reporter standing in
the queue at West Berlin airport. 'Kinda trailed away yesterday and
today,' said his colleague. 'Yeah, audience interest way down.' This
tells us something about America, but nothing about the story, which
has only just begun. It is, in fact, three concentric stories: those of
Berlin, Germany and Europe.

The surest part is the smallest: the reunification of Berlin. It will
probably be some time before the Potsdamer Platz becomes a Piccadilly Circus again, although there is already a fantastic plan to build a
huge department store — a *Kaufhaus des Ostens* — with entrances
from both sides. But the mental geography of both half-cities has
changed overnight. What was the edge has become the centre. And
practical convergence proceeds apace. Bus services will now run
through the Wall. Where previously a West Berlin underground line
ran through ghostly, sealed stations in East Berlin, the doors now open
and East Berliners leap aboard. East and West Berlin police co-operated
— at one point actually arm-in-arm — to restrain the crowds at the new
crossings.

There will be problems enough here. The warmth and generosity of the West Berliners' welcome was spectacular. 'I was really received like a brother,' one youth told me – and whether he was tipsy with *Sekt* or sheer excitement I could not tell. Probably both. The old, pathos-laden phrase about 'our brothers and sisters in the East' acquired a new reality. But for how long? Already by the end of the weekend there were complaints about the East Berliners causing traffic jams and the stink from the two-stroke engines of their little Trabant cars. What if they keep coming? And what if you get thousands of East Berliners coming over to do legal or illegal part-time jobs, taking work away from West Berliners? And then look at it from the other side. What on earth will an open border do to the East German economy? Won't the strong currency drive out the weak?

Here the Berlin story flows into the German story. These developments have thrown all the West German parties into turmoil. The Ostpolitik, says its father Willy Brandt, is over. It began with the building of the Wall; it has ended with the opening of the Wall. But for the next few weeks, at least, the crucial action will be in East Germany. Shattered by people's power, the Communist Party has embarked on a *Flucht nach vorn*, a flight forward. Previously subservient puppet parties, the rubber-stamp parliament, the media, all have suddenly come to life, like so many Pinocchios touched by the blue fairy of revolution. Hans Modrow, the new Prime Minister, should have announced his new coalition government by the time you read this. There is to be a special Party congress in the middle of next month. But can they begin to satisfy the hundreds of thousands of people on the streets demanding free elections and an end to Party power?

Beside the political crisis there is the economic crisis, which Monday's stormy session of the parliament revealed to be deeper even than many Western analysts had thought. The opening of the frontiers will immediately expose it to new pressures, with the East Germany mark, officially at parity with the deutschmark, now standing unofficially at one tenth of that. In terms of structural economic reform the country has much further to go than, say, Hungary. In any attempted marketisation, people are likely to get worse off initially. Worsening economic conditions would increase political discontent, and also the temptation to sell out – individually or collectively – to West Germany.

At the moment there is one thing on which the opposition and the Party agree: they don't want to sell out. On Sunday evening I took part in a discussion about reunification in an East Berlin church. Some 20 people spoke from the floor. Not one was for reunification. The new opposition groups – New Forum, Democracy Now, Democratic Awakening – want to make a different East Germany, a Third Way. But even if there is theoretically a third way – and their programmes are desperately vague – it is by no means clear that this is what the majority in East Germany will actually want, once they start to think about it. After all, they have seen West Germany – and it works. Despite the explicit wishes of all the politically articulate forces in East Germany at this moment, and the explicit or implicit desires of many in West Germany, the logic of events may therefore begin to pull both halves together at remarkable speed.

Here, at the latest, the German story becomes a European story, with fundamental implications for Britain. An East German foreign trade minister has already said that an application to join the EC could not be ruled out. Even intermediate steps of association pose major problems – as European leaders will be discussing at the emergency summit in Paris this weekend. Britain remains an occupying power in Berlin. Our representatives, along with those of France and the United States, had direct contacts with the Russians over the weekend. (They speak on the telephone, in German!) The West German and West Berlin governments recognise that this four-power framework is still a useful one for managing the reunification of Berlin, and reassuring the Russians. But it will be increasingly difficult to explain to German voters. Already the arch-strategist of social democratic Ostpolitik, Egon Bahr, is saying: 'all this rubbish with these old occupation rights must now be finished.'

And then there is the biggest question of all: the alliances. If you were Mr Gorbachev, and you saw East Germany falling into the West German embrace, what would you do? Would you cling for dear life to your military presence, with the residual control possibilities that offers? Or would you go for a bigger prize – Nato! A crude offer like that Stalin made in March 1952 – neutralisation in return for reunification – would almost certainly still be rejected by West Germany. But a more subtle package, under the sign of 'co-operative security', suggesting the removal of all nuclear weapons and Soviet and American troops from an area called 'Central Europe': this, I believe, could rapidly win powerful support in West Germany, and might well be accepted by the main opposition party, the Social Democrats. And next December there is a general election.

As the demolition of that famous platform on Potsdamer Platz followed swiftly on the opening of the Wall, so larger Western landmarks may soon follow Eastern ones, into history.

18 November 1989

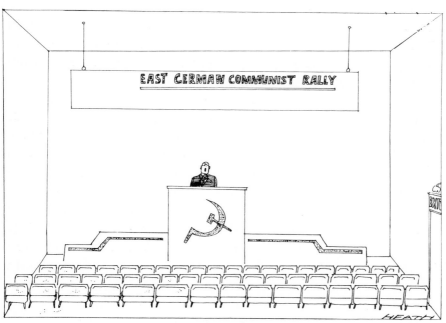

'Comrades.'

TEN DAYS THAT STIRRED
THE WORLD

Timothy Garton Ash

Prague

It has been a year of peaceful revolutions in Central Europe, but this is the fastest, merriest of them all. What in Poland took years of hard struggle, in Hungary months, in East Germany weeks, has happened here in days.

Only the very beginning was neither fast nor merry. On Friday 17 November, some 50,000 people, mainly students, turned out for an officially permitted demonstration to mark the 50th anniversary of the murder of a Czech student by the Nazis. It was a long, joyful march, with the chants and slogans directed increasingly against the present rulers in Prague Castle, and it wound its way to the traditional forum for national manifestations: Wenceslas Square. Here, however, most of

the demonstrators were surrounded and cut off by white helmeted riot police and, for the first time, by red-bereted anti-terrorist squads. The crowd placed candles before them and tried to give them flowers. People knelt on the ground and raised their arms, chanting, 'We have bare hands.' But the police, and especially the red berets, beat them nonetheless: truncheoning men, women and children.

This was the spark that set Czechoslovakia alight. In the night from Friday to Saturday — with reports of one student dead, and many certainly in hospital — the students determined to go on strike. Then they decided to call for a nationwide general strike in a week's time. The universities were joined by the theatres, which had already been active in the defence of the playwright, opposition leader and now national hero, Vaclav Havel. On Sunday evening Havel himself called a meeting of all the main opposition groups, and members of the formerly puppet Socialist and People's Parties, in a theatre. They joined together in what they called a Civil Forum, demanding the resignation of the Party leaders directly responsible for the Warsaw Pact invasion in 1968, a special commission to investigate the 'massacre' of 17 November, the punishment of those responsible for it, and the release of all prisoners of conscience.

Students, actors and intellectuals were thus the vanguard of this revolution. But, as in East Germany, the crucial difference was made by ordinary people coming out onto the streets: by People Power. For on Monday afternoon Wenceslas Square was filled by a huge crowd — 200,000 they say — supporting the students who spoke from beneath the equestrian statue of St Wenceslas, while behind it a banner on the huge and imposing national theatre declared 'the national theatre with the nation'. The moment had come. The most thoroughly Western of East Central European countries was demanding that its proper history should start again, as those of its neighbours, Hungary, Poland, Germany, already had. These children had shown them the way. As a friend explained to me, for 20 years people had kept quiet and knuckled under 'for the children's sake'. And now the police were beating even the children. 'Parents come with us,' said a banner on the Wenceslas statue, 'we are your children.' And so they did.

As in East Germany, when the Party leaders had woken up to what was happening, it was already too late. In Central Europe today, with Gorbachev in the Kremlin, the kind of violence needed to repress such masses of people appears simply not to be an available option. (But the prime minister, Adamec, subsequently emphasised that martial law would not be imposed, thus implying that the option had been seriously considered.) Once people saw the door to self-expression was open, they rushed through it with shouts of glee.

By midweek, the centre of Prague was plastered with improvised posters declaring 'Truth will prevail!' or 'Let the government resign!' or 'We support the general strike.' There were xeroxed photos of the prewar president, Thomas Garrigue Masaryk, and copies of the Civic Forum declaration (often computer-printed). Groups gathered in front of shop windows where televisions played over and over again a videotape of the 17 November events. Ever larger crowds gathered for the afternoon demonstrations in Wenceslas Square, waving their red, white and blue flags and chanting away as if this was the most usual thing in the world. Cars hooted in support as they drove across the top of the square, and small children gave V-for-Victory signs. Meanwhile, Adamec had his first meeting with representatives of the Civic Forum. The once puppet Socialist Party opened its newspaper, *Svobodné Slovo* (The Free Word), to fair reports of the protest movement, and its balcony, perfectly located halfway down Wenceslas Square, to the speakers organised by the Forum. Even the official radio and television began to report opposition demands.

On Friday came Dubcek. He looked as if he had stepped straight out of a black and white photograph from 1968. The same grey coat and paisley scarf, the same tentative smile, the same functionary's hat: all contributed to the illusion that we had just left a 20-year timewarp, with the clock that stopped in 1969 starting again in 1989. As we scuttled along the covered shopping arcades to reach the balcony, people simply gaped. It was as if the ghost of Winston Churchill were to be seen striding down the Burlington Arcade. But when he stepped out into the frosty evening air, illuminated by television spotlights, the crowd gave such a roar as I have never heard, 'DUBCEK! DUBCEK!' Many people mourn his ambiguous role after the Soviet invasion, and his failure to use the magic of his name to support the democratic opposition.

He has not changed with the times. His speeches still contain those wooden, prefabricated newspeak phrases. He still believes in socialism − that is, reformed communism − with a human face. The true leader of this movement is not Dubcek but Havel. But for the moment none of this matters. For the moment all that matters is that the legendary hero is really standing here, addressing a huge crowd on Wenceslas Square, while the emergency session of the Central Committee has, we are told, been removed to a distant suburb. They have fled. 'Dubcek to the castle!' cries the crowd: that is, Dubcek for President.

Later in the evening, Dubcek and Havel again share the stage. Literally so, for the Civic Forum has its headquarters in a theatre, called, appropriately enough, the Magic Lantern, and the press conference is held on a stage, complete with set. Dubcek and Havel are just telling us their different ideas about socialism when the conference is interrupted by the news that the whole Politburo and Central Committee secretariat have resigned. The theatre erupts in applause. Havel embraces Dubcek, and makes the V-for-Victory sign. Someone brings them champagne. Havel raises his glass and toasts 'a free Czechoslovakia!' For 20 years his work has been banned from Czechoslovak stages. But he has been saving it up. And this production will certainly go into the history books. Cry your eyes out, Bertolt Brecht.

Next morning, the waiter in my hotel sees me reading *Svobodné Slovo*. 'Ah, victoria!' he says, pointing to the blue, white and red ribbon in his lapel. Then he leans over and whispers in my ear: 'finished communism'. Straightening up, he rubs his shoe across the floor, as if crushing a beetle. Then he takes my newspaper, but not my breakfast order, and disappears into the kitchen.

This Saturday there is, by happy chance, a festive mass in the cathedral to celebrate the canonisation of Agnes of Bohemia. The 89-year-old Cardinal Frantisek Tomasek is the symbol of a resistance older than that represented by either Havel or Dubcek: some two thousand years older. The Church here is nothing like the force that it is in Poland, for Czechoslovakia has been historically (and bitterly) divided between Roman Catholics and Protestants, and both Churches were ruthlessly suppressed in the Stalinist period. Much of the crowd on Wenceslas Square did not know the words of the old Wenceslas hymn. But Catholics play a crucial part in the opposition. And Tomasek has declared, 'The Catholic Church stands entirely on the side of the people in this present struggle. . . . I trust completely the Civic Forum, which has become a spokesman for the whole nation.' So there is a goodly crowd here too, overflowing into the castle square. In front of the Archbishop's Palace they chant 'Frantsi Tomasek, Frantsi Tomasek', a marvellously chummy way to address a Cardinal (as it might be, ' "Basi" Hume'). And the mass for the patron saint of

Bohemia, the king's daughter who came down to live among the poor, is a further celebration of national renewal. Angels at work.

Later, in freezing snow, there is the biggest demonstration of all: perhaps half a million people, in a park before a football stadium. Again there are cries for the government to resign, expressions of support for the general strike, and, most important, for free elections. The Civic Forum, for its part, expresses dismay at the composition of the new Party leadership, and calls for the general strike to be an 'informal nationwide referendum on whether or not we want to go on being humiliated and also whether the leaders of the one political party, permanently monopolising the leading role, should continue to ruin this country.'

On Sunday morning, Adamec had a fully official meeting with a Civic Forum delegation led by Vaclav Havel. In the afternoon, there is yet another huge demonstration from the stadium, to which Adamec agrees to speak. 'Adamec, Adamec', chants the crowd, but when he calls for discipline, no more strikes, and economic rather than political change, the reception is as cold as the weather itself. All the greater is the enthusiasm for Havel and his concise description of the Civic Forum as a bridge from totalitarianism to democracy. 'Free elections' is again the cry.

The crowd has developed an extraordinary capacity to talk to the speakers, in rhythmic chant. 'Make way for the ambulance!' they chant, when one is needed, or 'turn up the volume!' When a long list of political prisoners is read out they chant 'Stepan to prison!' (Miroslav Stepan is the much disliked Prague Party secretary, also held partly responsible for the 17 November action.) 'Perhaps we should give him a spade,' says a voice from the platform. 'He'd steal it!' comes the almost immediate response from the crowd, half a million speaking as one. And then 'Here it comes!' And sure enough, there is a spade held aloft at the front of the crowd. 'Stepan, Stepan,' they cry, as in a funeral chant, and then they take out their keys and ring them like Chinese bells.

Next morning we have the news that Stepan, along with further discredited leaders, has resigned at an extraordinary session of the Central Committee. The same session voted for a special Party congress in January 1990, and a small catalogue of good intentions. Western journalists obsessively ask the Civic Forum what they think of the latest Party moves, and what the Party will do next. Of course they don't know, and anyway that is not the point. The point is to try to organise what has in ten days become a civic crusade for national renewal.

By the start of the general strike, at noon on Monday, it is already clear that it will be a success. The media, and above all the television, had given it extensive and mainly positive coverage. Many communists seem to have decided 'if you can't beat them, join them' — at least for the duration of the strike. Television reports of large, peaceful strike meetings all over the country had subtitles explaining that these reports were the television team's contribution to the strike.

I was driven by Petr Miller, a technician and workers' leader from one of the largest Prague factories, to a meeting at the factory gate. On the way we passed an incredible sight: a line of taxis at least one mile long, taxi after taxi, crawling out up to the hills, hooting. It was the taxi-drivers' strike demonstration. At the factory gate, the workers listened patiently to a long lecture about political and economic reform from the well known head of a particularly outspoken research institute, Dr Valtr Komarek. 'Komarek, Komarek,' they chanted. The meeting ended at half past one so they could be back at work by two. So the general strike was a triumph.

And now there is yet another demonstration on Wenceslas Square. Here an emerging star of the Civic Forum, Dr Vaclav Klaus, reads the text of the latest declaration, announcing the formation of a co-ordinating centre for Forum groups throughout the country. If Adamec is not ready to meet the Forum's demands, they will demand the government's resignation. 'Resignation!' chants the crowd. All this concerns only the transitional phase to the indispensable free elections. Then comes the portly and bespectacled Dr Komarek, who offers what amounts to a new government programme. 'Komarek! Komarek!' cry the people. Then a girl student reads, very slowly and clearly, as if in school dictation, a letter from the students asking the President of the Republic to replace Adamec with Komarek. Oh yes, and incidentally the Forum has produced a statement of basic principles: the rule of law, democracy, European integration, market economy.

Just ten days ago, the police were truncheoning children on this very square. Czechoslovakia still seemed lost under the Brezhnevite ice of the last 20 years. Now the opposition, having organised a nationwide general strike, has just presented an alternative candidate for prime minister, and a programme for the end of communism in Czechoslovakia. And the people in the square applaud as if they would never have thought of anything else. 'That's it,' they chant, 'that's it!' On Tuesday, a Civic Forum delegation had another hectic meeting with the Prime Minister, Mr Adamec, and a group representing the government and the so-called National Front of parties previously tied to the communists' apron strings. Adamec agreed to present a new government based on a 'broad coalition', a 'government of experts', by the end of the week. He will propose to the Federal Assembly (the pseudo-parliament) that the clauses concerning the leading role of the communist party and the grounding of education in Marxism-Leninism be deleted from the constitution (as done already in Poland and Hungary, and suggested in East Germany). The Civic Forum called on the authorities to release all prisoners of conscience by 10 December, international human rights day. They also called on Gustav Husak, the President and ultimate symbol of the lost 20 years since 1969, to resign by the same date.

The Prime Minister has until the end of the year to introduce a credible programme including the legal conditions for free elections, free assembly, speech and press, an end to state control over the churches, and amending the defence law. If the new government does not make satisfactory progress by the end of the year, the Civic Forum will call on the Prime Minister to resign, and suggest a new one! Regional and local committees throughout the country, and students and workers on 'strike alert', will provide the national backing for their negotiation of this transition. But for the time being, there will be no more strikes or mass demonstrations.

The first and, so to speak, heroic phase of the revolution is thus over. Symbolically, the Civic Forum now moves from its improvised quarters in the Magic Lantern to more normal offices provided by the City Council. These were perhaps not 'ten days that shook the world', but they were certainly ten days that delighted the world, changed the political face of Europe (for all of East Central Europe is now sailing towards democracy), and, above all, offered, as one of the earliest demonstration banners said, 'a chance for 15 million' Czechs and Slovaks. 'The heart of Europe cries for freedom,' declared another homemade poster. The second phase that now opens bids fair to be one of tortuous, complex negotiation, with not a few divisions, ambiguities and compromises. The revolution inside the Communist Party itself has only just begun. This is no time or place for prediction. By the time you read this, four or five more extraordinary, unprecedented and unpredictable events will probably have occurred. The clocks have started again in Czechoslovakia, and they are racing to make up lost time.

2 December 1989

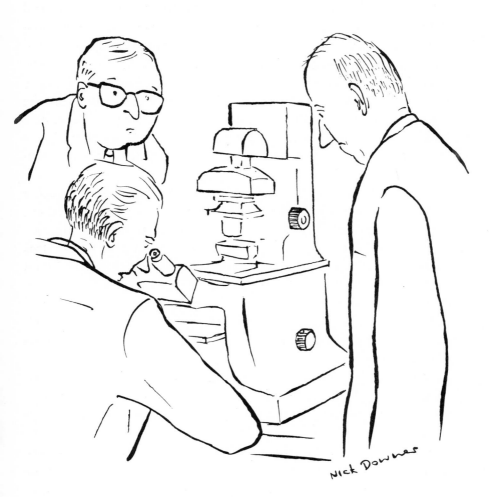

'*By God, you're right, Harris, extremely miniature golf.*'

THE EDWARD LEAR POEM

John Mole

He kept his wife in a box he did
And she never complained though the neighbours did
Because of the size of the box and the way
He tried to behave in a neighbourly way
But smiled too much of a satisfied smile
For a body to know what to make of his smile.

Then there came such a terrible cry one night
Of the kind you don't like to hear in the night
Though the silence that followed was broken at last
By the blows of a hammer which seemed to last
For ever and ever and ever and ever
And no one set eyes on that man again ever.

2 December 1989

THE KING OF BOHEMIA

Timothy Garton Ash

Prague

A more unlikely leader of a revolution it would be hard to imagine.
The playwright and essayist Vaclav Havel is a Bohemian in both senses
of the word. He is a Czech intellectual from Bohemia, with a deep
feeling for his native land. He is an artist, nowhere happier than in a
tavern with a glass of beer or becherovka, and the company of pretty
and amusing friends.

Short, with light hair and moustache, and a thick body perched on
small feet, he looks younger than his 53 years. Even in quieter times,
he is a bundle of nervous energy, with hands waving like twin

propellers, and a quite distinctive, almost Chaplinesque walk: short steps, slightly stooping, a kind of racing shuffle. He wears jeans, open shirts, perhaps a corduroy jacket, only putting on a suit and tie under extreme duress: for example, when receiving some international prize. (He has had two in the last fortnight.) Negotiations with the government, by contrast, do not qualify for suit and tie. His lined yet boyish face is constantly breaking into a winning smile, while from inside this small frame a surprisingly deep voice rumbles out some wry remark. Despite appearances, he has enormous stamina: few men could have done half of what he has in the last fortnight, and come out walking, let alone talking. Yet here he is, at one o'clock in the morning in his favourite pub, laughing as if he made revolutions every week.

His charm, eloquence and stamina have carried him thus far through a life deeply marked by the sufferings of his country. He was born just two years before Britain and France sold Czechoslovakia down the river, at Munich in 1938. He was 12 when the communists seized power in the Prague coup of 1948. As punishment for his *haut bourgeois* social origins − his father was a well-known pre-war millionaire − he was barred from secondary and higher education in the humanities. After a makeshift technical education, he gravitated to the theatre, first as stage manager, then as playwright, working in those Prague theatres which have now been turned into political debating chambers.

Even in the 1950s he was involved in the first attempts to produce a sort of rudimentary *samizdat*, and in informal discussion groups. One, which met in the famous Café Slavia, called itself the 'Generation of '36'. While never neglecting the bohemian side of life, he nonetheless played an active intellectual role − with his plays and occasional writings − in the preparation of the Prague spring. His dramatic work also began to be known and performed in the West. Czechoslovakia's third 'year of 8' − 1968 − was a drastic turning-point in his, as in all his compatriots', lives. Within a few years, his plays were being performed everywhere except in his own country. When, at the age of 41, he became one of Charter 77's first spokesmen, even his name was banished from the Czechoslovak media − except when they denounced him as a millionaire's son and agent of Western imperialism.

The next period, from 1977 until almost the day before yesterday, was of hard, isolated struggle. Support for the Chartists grew only very slowly. The repression was harsh. Havel himself spent nearly five years in prison. To be sure, there were compensations. There was the comradeship of a small circle of persecuted idealists. There was his growing fame in the world, both as a writer and as a campaigner for human and civil rights. And there was, for the last year or two, the sense that at last other people were beginning to wake up and stand up: Christians, with their petition for religious freedom, students, actors.

It is difficult to say precisely why Havel became such a central figure in the, so to speak, pre-revolutionary opposition. He was not an obvious leader, like the grave and princely philosopher Jan Patocka. His international reputation surely had something to do with it – his fame and his leading role in the opposition each reinforcing the other. So did his personality: that mixture of stamina and determination with charm and great courtesy. He also had the advantage of not being closely identified with any particular political, religious or ideological tendency. In any case, it seemed natural that when the revolution began it was Havel who, dashing back to Prague from his farmhouse in northern Bohemia, summoned a meeting of all the main opposition groups – in a theatre, of course – led the formation of the Civic Forum, and drafted its first declaration.

Since then he has been the epicentre of the revolution: at once playwright, stage manager, director and leading actor in this theatre of the fantastic. To be sure, much happens without him. The students who actually started the revolution are still in the vanguard, and fiercely independent. The workers have their strike committees. Civic Forum groups are sprouting spontaneously in institutes, schools, shops, hospitals, even in government offices. The Forum's central 'co-ordinating' body meets in plenary session and in working groups. But his presence gives a special quality to each meeting he attends. And there is no doubt that all the crucial political decisions and statements of the Forum are, at the very least, made in consultation with him.

Future historians may detect in some of those early moves and statements the hand of the dramatist and moralist rather than the politician. The ten days up to the general strike were almost perfect. But the second week perhaps saw the Forum dispersing its energies in too many directions at once, while various powers-that-be (or were) deliberately muddied the waters. But if anyone kept the opposition centre in Prague together, balancing the very diverse tendencies inside the Forum with an almost charismatic authority, it was Havel.

Those future historians must also try to imagine the extraordinary physical circumstances in which these decisions were made, in the subterranean Magic Lantern theatre. Havel had his personal headquarters in dressing room number 10, in a desperately stuffy and overheated corridor, with a permanent scrum before the door. Everyone was exhausted. Everyone, but everyone, wanted just a minute of his time. For the duration of the revolution he has a bodyguard, a posse of beefy youths led by the dynamic son of a Czech wartime RAF pilot. But people got through to the great man nonetheless.

One moment he was dashing off to speak on television, the next to a meeting of the 'crisis staff' in the theatre's 'smoking room'; then on to negotiate with the Prime Minister. In between he popped out to receive the Olaf Palme Prize and the Peace Prize of the German book trade. Now he had to placate the students, now to attend the inaugural meeting of a new independent writers' union. He was just slipping away from that when they hauled him back on stage (it was in a theatre, of course) and told him he must be chairman. Elected by acclamation, he made his racing shuffle to the microphone and said thank you, yes, thank you, and he was frightfully sorry but he really had to dash . . . and so he did, for they were about to tell him the composition of the new government. This was the atmosphere in which decisions were made.

Last Saturday evening there was a ceremony on the stage of the Magic Lantern to thank the staff for their help. After short speeches the lights went down, a fireworks display was projected onto the backdrop, and everyone joined in singing the Czech version of 'We shall Overcome', swaying from side to side with hands raised in the V-for-Victory sign. Then we drank pink champagne. Emerging from the auditorium, I saw a solitary figure standing in the foyer with half-raised glass, indecisively, as if pulled in four directions at once by invisible arms. It was Havel. We sat down on a bench and he rumbled confidentially: 'I am just engaged in very important negotiations about . . .' — at which point a pretty girl came up with another bottle of champagne. Then someone with an urgent message. Then another pretty girl. Then Prince Schwarzenberg from Vienna. I never did get his account of those vital negotiations.

Suddenly everyone was wearing blue, white and red badges declaring 'Havel for President'. Well, more improbable things have happened in Central Europe. From what I know of him, he really would not like the job. Too much suit-and-tie. And if he had the greatness thrust upon him, he would still more likely be found in the pub at the bottom of the castle hill, rather than in the palace atop it. But whatever happens, for today he is the uncrowned King of Bohemia.

9 December 1989

LAND OF LOST VILLAGES

Simon Jenkins

Every village along the Iron Curtain now has its November 1989 story. On the 19th, the little town of Hornburg, west of the fence near Brunswick, was awakened at 6 a.m. to the sound of its fire engine racing down the lane towards the wall of steel, wire and machine guns across the fields one kilometre to the east. The villagers rose and followed it. In the old days, the only event to bring out the engine like this was an escapee being shot.

As they crested the small hill which marks the parish boundary between Hornburg and Rhoden, and between East and West, the villagers were astonished. There in the lights of their fire engine, East German border guards were cutting through the metal and wire and laying duckboards in the mud of no-man's-land. Behind them, an eerie crowd of some 5,000 people, drawn as if by some magnetic herd instinct, was gathering in the freezing dawn, ready to walk across.

These were not the sophisticates of East Berlin or Leipzig. They were simple farmers from the frontier villages, from Rhoden and Bühne and Osterwieck, entombed for the bulk of their lives in the border zone. Like Fidelio's prisoners, they could scarcely believe what was happening. They streamed through the gap in the fence, tears in their eyes, to the embraces of the Hornburgers. After four decades, their VE day had come at last.

Last week, I passed through the same gap in the opposite direction. I went in the company of a Hornburg farmer's daughter, 31-year-old Karolina Arnold, proud to have ploughed 'the last furrow' against the Iron Curtain and eager to meet the inhabitants of the villages over the valley, ploughmen she could see from her bedroom window but never met. As a child, she had played games of 'dare' right up to the edge of no-man's-land. She had stood with elderly villagers gazing through binoculars at the funerals of their friends in the East. They were Germans too, separated by some mediaeval baron into another parish, and by the cruel cartography of 1945 into another state, another ideology and another hemisphere. To Karolina they were now total aliens.

We thus entered the East German border security zone, until now utterly forbidden to foreigners. The strip runs from the sea at Lübeck down through the Harz mountains to the Czechoslovak border. It must rank as one of the great lost corners of Europe. With commercial activity frozen since 1945, it has been inaccessible to non-locals even from the east since the fence was built in 1961. Here, villages have been left undisturbed, ageing, rotting, their young draining away and the land degenerating into collectivised exhaustion. Here are hills and plains where soldiers plot atomic minefields and tank deployments, where every living thing was expected to vanish in the first puff of a battlefield nuclear exchange.

We wandered along the east side of the fence uninterrupted. Youthful border guards shook hands, exchanged souvenirs and addresses and pointed out the features of no-man's-land like practised tour guides. Soldiers Hendrick and Olaf, unborn when the fence went up, posed for pictures against watchtowers and free-fire zones. The Cold War they had known all their lives was at an end. This was their own personal armistice. We were their first Westerners. They were elated.

In the frontier villages of Rhoden and Bühne, we found villagers still reeling from that night of 19 November, when they grabbed every sack they had, and every baby (to qualify for West Germany's gift of 100 deutschmarks per head), and made the mile-long trek over the hill to Hornburg. They returned the following evening dazed by the cars, the colour of the advertising, the wealth, the shops, the prices. No amount of Western television had prepared them for the culture shock. It was like mainland Chinese visiting Hong Kong.

I met one old man quite shattered by the experience. He found the West intolerably 'noisy'. He was shocked to discover that food was a different price in different shops and felt constantly cheated. Another old man, who had farmed the village fields since 1936 and had cousins in the West, could not face the trauma of the encounter. He was happy to go on ploughing his smallholding with his two shire horses.

At a bus stop, I was assailed by a local who had fought with Rommel and been imprisoned by Montgomery at El Alamein. The English had ruined his 'prime of life'. Repatriated here to Rhoden in 1945, his anti-British resentment had been unsoothed by time; he finally unleashed it on me, an enraged Rip van Winkel, stamping on the cold muddy pavement.

On all sides, there was nervous pride. The keeper of the one shop in Rhoden simply would not sell any of the cakes in her window, ashamed of their quality. She insisted on giving me gifts instead. These are Europe's mental refugees, forgotten, bitter, threatened not by economic distress − they are used to that − but by the humiliation that all their deprivation has been in vain. This is what drove Egon Krenz from power last week.

These villages are not poor historically. This is not Silesia or East Prussia. Here in Lower Saxony was the richest country in Europe. The people speak the same German, with the same accent, as their neighbours in the West. Only the vocabulary is now different − permeated by decades of Eastern propaganda, insulated from the words and phrases of Western capitalism.

More important, they can still share their finest asset, their landscape and townscape. The villages are remarkably unscarred by war and are visibly of the 16th and 17th centuries. Their sweeping tile roofs, half-timbering, pointed church spires and smoking chimneys might be Pied Piper stage sets. Many of the older houses, starved of restoration, are deserted, some with roofs caved in. Churches are ruined, their graveyards overgrown. But the coloured fantail decoration, known as *Fachwerk*, is still discernible on the façades. The huge old barns and farmyards are museums of industrial archaeology. The streets are still cobbled and strewn with straw.

East Germany is now agonising over its economic future, obsessed by West Germany's manufacturing strength. If it can bring itself to be truly radical, I see no problem, at least in this land of lost villages. The countryside offers precisely the qualities in shortest supply in the West: cheap and attractive old houses and an accompaniment of peace and quiet.

These villages could leap direct from the last century into the next. They could, restored with careful planning control, skip an entire era of countryside ruination, of commercial tattiness, of ribbon development, of pylons and advertisement hoardings, unnecessary roadworks and grotesque garages. Here are settlements where cobbled squares lead into mediaeval alleys and out into the woods and fields in complete harmony. This is not kitsch nostalgia, but the most intense scenic beauty.

In Halberstadt, three great churches, one of them pure romanesque, soar over a renaissance town hall, a bishop's palace and a complete old town of half-timbered streets that would outrank Chester or York – and certainly rival Goslar or Celle over the border. Six hundred timber-framed houses were listed in 1930, and most seemed to me still standing, just. Yet the great Lutheran cathedral is utterly dejected. The old town is largely unoccupied, lost in time, waiting.

East Germans are now flowing west, the new *Gastarbeiter* of the West German economic miracle. I see no reason why their bosses should not flow in the opposite direction, in search of holiday homes and long-distance commuting. One plan, from the Bonn economic expert, Ulrich Pfeiffer, has already proposed that the East German government should sell off all its public housing (80% of the total) to mop up ostmark savings and generate a free property market. This is no fanciful reform. (Though it will need swift action: in Osterwieck I hear that spivs are already selling street cobbles to West German villages who want to be more old-fashioned.)

Releasing thousands of renaissance *Fachwerkhäuser* in Lower Saxony onto the West German property market would, I predict, yield a swift inflow of deutschmarks. The border country is less than an hour from Hamburg, Hanover, Kassel, even Berlin. This would lead to a further inflow of spending on builders, decorators, artists, even cooks, cleaners, au pairs. It has the advantage over the '*Gastarbeiter* option' of concentrating hard currency spending in the East, not the West. Historic architecture is a true invisible export. Nor would the newcomers be foreigners: these are all Saxons, Prussians, heirs of Bismarck. Besides, beggars can't be choosers. East Germany, crippled by communism, is about to be no longer the rich man of eastern Europe but the poor man of the West. It is a beggar indeed. But there are worse places to start begging than the cottages of Rhoden or the great cathedral close of Halberstadt.

9 December 1989

CHESS

ROARING 80s

Raymond Keene

This column is my final one of the 1980s, and marks the close of a decade which has witnessed some remarkable developments on the world chess scene. As I noted last week, the most important of these has been the rise of Gary Kasparov, first as challenger and then as world champion. In 1980, Karpov reigned as world champion, but in spite of his brilliant successes in tournaments and matches, he somehow failed to recapture the charisma of Bobby Fischer.

Kasparov changed all that. He is widely perceived as a rebel within the Soviet system, a chessboard equivalent of glasnost and perestroika, in perpetual opposition to the old-style Soviet Chess Federation. His popularity has been boosted by his recent rating Everest, now expected to be 2810, which has finally laid the ghost of Bobby Fischer.

Kasparov has also been heavily involved in one of the other major upheavals of the 1980s, the clash between Fidé, the World Chess Federation, and the Grandmaster Association, essentially a trade union for top players, formed in 1986. The impetus for the split between Fidé and the Grandmasters came in February 1985, when Campomanes, the Fidé President, halted 'without result' the first Karpov–Kasparov world championship match, just as Kasparov had won two consecutive games. Since then, Fidé and Kasparov have been at daggers drawn. The GMA World Cup series (won by Kasparov ahead of Karpov) has become one of the positive results of this tension. Nevertheless, the two bodies are still fighting over who should control rights to the world championship match itself.

Since 1980 unexpected challenges to Soviet domination of world chess have come from three separate directions. Perhaps the most remarkable is the advent of the three gifted Polgar sisters from Budapest. All of them have the potential to become Grandmasters, while the youngest, Judit, aged 13, has been tipped by many as a future world champion. The days when Bobby Fischer claimed he could give knight odds to any female player are long gone.

Hardly less surprising has been the resurgence of chess in England. In the days of Howard Staunton, who founded the first ever international tournament at London in 1851, London was the capital of world chess. This eminent position was substantially eroded over the next century or so, but in 1980 the first Phillips & Drew/GLC international tournament heralded a new period of English chess success on a world scale. Heavily increased sponsorship culminated in the staging of the first half of the 1986 world championship in London. Meanwhile, English players seized the number two position behind the Russians by winning the silver medals in the Olympics of 1984, 1986 and 1988. On the individual front, Jon Speelman qualified for the semi-final of the world championship, Nigel Short developed into one of the foremost tournament competitors and has pushed his rating up to third in the world, while Michael Adams, aged 18, has become the world's youngest Grandmaster and the youngest ever British Champion. These are achievements of which we can be justly proud.

If American players cannot defeat the Russians, their technology may well do so in the future. The 1980s have seen the birth of the very dangerous computer Deep Thought, which has already beaten Grand-masters Larsen, Byrne and Miles. So far, only Kasparov has been able to

'The crowd has turned ugly.'

dominate it, but for how much longer? Deep Thought sees a million positions a second and its boffins predict this will increase to one billion within two years.

I bid goodbye to my readers at the end of this decade with a pointer to the future, one of Deep Thought's wins from its crushing 4-0 victory in last week's Infolink Challenge in aid of the Royal London Society for the Blind. As the 1990s dawn, I imagine I shall be presenting you with many more such wins by the computer:

Deep Thought-David Levy: *Game 4, Infolink Challenge; King's Indian Defence.*

1 c4 d6 2 Nc3 Nd7 3 d4 g6 4 Nf3 Bg7 5 e4 c5 6 Be2 cxd4 7 Nxd4 Ngf6 8 Be3 0-0 9 0-0 a6 10 f3 Re8 11 Qd2 Ne5 12 h3 Bd7 13 f4 Nc6 14 Nf3 Qa5 15 a3 Rad8 16 b4 Qc7 17 Rac1 b6 18 Bd3 Qb7 19 Qf2 Rb8 20 e5 Nh5 21 b5 axb5 22 axb5 Nd8 23 g4 Bh8 24 gxh5 Bxh3 25 hxg6 hxg6 26 Rfd1 Qd7 27 Ng5 Bg4 28 Qh4 Bg7 29 Rd2 Bh5 30 Nd5 Qa7 31 Rc7 Rb7 32 exd6 exd6 33 Rc8 Qxa3 34 Ne4 Black resigns.

23/30 December 1989

FIRST-CLASS FREE LOAD

Patrick Skene Catling

In every metropolis, I suppose, there are tycoons whose style may be cramped temporarily by an impediment in the cash flow, between one big deal and another. My friend Vincent, having painfully stubbed his toe in the City, has recently been resting longer than usual while considering what to get into next.

'During the present hiatus,' he said on the telephone the other morning, 'it is important to maintain one's morale, keep the wits well honed, and so on. Are you doing anything for lunch?'

As it happened, I was not busy. In memory of his lavish hospitality in the past, I was glad to be able to treat him to a meal.

'The Connaught?' I suggested, not without a certain apprehensiveness, for I have never been as rich as he sometimes is.

'No, no, no!' he protested genially. 'I'm not asking you to ask me to lunch. This expedition was my idea. All I want from you is your company. Almost all.'

'But surely it's my turn,' I murmured.

'No. This little outing is something I thought up just today in the bath. It'll do both of us a lot of good. It may well change the pattern of social life as we know it. In addition to your presence, actually there is one contribution I need from you.'

Oh, I thought. Here it comes.

'Are you still there?' he asked.

'Yes,' I admitted.

'You have to bring some cash.'

'Yes,' I said with a sigh. 'How much?'

'Enough for two tickets from London to Paris.'

'Paris!' That must mean the Tour d'Argent or the Grand Véfour or at least the Crillon. Wasn't that rather extravagant, even for someone whose morale needed a boost?

'Paris,' he confirmed. 'First class.'

'London–Paris first-class return must be – ' I could only hazard a guess. I fly to Paris only infrequently, and then always executive class or even economy.

'First class,' he repeated emphatically. 'But not return. I've checked on the one-way fare.' This was in the peak season. 'It's £167 – £334 for the two of us.' Some lunch! And that was what it would cost the *guest*.

'But Vincent – '

'Why only one way?' he said, as if reading my mind. Even over the telephone, I could detect his characteristically cryptic smile. He enjoys mystifying others. 'That's all you have to bring,' he assured me. 'In cash, please. You'll see soon enough how it's all going to work out. You'll get your money back.'

How and when? I wondered, not very optimistically. I trust him but there are times when he seems mañana-orientated. Was he counting on funds from some French business associate? As far as I knew, he had dealings with only a charming but languid marquis, whose principal function was to add Continental *éclat* to Vincent's letterhead.

Having pocketed my passport and visited my bank, I took a taxi to Vincent's mews house in Belgravia. He was already outside the yellow door, dressed in a cheerful tweed suit, a soft brown hat and brown suede shoes, as if going to an informal race meeting. He was wearing a red carnation in his button-hole and a grin on his roundish, pink face, so I realised he was in a playful mood. I wished I were too. Slamming the taxi door behind him, he told the driver to take us to Heathrow.

'Which terminal, guv?'

Vincent said he wanted the one from which planes left for Paris, and told him the name of the airline.

'Why that one?' I asked. I wasn't objecting; I was merely curious. It was a long-established, reputable national airline, but not the one that would first have sprung to mind.

'Their new advertising campaign is incomparably superior to the others',' Vincent replied. 'They are really trying to please. Haven't you noticed? They obviously understand about food and drink. They sympathise with gluttons. Their stewardesses are the prettiest.'

At the airport, I gave Vincent the money. He went to get the tickets, while I looked at magazines.

'What's our flight?' I asked. I like to be on time. He smiled complacently.

'The 4.50,' he said.

'4.50! I thought we were going to have lunch.'

'We are. Oh, we are!'

He led the way to the newly redecorated first-class departure lounge, whose luxurious facilities are open, of course, only to bearers of first-class tickets. Vincent uttered a conventional pleasantry or two as he showed our tickets, and the beautiful hostess beamed as warmly as a breakfast-show presenter. The lounge was gently animated by the small talk of elegant men and women. The place was not crowded. Everything about it was pleasantly soft: the lighting was soft; the music was soft; softly upholstered, dull-golden armchairs were disposed here and there in discreetly separated groups; the dark-saffron carpet was soft on the way to the long, richly-stocked bar and buffet.

'Champagne first, don't you agree?' Vincent suggested. 'I always say it's the best thing to rinse the taste-buds with, early in the day.' A softly illuminated golden clock on the wall indicated that the time was 11.40, five hours and ten minutes to our scheduled time of take-off. Champagne, I thought, was a good idea.

'Have you any Bollinger?' Vincent enquired of the young blonde barmaid, whose voluptuousness mocked the restriction of her well-cut uniform. 'Or Veuve Clicquot would do.' Thus began the first of many interesting discussions which enlivened the hours.

'The champagne is Piper-Heidsieck,' the barmaid informed us. 'Is that all right?'

'Quite all right,' Vincent assured her encouragingly. 'I like its fullness and dryness and all-round friendly demeanour. Let us, by all means, have some of that.'

We found that we were thirsty. The first bottle went fast. As we thoughtfully sipped a second, Vincent moved, and I followed, in a leisurely fashion along the bar to inspect the buffet counter. We found a tempting array of hors d'oeuvres, smoked salmon and trout, shrimps and lobster, cold turkey, ham and rare roast beef, salads, fresh fruit and an assortment of classic cheeses.

'It all looks eminently satisfactory,' he commented approvingly, spearing an anchovy-stuffed olive with a pointed swizzle-stick. 'There's absolutely no rush, mind you, but it's nice to know it's all here. For the moment, perhaps just some of this pâté.' He tasted it. 'Mmm! Smoked mackerel. Delicious. At this point, I do believe I'll switch to Chablis.'

After a time passed sampling various excellent white burgundies, we took a series of carefully laden dishes to a convenient table for two.

'How do they keep track of all we're having?' I asked — naïvely, I know now.

' "Keep track"?' he echoed with a frown of aesthetic distress. 'Why would they wish to do that? There is no time limit here for passengers awaiting their flights. There's no limit to what they may eat and drink. And, of course, there is no charge.'

These considerations greatly stimulated my appetite. When sated with sea-food, I helped myself to a generous selection of cold meats. The beef was perfectly moist and tender. Vincent, also having progressed to the more serious viands, soon announced his approval of the claret. 'This,' he solemnly averred, 'is a quite exceptionally jolly Pauillac. Call me sentimental if you will, but Lynch-Bages has always been a favourite of mine.'

The afternoon gradually latened and we noticeably mellowed, and I suddenly became concerned about the time. It was 4.05.

'Yes,' Vincent acknowledged, 'it is almost time to go. I'll have only one more port with this splendid Stilton. We can leave the Armagnac for another time.' He paused at the reception desk to give the hostess our compliments, some of which were to be conveyed to the chef and the sommelier, our congratulations to the airline and our warmest thanks.

'I don't see how we'll be able to appreciate Paris after all that,' I said. Vincent smiled, a bit sleepily.

'Nor do I,' he said.

Then, to my surprise, he led the way back to the ticket counter. They honoured without question our request for cancellation and immediately gave us a full refund.

'Here you are,' Vincent said smugly. 'Your £334 as good as new.' I gratefully stuffed the money into a pocket, and didn't mind when he stuck me for the cab home.

23/30 December 1989

DIARY

Ferdinand Mount

As you approach the Berlin Wall, you hear, from 200 yards away or more, the sound of hammers tapping. They say Erich Honecker can hear it from his hospital bed in La Charité, overlooking Checkpoint Charlie. The sound is both eerie and cheerful, a mixture of Wagner's dwarfs and Walt Disney's. The souvenir-hunters leave holes in the shape of swelling clefts which expose the bars reinforcing the concrete. The effect is not unlike those anti-totalitarian sculptures of the Reg Butler period – Life limping after Art again, not even very good Art either.

Crossing back into the West at Trieste, I felt none of the old sense of liberation. These days, that sort of relief would probably be experienced only on coming out of Albania. Or perhaps not even there, if one

is to judge by a recent article in the *Garden*, the journal of the Royal Horticultural Society, by Primrose Peacock, entitled 'Exemplary Albania'. She records that:

> the Albanians' fondness for flowers was immediately apparent. . . . I saw individuals carefully cutting a buttonhole, but there was no pillaging, vandalism or litter. I was told that the garden belonged to the people to enjoy the beauty and scent of the flowers. . . . No serious visitor to Albania can leave without admiring the national spirit of independent self-sufficiency.

Her only problem was that 'I found that most people dislike cameras, so I had to be careful and not get too close to them.' Even in Albania, it seems, there is buttonholing and buttonholing.

In a crowded Trieste fish restaurant (they are all crowded and the gentle, elderly waiters have scarcely room to push their steel trolleys of skate, squid and mullet between the Triestines who eat in a serious fashion, their droopy moustaches sweeping the plate), I found myself next to a hunched old man, in his late seventies at least but dressed in a careful, old-fashioned, bohemian style − soft leather jacket, floppy collar and cravat, spectacles propped high on his ancient brow. Surely this must be some lingering remnant of the Trieste intelligentsia, one of those 80-year-old *baroni* described in Richard Bassett's *Guide to Central Europe* who spend their time at the Café Tommaseo disputing points of Virgil with the waiter. With his air of exasperated gloom, he seemed to have tottered straight out of the pages of a novel by Italo Svevo, perhaps Trieste's most famous son (there is not much competition). What, I enquired, was his profession? 'I am electronics engineer but I not decide yet how to live life.' A real Svevo character in fact, and pretty drunk too. 'Did you happen to know Italo Svevo?' 'Of course, my uncle was his brother-in-law.' Excited by what must be nearly the last surviving link with that charming and melancholy writer, I asked if he had any recollection of him. 'Svevo was nothing. Trieste is nothing. But Svevo nothing, nothing. Shakespeare is good. I see Sir Laurence Olivier *Amleto* 15 times.' I had one more go. 'Why you want to know about Svevo? Svevo nothing.' Which is what Svevo himself was told nearly all his life and why he spent most of it running his wife's paint business, but it is just what a Svevo character ought to think about his creator.

27 January 1990

THE FULL TEXT OF THE FIRST SPEECH BY **VACLAV HAVEL** *AS PRESIDENT OF CZECHOSLOVAKIA*

'THE ART OF THE IMPOSSIBLE'

My dear fellow citizens.

For 40 years you heard from my predecessors on this day different variations of the same theme: how our country flourished, how many millions of steel we produced, how happy we all were, how we trusted our government and what bright perspectives were unfolding in front of us.

'I'm helping to improve the pupil teacher ratio!'

I assume you did not propose me for this office so that I, too, would lie to you.

Our country is not flourishing. The enormous creative and spiritual potential of our nations is not used sensibly. Entire branches of industry are producing goods which are of no interest to anyone, while we are lacking the things that we need. A state which calls itself a workers' state humiliates and exploits workers. Our obsolete economy is wasting the little energy we have available. A country that once could be proud of the educational level of its citizens spends so little on education that it ranks today as 72nd in the world. We have polluted our soil, our rivers and forests, bequeathed to us by our ancestors, and we have today the most contaminated environment in Europe. Adult people in our country die earlier than in most European countries.

Allow me a little personal observation: when I flew recently to Bratislava, I found time during various discussions to look out of the plane window. I saw the industrial complex of Slovnaft chemical factory and the giant Petrzalka housing estate right behind it. The view was enough for me to understand that for decades our statesmen and political leaders did not look or did not want to look out of the windows of their aeroplanes. No study of statistics available to me would enable me to understand faster and better the situation into which we had got ourselves.

But all this is still not the main problem. The worst thing is that we live in a contaminated moral environment. We felt morally ill because we became used to saying something different from what we thought. We learned not to believe in anything, to ignore each other, to care only about ourselves. Concepts such as love, friendship, compassion, humility or forgiveness lost their depth and dimensions and for many of us they represented only psychological peculiarities, or they resembled gone astray greetings from ancient times, a little ridiculous in the era of computers and spaceships. Only a few of us were able to cry out loud that the powers that be should not be all-powerful, and that special farms, which produce ecologically pure and top-quality food just for them, should send their produce to schools, children's homes and hospitals if our agriculture was so far unable to offer them to all. The previous régime – armed with its arrogant and intolerant ideology – reduced Man to a force of production and Nature to a tool of production. In this it attacked both their very substance and their mutual relationship. It reduced gifted and autonomous people, skil-

fully working in their own country, to nuts and bolts of some mon-
strously huge, noisy and stinking machine, whose real meaning is not
clear to anyone. It cannot do more than slowly but inexorably wear
down itself and all its nuts and bolts.

When I talk about contaminated moral atmosphere, I am not talking
just about the gentlemen who eat organic vegetables and do not look
out of the plane windows. I am talking about all of us. We had all
become used to the totalitarian system and accepted it as an unchange-
able fact and thus helped to perpetuate it. In other words, we are all —
though naturally to differing extents — responsible for the operation of
the totalitarian machinery, none of us is just its victim: we are all also
its co-creators.

Why do I say this? It would be very unreasonable to understand the
sad legacy of the last 40 years as something alien, which some distant
relative bequeathed us. On the contrary, we have to accept this legacy
as something we committed against ourselves. If we accept it as such,
we will understand that it is up to us all, and up to us only, to do
something about it. We cannot blame the previous rulers for everything, not only because it would be untrue but also because it could
weaken the duty that each of us faces today, namely the obligation to
act independently, freely, reasonably and quickly. Let us not be
mistaken: the best government in the world, the best parliament and
the best president cannot achieve much on their own. And it would
also be wrong to expect a general remedy from them only. Freedom and
democracy include participation and therefore responsibility from us
all.

If we realise this, then all the horrors that the new Czechoslovak
democracy inherited will cease to appear so terrible. If we realise this,
hope will return to our hearts.

In the effort to rectify matters of common concern we have something to lean on. The recent period — and in particular the last six
weeks of our peaceful revolution — have shown the enormous human,
moral and spiritual potential and civic culture that had slumbered in
our society under the enforced mask of apathy. Whenever someone
categorically claimed that we were this or that, I always objected that
society is a very mysterious creature and that it is not wise to trust
only the face it presents to you. I am happy that I was not mistaken.
Everywhere in the world people wonder where those meek, humiliated, sceptical and seemingly cynical citizens of Czechoslovakia found

the marvellous strength to shake from their shoulders in several weeks and in a decent and peaceful way the totalitarian yoke. And let us ask: from where did the young people who never knew another system take their desire for truth, their love of free thought, their political ideas, their civic courage and civic prudence? How did it happen that their parents – the very generation that had been considered as lost – joined them? How is it possible that so many people immediately knew what to do and none of them needed any advice or instruction?

I think that there are two main reasons for this hopeful face of our present situation: first of all, people are never just a product of the external world, but are also always able to relate themselves to something superior, however systematically the external world tries to kill that ability in them; secondly, the humanistic and democratic traditions, about which there had been so much idle talk, did after all slumber in the unconsciousness of our nations and ethnic minorities and were inconspicuously passed from one generation to another so that each of us could discover them at the right time and transform them into deeds.

We had to pay, however, for our present freedom. Many citizens perished in jails in the Fifties, many were executed, thousands of human lives were destroyed, hundreds of thousands of talented people were forced to leave the country. Those who defended the honour of our nations during the Second World War, those who rebelled against totalitarian rule and those who simply managed to remain themselves and think freely were all persecuted. We should not forget any of those who paid for our present freedom in one way or another. Independent courts should impartially consider the possible guilt of those who were responsible for the persecutions, so that the truth about our recent past is fully revealed.

We must also bear in mind that other nations have paid even more dearly for their present freedom and that indirectly they have also paid for ours. The rivers of blood which flowed in Hungary, Poland, Germany and not long ago in such a horrific manner in Rumania, as well as the sea of blood shed by the nations of the Soviet Union, must not be forgotten. First of all because every human suffering concerns every other human being; but more than this: they must also not be forgotten because it is these great sacrifices which form the tragic background of today's freedom, and of the gradual emancipation of the nations of the Soviet bloc. They also form the background of our own newfound freedom: without the changes in the Soviet Union, Poland, Hungary and the German Democratic Republic what has happened in our country could scarcely have happened. In any event, it would not have followed such a peaceful course.

The fact that we enjoyed optimal international conditions does not mean that anyone else has directly helped us during the recent weeks. In fact, after hundreds of years, both our nations have raised their heads high of their own initiative without relying on the help of stronger nations or powers. It seems to me that this constitutes the great moral asset of the present moment. This moment holds within itself the hope that in future we will no longer suffer from the complex of those who must always be expressing their gratitude to somebody. It now depends only on us whether this hope will be realised and whether our civic, national and political self-confidence will be awakened in a historically new way.

Self-confidence is not pride. Just the contrary: only a person or a nation that is self-confident in the best sense of the word is capable of listening to others, accepting them as equals, forgiving its enemies and regretting its own guilt. Let us try to introduce this kind of self-confidence into the life of our community and, as nations, into our behaviour on the international stage. Only thus can we restore our self-respect and our respect for one another as well as the respect of other nations.

Our state should never again be an appendage or a poor relation of anyone else. It is true we must accept and learn many things from others, but we must do this again as their equal partners who also have something to offer.

Our first president wrote: 'Jesus, not Caesar.' In this he followed our philosophers Chelcicky and Comenius. I dare to say that we may even have an opportunity to spread this idea further and introduce a new element into European and global politics. Our country, if that is what we want, can now permanently radiate love, understanding, the power of spirit and ideas. It is precisely this glow that we can offer as our specific contribution to international politics.

Masaryk based his politics on morality. Let us try in a new time and in a new way to restore this concept of politics. Let us teach ourselves and others that politics should be an expression of a desire to contribute to the happiness of the community rather than of a need to cheat or rape the community. Let us teach ourselves and others that politics can be not only the art of the possible, especially if this means the art of speculation, calculation, intrigue, secret deals and pragmatic manoeuvring, but that it can even be the art of the impossible, namely the art of improving ourselves and the world.

We are a small country, yet at one time we were the spiritual crossroads of Europe. Is there any reason why we could not again become one? Would it not be another asset with which to repay the help of others that we are going to need?

Our home-grown mafia of those who do not look out of plane windows and eat specially fed pigs may still be around and at times muddy waters, but they are no longer our main enemy. Even less so is our main enemy the international mafia. Our main enemy today is our own bad traits: indifference to the common good, vanity, personal ambition, selfishness and rivalry. The main struggle will have to be fought on this field.

There are free elections and an election campaign ahead of us. Let us not allow this struggle to dirty the so far clean face of our gentle revolution. Let us not allow the sympathies of the world which we have won so fast to be equally rapidly lost through our becoming entangled in the jungle of skirmishes for power. Let us not allow the desire to serve oneself to bloom once again under the fair mask of the desire to serve the common good. It is not really important now which party, club or group will prevail in the elections. The important thing is that the winners will be the best of us, in the moral, civic, political and professional sense, regardless of their political affiliations. The future policies and prestige of our state will depend on the personalities we select and later elect to our representative bodies.

We succeeded before the elections in establishing diplomatic relations with the Vatican and Israel. I would also like to contribute to peace by my brief visit tomorrow to our mutually close neighbours, namely the German Democratic Republic and the Federal Republic of Germany. Neither shall I forget our other neighbours – fraternal Poland and ever closer Hungary and Austria.

In conclusion, I would like to say that I want to be a president who will speak less and work more. To be a president who will not only look out of the windows of his aeroplane but who, first and foremost, will always be present among his fellow citizens and listen to them well.

You may ask what kind of a republic I dream of. Let me reply: I

dream of a republic independent, free and democratic, of a republic
economically prosperous and yet socially just, in short of a humane
republic which serves the individual and which therefore holds the
hope that the individual will serve it in turn. Of a republic of
well-rounded people, because without such it is impossible to solve
any of our problems, human, economic, ecological, social or political.

The most distinguished of my predecessors opened his first speech
with a quotation from the great Czech educator Comenius. Allow me
to round off my first speech with my own paraphrase of the same
statement:

People, your Government has returned to you!

27 January 1990

'You're carrying an awful lot of luggage from your childhood.'

PUBLISH AND BE POPULAR

David Nokes

BOSWELL, THE GREAT BIOGRAPHER, 1789-1795
edited by Marlies K. Danziger and Frank Brady
Heinemann

The publication of this final volume of Boswell's journals brings to a triumphant conclusion a scholarly detective story which began over 60 years ago in the cobwebbed attics and dank out-houses of Malahide Castle where Boswell's private papers were first uncovered in such unlikely hiding-places as an abandoned croquet-box and disused granary. From the start, the 13 volumes of the Yale-Heinemann edition have been remarkable both for the engaging candour of Boswell's irrepressible self-conceit, and for the editors' adroitness in combining scholarly thoroughness with an imaginative sympathy for Boswell's own beguiling tone. Typical of this editorial flair is one celebrated entry in the index to *The London Journal* which beautifully encapsulates Boswell's affair with the actress 'Louisa' as an ironic comedy of manners, beginning with protestations of eternal love and offers of financial help, but concluding with a dose of clap and demands for his money back.

*'Looks like they'll have to shoot
Mrs Thatcher.'*

That first volume of the series, *The London Journal*, published 40 years ago, revealed the youthful Boswell revelling in his release from his dour Scottish upbringing, and taking an almost manic delight in the pleasures of the town. In a characteristically hedonistic expression of his political principles, he chose to celebrate the king's birthday with an heroic sexual odyssey. Starting in St James's Park, he picked up 'a low brimstone' with whom he performed 'most manfully', having first taken the unlikely precaution of 'dipping my machine in the canal'. Thence to the Strand, where a 'little profligate' allowed him entrance but refused performance, even after his appeal to a crowd of onlookers to uphold his right 'to roger for sixpence'. Finally to Whitehall, where he demanded, but was refused, sex on credit. Typically, in preparing for this escapade, Boswell dressed in his shabbiest clothes to corroborate his pleas of poverty. Yet he confessed: 'My vanity was somewhat gratified tonight that, notwithstanding of my dress, I was always taken for a gentleman in disguise'. This cool blend of vanity, parsimony and promiscuity is quintessential Boswell.

Thirty years on, the Boswell of this final volume is older but not wiser, though by now the theatre of his vanities includes more tragedy than comedy in its repertoire. Depression and dyspepsia, melancholia and mortification cast an almost perpetual gloom over his spirits, relieved only by a regular intake of alcohol, the occasional spectacle of executions at Newgate, and a succession of sexual adventures. The volume begins with the death of his wife Margaret in 1789, a blow which leaves Boswell declaring his own 'avidity for death'. Thereafter, while constantly reiterating that it is 'impossible I could ever again love a woman', Boswell indulges in a bewildering variety of amorous fantasies. The daughter of a close friend describes, with evident dismay, the absurd spectacle of this man 'of more than 50 . . . perpetually falling in love, as he calls it, and then he can do nothing but talk of the angelic creature'.

What is most obvious and most poignant about Boswell in these final years is his increasingly desperate need for distractions. He wanders the streets of London in pursuit not of sex but of friendship. One night he scours the coffee-houses of Covent Garden in search of congenial companions, but 'I knew nobody'. He saunters down Bond Street and St James's Street in hopes of dinner invitations, 'but in vain'. Another night, declaring 'I wished to dine with somebody, but I knew not with whom', he makes a circuit of his friends' houses, but finds them not at home. Behind this restless desire for companionship lurks a nostalgia for the conviviality of an earlier time, when Boswell knew everybody and when the doors of his many London friends were always open with a welcome. Much of this final journal reads like an attempt to recapture the spirit of an age which had vanished forever with the death of Johnson in 1784. The completion and publication of Boswell's most enduring tribute to that spirit, his great *Life of Johnson*, dominates this volume which is appropriately entitled 'The Great Biographer'. The success of that work brought Boswell precisely the kind of rewards he most relished. *The Public Advertiser* for 27 May 1791 – ten days after publication – announced that 'Boswell has so many invitations in consequence of his *Life of Johnson* that he may be literally said to live upon his deceased friend'. There were, however, certain drawbacks to his new celebrity status. One host warned him that fellow guests were anxious lest their conversations might be published without their consent. Boswell was probably the first man to experience the uneasy welcome accorded to the gossip writer.

Not content with merely recording the life and words of his great friend and mentor, Boswell's later journals reveal his growing tendency to refashion himself in his master's image. Often one finds the Boswell of the journals expressing sentiments which bear a striking resemblance to some of the more celebrated utterances attributed to Johnson in the *Life*. Johnson's witticisms at the expense of all things Scottish, a notorious feature of the *Life*, are echoed in Boswell's ridicule of 'the Scotch' throughout this journal. It is Boswell's *Life* which created the image of Johnson as perpetual Londoner, proclaiming 'When a man is tired of London, he is tired of life'. Similarly, in the journal, Boswell expresses his love of the metropolis and contempt for the country. Dining high above Green Park, with views over St James's Park and

towards the Surrey Hills, he exclaims, 'how delightful it is to see the country and be sure you are not in it! Piccadilly is between us and it!' On a visit to Cornwall he complains, 'my mind *rusts* in the country', but he is quickly revived by a Newgate feast at which 'our conversation was chiefly of London'. Yet in mimicking Johnson's manner, Boswell merely underlines the essential differences between them. The humanity of Johnson's conservatism is founded upon principles of morality and social justice which Boswell, with his narrower concerns for social status, could never achieve. Johnson raised a toast 'to the next insurrection of the negroes in the West Indies', but Boswell, in 1791, penned a polemical verse pamphlet, *No Abolition of Slavery*, opposing Wilberforce's Bill.

Where Boswell is most clearly his own man is in the mechanical operations of his spirits, determined as they are by the ebb and flow of appetite. Wine revives his spirits as surely as water drowns them. 'My spirits are vigorous and elastic', he declares, after a succession of good dinners; or again, 'I became pretty hearty by means of turbot, venison, and a liberal dose of wine'. Tea and chocolate had directly contrary effects upon his volatile spirits. One morning he enjoyed a breakfast of 'good chocolate and important conversation' with General Paoli which left him 'floating upon life with really pleasing sensations'. Later that same day he drank tea with his daughter Veronica and 'felt myself sink'. 'How mechanical is man!' he observes, which seems a fitting conclusion. Where Johnson's philosophy is a strenuous triumph of mind over matter, Boswell's journals reveal the irresistible influences of matter over mind.

3 February 1990

A DICTIONARY OF CANT

Nigel Burke

RELATIONSHIP. Stereotype rejecting, personal space respecting, trusting, caring and equal, a relationship is a love affair designed by a committee of social workers.

*'I know they're fashionable now — but will
they be in nine months' time?'*

OPERA

ALL WORTH IT

Rodney Milnes

PRINCE IGOR
(Covent Garden)

A great deal depended on this production. Both Jeremy Isaacs, who is starting to be seen as the Hard Man of the arts world, and the music director Bernard Haitink were determined that Borodin's sprawling (and expensive) epic should be staged as a collaboration between the

Royal Opera and the Royal Ballet. The latter body cannily saw this as a
strong bargaining point in their pursuit of better pay and status, and in
the event a settlement was reached only a week before the first night.
The Polovtsian Dances went on — no more than that, honestly, but
they were there. Was it all worth it? Emphatically yes: orchestrally and
vocally this was an evening of great distinction.

The work itself is one of opera's great problem pieces. Left un-
finished by Borodin, completed by who knows who and to what extent,
virtually plotless, potentially inconsequential, by all the rules of opera
it shouldn't work — and indeed has been seen not to work. On this
occasion it did, shatteringly. Its collective provenance was made to
match its collective impact as something slightly more than a great
Russian epic: a great Eastern European epic, a great world epic. In
amongst its plotlessness a very great deal is said about war, peace,
political opportunism, the profound power of human love, the nobility
and strength of womankind, and much else.

All this shone through thanks to the presiding genius of Haitink,
who brought to the score a convincing unity and a shape, an overall
achievement far outshining some uneasy moments of ensemble (the

'I'm tempted to ditch the lawn chairs.'

unusually sluggish chorus seemed about half a beat behind him for most of the evening). Above all, he and the definitely unsluggish orchestra created a sound-world that equally convincingly drew together the craggy simplicity of Borodin's writing for the Russian characters – it sounds like cleaned-up Tchaikovsky – and the exoticism of the Polovtsians, in which one cannot help detecting the hands of Glazunov and Rimsky. The playing was quite wonderful.

And the singing was amongst the most inspiring I have heard at Covent Garden in 35 years of opera-going. This was not in any sense to do with King of the High Cs showmanship, but with serious, dedicated artists singing in a language that they understood even if it was not their native tongue (which in many cases it was) and singing as if they understood the importance of the words. When this is combined with technical prowess on the scale manifested here, one's faith in the future of opera is restored.

Sergey Leiferkus, who sang the title role, may not have the most densely coloured of baritone voices, but he sings with an intelligence and understanding virtually unique in the world today. Among the many benefits of *glasnost*, I trust the swift importing of aspiring Western students to the Leningrad Conservatory, or the swift exporting of their professors, are high on the list. I have long thought Anna Tomowa-Sintow one of the world's great sopranos and been mystified that this should not be universally recognised, but after her Yaroslavna there can surely no longer be doubts. The vibrant lusciousness of her voice, the extraordinary dignity and beauty of her person, her infallible technique, all came together in an impersonation of soul-searching intensity. For as long as I live I shall remember the last note of her Lament, launched high above the stave with a sword-like forte and fined down, what seemed like five minutes later, into the sweetest thread of sound. Unbelievable!

Add Paata Burchuladze (Konchak), whose incursions into Italian opera have been less than wholly convincing, as if reborn singing his own language and his own music; Elena Zaremba (Konchakovna), a mezzo with authentic Russian rasp and warmth; Alexey Steblyanko (Vladimir) erasing unhappy memories of his Jason-Napoleon; Nicola Ghiuselev (Galitsky) singing better than ever, and you have an evening with which to bore your grandchildren to death in years to come.

I admired the thinking behind Andrei Serban's production – the reference to present-day Eastern Europe in the last act was tactfully achieved — but its execution rather less. I was not alone in sensing a rather creepy sexist approach to the much-interfered-with female captive (who added to the general topicality by bearing a striking resemblance to Pamella Bordes) and the Polovtsian bathing beauties; a respectably married lady friend remarked in the second interval that the balance would only be restored if Mr Leiferkus took his clothes off in the finale (he didn't). Serban's use of an army of extras to carry the action, none too convincingly, reduced the chorus to the status of the Polovtsian Choral Society standing motionless in serried ranks, albeit in more interesting frocks than their colleagues in Huddersfield. The ludicrous business with papier mâché trumpets should have been discarded at an early rehearsal.

Mr Serban has said that he is thinking of forsaking opera — temporarily I trust, since his own WNO *Onegin* and Royal Opera *Turandot* have shown rare understanding of the genre. But if his *Igor* is not quite worthy of him, everything else about the evening is definitely worthy of Borodin.

10 February 1990

DIARY

Charles Moore

Bishop John Spong is not an invention of Peter Simple, but the real-life Episcopalian Bishop of Newark, New Jersey. Bishop Spong is the most radical of that most radical bench of bishops. He recently ran to form by ordaining an openly practising homosexual as a priest, the first time, allegedly, that this had been done. This priest, the Revd Robert Williams, was appointed to run Oasis, the diocese's 'ministry to gays and lesbians'. But then something really extraordinary happened. Bishop Spong discovered that there was something which he would not tolerate. At a 'public forum' in Detroit last month, Mr Williams delivered his views on sexual morality. He said, according to a report in the *Church Times*, that 'monogamy was basically a crazy idea that most people just didn't believe in, and that it was just as unnatural as celibacy'. He also said: 'If you're asking me whether Mother Teresa would be better off getting laid, my answer is yes.' Bishop Spong could not stand for this. He wrote to the House of Bishops saying, 'Ordaining Robert Williams, with the assurance that his life could offer to the homosexual population of our metropolitan area a model of holiness, fidelity and monogamy with which we could counter promiscuity and other forms of predatory or casual sexual behaviour, was our fervent hope. We do not affirm sexual immorality. . . .' Mr Williams says, '. . . I have put myself in the position of convenient scapegoat. The diocese wanted me to be a cardboard cut-out gay priest.' One can see why Mr Williams is rather confused. For it is not clear why the Church should approve monogamy, fidelity etc in homosexual relationships. The Christian doctrine of marriage has a theological aspect – it signifies 'the mystical union which is betwixt Christ and his Church' – and a practical one – the best way of bringing up children. Where neither of these considerations applies, why should the moral constraints? What is the basis of Bishop Spong's belief in homosexual monogamy and fidelity? Since there is no Biblical or traditional support for such a thing, he must simply be extrapolating it from the Biblical teaching about heterosexual love, and what are his grounds for doing that? Mr Williams must quite reasonably have assumed that since Bishop Spong had made up his sexual morality without giving it a distinctively Christian base, he, Mr Williams, was entitled to do the same. If you accept homosexuality, he must have argued to himself, what makes you want to keep monogamy, let alone celibacy? Why *shouldn't* Mother Teresa get laid? It is a serious question, and I cannot imagine what the radical answer to it might be. Come on, Bishop Spong, why shouldn't Mother Teresa get laid? Have you got a reason, or are you really just a miserable old puritan underneath your New Age vestments?

Six years ago this month, my predecessor Alexander Chancellor announced on this page that I was to be his successor with the words: 'Mr Moore is only 27 years old and with luck should still be occupying the editorial chair many decades from now.' There have been times, I confess, when I have been tempted to try to follow one of those great Victorian editors like R. H. Hutton and see if I could stay in the chair for 40 years. Much more often, however, I have felt the reverse, and dreaded outstaying my welcome. Modern times do not seem well adapted to very long stints at anything. It is interesting that *The Spectator* had six editors from 1828 to 1953, and has had ten from 1953 to the present. From April it will have an eleventh. I have decided to resign, and am delighted that my successor is to be my deputy, Dominic Lawson, an outcome for which I hoped when I appointed him in 1987. The editor's job is sometimes described as a 'bed of nails'. In my case, this is literally half-true. I have no bed in the office, but my editorial chair has several nails which are now coming through the seat. In recent weeks, they have twice torn my trousers. It is time to go.

17 February 1990

'EVERYTHING WILL GET BETTER'

Ambrose Evans-Pritchard

Managua, Nicaragua (eve of the election)

The old poor, the new poor, and the barefoot waited patiently in the Plaza de la Republica. Some sat perched on the cracked ledges of the derelict cathedral, waving the blue and white flags of the united opposition. Every now and then the crowd began to chant abuse against the Sandinista Front, fearless in the safety of numbers. But there were no cheer-leaders to keep the chants alive. There was no music, no ceremony, nothing to ignite the closing rally of the campaign, the biggest gathering of the opposition since Marxist students seized the country ten years ago. The rally went from bad to worse. When the time came to sing the national anthem – the old anthem, not the Sandinista version with its fanatical lyrics about 'the Yankees, enemies of humanity' – almost nobody could remember the words. Muffled humming was all that could be heard, fading into an embarrassed silence after a couple of verses. Still there was no music. Only later did I learn that the Sandinistas had sabotaged the rally by confiscating the sound system.

At long last the wheelchair of 'La Candidata' was raised onto the stage by an industrial fork-lift. She struggled to her feet for a moment to accept the ovation, in spite of her fractured knee, a tall, slender, aristocratic figure dressed in white from head to toe. She read from cue cards in her innocent voice, stumbling over the words and never once daring to depart from the prepared text. It was obvious that 'La Candidata' was hopelessly out of her depth, but equally obvious that she meant well, that she saw herself as the mother of Nicaragua. The tattered people around me listened respectfully, a stern expression on their inscrutable leather faces. 'Viva,' they shouted from time to time, for no apparent reason. 'Viva Dona Violeta.'

If Violeta Barrios de Chamorro wins the vote on Sunday she will become the first woman to be elected president in the history of Latin America. For years it has been an article of faith in Washington that Chamorro would trounce the Sandinistas in free elections if she could ever be persuaded to run for the presidency. She was a living symbol of resistance against the Somoza dictatorship, widow of the first Sandinista junta, before resigning in protest over the totalitarian bent of the régime and returning to her old post as publisher of the family newspaper *La Prensa*.

Washington has got everything it wanted. Dona Violeta reluctantly agreed to run, and 14 opposition parties miraculously agreed to suspend their squabbles until after the vote. The Communists, Socialists, Liberals, and Conservatives have rallied around Chamorro offering a 'government of national salvation'. It is hard to imagine more advantageous circumstances for getting the dead weight of Sandinismo off the backs of the Nicaraguan people, yet the Congress and the White House have lost their nerve. Over the last two months a consensus has emerged in Washington that the Sandinista Front is bound to win the election, and probably by a large margin.

I do not share that assessment, which seems to be based entirely on opinion polls conducted by foreign firms. It is impossible to poll opposition sentiment in a Marxist state like Nicaragua, where informers are ubiquitous and where, until recently, ration cards for rice, beans and sugar were used as a tool of political subjugation. True, the society is more open now than it was two years ago, and there is less palpable fear and suspicion. But Nicaraguans continue to dissemble reflexively with strangers, sometimes putting on a brilliant show of Sandinista sympathies until they are sure they're not talking to a 'toad' of the régime. It is therefore ludicrous how much solemn attention has been given to a poll in January by the Boston firm Greenberg-Lake, which gave the Sandinistas a lead of 27 points. The door-to-door questioning was contracted out to Itztani, a Nicaraguan group with a Trotskyist past.

Nevertheless, it is clear that Nicaragua is not going the way of eastern Europe. Sandinismo, though poisoned by Leninism, is an indigenous movement, born out of a struggle against a seedy, brutal family kept in power by the United States. It still commands the loyalty of Nicaragua's best and brightest, who gave the passion of their youth to the cause. It has not been undermined by massive venality. The Sandinista police and border guards, paid a miserable salary of $30 a month, have not become, not yet at least, licensed extortioners like their colleagues in the rest of Central America. Sandinismo is still young.

I gave a ride to a young doctor yesterday who talked breathlessly for half an hour about all the abuses of the Sandinistas: their arrogance, their Napoleonic adventurism, their insufferable bureaucracy, their economic madness. Yet as he got out of the car he leant over and said with a huge grin, 'You know, in spite of everything I'm going to vote for the [Sandinista] Front.' 'And what about the opposition?' 'I can't,' he replied, 'I just can't.'

Looking up at the platform of La Candidata, I could see why so many Nicaraguans cannot quite bring themselves to cross the great emotional dividing line. For there, among the inner councillors of 'La Candidata', was the round white face of Alfredo Cesar, a former director of the Contras. And there, too, part of the inner core, was La Candidata's

'He's very good but he refuses to play the white keys.'

son, Pedro Joaquin Chamorro, another former Contra. And then, horror of horrors, I began to make out the features of the fat, pock-marked Frank Arana, spokesman of the Contra forces in Honduras.

The Sandinistas have used the state propaganda machine day and night, month after month, to convince the people that Violeta Chamorro is the figurehead of the Contras. Her electoral campaign has played straight into their hands. At a rally in the mountain town of Matagalpa two Contra field commanders even appeared on stage and were introduced by name to the crowd, which cheered enthusiastically. Chamorro's message of reconciliation and forgiveness has been eclipsed, replaced by a suspicion that she leads a revanchiste movement of the old élite.

While Chamorro has stumbled, the Sandinistas have recovered ground, chiefly by abandoning military communism and reverting to the system of the Somozas. The collective image of nine *comman-dantes* has been replaced by the personality cult of President Daniel Ortega. Tens of thousands of state workers are brought in trucks to vast fascist rallies to watch Ortega play the role of pop star. He is very good at it. But he offers nothing to the famished, shirtless, unemployed except a feeble promise that everything will get better: 'todo sera mejor' – the election slogan of the Sandinista Front.

This is the most polarised country I have ever known. It is a mystery how the voters will behave on Sunday as they queue outside the polls contemplating six more years of 'continuismo' under the Sandinistas. The temptation to vote, secretly, for the party of the Americans, for the party that will end the war, the shortages, the misery of hyperinflation, will be irresistible I believe.

24 February 1990

THE SPY WHO DIDN'T LOVE ME

John Simpson

Prague

I walked through the familiar double doors with a certain apprehension. This was not the kind of assignment I was used to. Inside there was a lot of varnished wood and ugly copperwork. The windows rattled in the February wind. Once it was one of Prague's better places to stay. But now that hotels have been built with direct-dial telephones and doormen with top-hats, it has been colonised by visitors from the farther reaches of Moravia and Slovakia. Round the bar there was a convivial group of communist Third Worlders. History had stripped the establishment of its star-rating.

But it was a great deal livelier than when I had last been here, six years before. The showcases which had once been full of dusty Bohemian glassware and the marvels of Czechoslovak heavy engineering now contained jewellery and perfume. The former President, Gustav Husak, no longer stared gloomily out at you from his picture like an undertaker. I didn't even mind the canned music. In the old days it was so quiet your shoes creaked.

Better still, now that the revolution had taken place the hotel had dismantled the surveillance cameras that once kept an automatic eye on all the exits. And the two bulky secret policemen were gone from their seats by the door. My colleagues used to call them Bill and Ben, but, following Wagner and Somerset Maugham, I preferred to think of them as Fafner and Fasolt. Now, since the start of this month, Fafner and Fasolt have been out of a job. The Interior Ministry has disbanded the STB, the nasty, efficient Czechoslovak version of the KGB. The personnel files will be inspected to see which, if any, of the STB men might be suitable for ordinary police work.

I walked over to the counter, where a guest was arguing about his bill with the receptionist. This was the difficult part. I was a little surprised to see her there. Six years is a long time to be in one job, even in Czechoslovakia. She was still remarkably beautiful. The years had merely made her look more vulnerable, less disdainful. Her hair was blonder now. There was a ring of ambiguous meaning with a green

stone on the third finger of her long left hand. Perhaps it was to fend off
tiresome guests. The complainant paid up, and left. It was my turn.
'*Prosim?*'

She didn't recognise me. Under her clear gaze my prepared phrases
evaporated. I just said my name, and the organisation I work for. She
looked away for a moment, in the direction where there had once been
a remote camera. Then the gaze came slowly back to me. Her cheeks
went a delicate pink. She made a sound like a murmured cough,
turned, and headed away from the desk fast. The varnished door
slammed shut with the unconvincing sound cheap wood makes. It
didn't reopen. I was left there, alone.

The last time I had seen her was the day I was thrown out of
Czechoslovakia. I had been interviewing people like the future presi-
dent, Vaclav Havel, and the future foreign minister, Jiri Dienstbier.
They were anti-social elements then, agents of bourgeois interests.
During my time at the hotel she and I had smiled at each other and
made a couple of jokes; nothing more. But soon after I had returned to
London she started writing to me. I had replied as cautiously as a
lawyer. Entrapment, as everyone knows, is the favoured tactic of secret
policemen. But of course there was always another faint possibility. . . .
Men approaching 40 are more given to self-flattery than most.

Her tone soon became startlingly warm. I was, it seemed, the only
man who could understand her private thoughts. Her letters in which
those thoughts were contained were always sent to me at the BBC,
where I worked, and were always posted in West Germany. Since the
BBC was high on the list of organisations which the Czechoslovak
government disliked, letters addressed to it were liable to be inter-
cepted. She could have asked visiting German businessmen to take her
letters and post them when they got home. That's what I told myself.
Then one day I had a letter from her with a GDR postmark. The
chances of a letter getting through to the BBC from East Germany were
no greater than those of one from Prague. I liked it even less when I
read the letter inside. It spoke about sending me some special photographs. Photographs of what?

Soon after, a man with a Central European accent telephoned. He
was insinuating and over-familiar. He wanted to know where he could
send the photographs. I gave him the address. Presumably he knew it
anyway.

'What sort of business are you in?' I asked, to embarrass him.

There was a pause.

'Import/export,' he said. I laughed, and he rang off.

The photographs arrived. They turned out to be of her, on her own, and they weren't subtle. She was fully clothed, but with intent. Sometimes she leaned forward, bosom first. Sometimes she lay on a bed, a copy of *Playboy* beside her. It was a secret policeman's notion of erotic promise. Some lip-smacking Fafner, no doubt, had put this package together. I was annoyed that he should have expected to hook me by something so lacking in finesse. I rang a man who rang a man who rang MI5.

'I say,' said the man from MI5 a couple of days later. 'She's quite something, isn't she?'

She was. But she, or the Fafner figure, had made a mistake. On the back of one of the photographs she had written, 'I'm sorry this is so bad but I took it myself.' A magnifying glass revealed the reflection in a glass lampshade of the real photographer, hunched professionally over a tripod.

Patiently, the MI5 man explained to me about agents of influence: people whom intelligence organisations could manoeuvre into some embarrassing lapse. She had been talking about taking a holiday in Yugoslavia soon, with the hint that I should join her. Maybe, the MI5 man said, an incident would be engineered there which the STB could use against me. After that I might be asked to deliver a package to someone, or make a favourable reference in a broadcast to some policy of the Czechoslovak government. I reflected that no doubt our side was busy doing something of the same sort.

Later I was told that the over-familiar import/export man had been of some interest to MI5. When I rang his number, it seemed he'd left the country in a hurry. Others had gone with him. After that, of course, there were no more letters. I missed them. Few of us are proof against the hint of sexual flattery, even when we know it is synthetic.

And now here I was, six years later, standing by the reception desk where it had all started. The door stayed closed for some minutes. I could hear the faint sound of talking behind it: a well-modulated, low voice, 'an excellent thing in woman', and a harsher, higher one. Then the door opened and shut. A squat blonde figure in her fifties emerged and stood behind the desk. Her bust was vast and cunningly canti-levered. She pointed this particular marvel of Czechoslovak heavy engineering in my direction.

'*Prosim*?' The tone was harsh and high.

'Is Anna there?'

'Sorry, is not here.'

'When will she be back?'

'*Prosim*?'

I gave up eventually. No one stonewalls better than a hotel receptionist trained under Marxism-Leninism. I walked out, unwatched by remote television cameras, unfollowed by secret policemen, into the streets of a city which was still enjoying the feeling of having liberated itself from such things. There were smiling portraits of President Havel in every shop window. People looked relaxed and happy. They even apologised now if they got in each other's way. Forty-two years of surveillance, tale-telling and entrapment had come to an end. Anna's job with the secret police was over. From now on, she needn't write to foreign guests any more. Unless, of course, she chose to.

3 March 1990

A DICTIONARY OF CANT

Nigel Burke

CONSERVATIVE. A word now used by television announcers and in the press to describe hard-line Marxists and socialists in the Soviet Union and other communist countries.

NEW FACES FOR OLD IN EASTERN EUROPE

Timothy Garton Ash

Orwell once wrote that at 50 everyone has the face he deserves. I thought of this remark the other day when comparing the features of two men in their early fifties: the wooden, large-toothed face of Egon Krenz, briefly leader of East Germany's once ruling communist party, and the vivid, laughter-lined face of Vaclav Havel, the playwright-President of Czechoslovakia, who pays an official visit to Britain next week.

Professional politicians of Left and Right in contemporary Western democracies do not generally look very different from each other, because their life experience is usually not so different. To be 'in or out of office' means to be sitting in one office rather than another, not in jail rather than in a palace. In Prague, Warsaw or Budapest, the difference between the old and the new ruling élites is instantly visible — even when the new leaders have replaced their opposition jeans and sweaters with unfamiliar suits and ties.

Most politicians — most public figures — are less impressive close up than seen from afar. But even measured against low expectations the last generation of communist leaders in Eastern Europe was particularly unimpressive. The first generation of post-war communist leaders, though often ignorant and ruthless, could at least boast some real experience of adversity, of struggle, and often of long imprisonment. Most could legitimately claim to have had, at least in their early days, the courage of their convictions. By contrast, the second generation — and there were only two! — was very largely comprised of careerists and opportunists, fat-faced men delivering endless speeches about heroism and justice and equality while thinking only of lunch.

In terms of physiognomy, Roy Hattersley is the comparison that comes to mind. (This is not for a moment to suggest that Mr Hattersley is anything but a statesman of profound conviction, integrity and courage — witness his dauntless stand in defence of Salman Rushdie.) The Hungarian Karoly Grosz had slightly more brain than the others, and slightly less Apparatchik's Jowl, but he certainly did not deserve half the praise initially lavished upon him by, amongst others, the British Government. The Czechoslovak Communist Party's Milos Jakes was a bad joke. In Prague these days you see crowds standing in front of televisions in shop windows and howling with laughter. They are watching a video-recording of Jakes speaking off the cuff to a closed Party meeting, explaining why he had to lock up Vaclav Havel. His Czech is abysmal.

And then there was Egon Krenz, to whom I spoke last month in East Berlin. He received me cordially in the villa to which he had moved from the guarded compound at Wandlitz, where he previously lived with the country's other top leaders. In real life, his white teeth are every bit as distractingly large as in the photographs. The villa is light and comfortable, with good modern furniture. On one wall there is a large oil painting, with an effusive dedication from the artist to Herr Krenz on his 50th birthday, in 1987. Curiously enough the picture is entitled 'against fear'.

Herr Krenz now had time to spare: we spoke for nearly two hours. He told me he was worried that no one would give him a job. After 30 years, he said, he probably could not return to his original profession of . . . teacher. However, he was writing the memoirs of his brief time at the top. 'It's a welcome distraction,' he confided. He was also pub-

'Really? Which lodge?'

lishing advance titbits in the *Bild-Zeitung*. So just a few weeks after being deposed as communist party leader, he had sold himself to a right-wing West German tabloid which stands for everything that he had supposedly worked and fought against for 40 years.

'Granny, what large teeth you have!' said one placard in the popular demonstrations that brought him down. But close up he was no wolf: rather a sheep in wolf's clothing. The illegitimate son of a Pomeranian peasant woman, he grew up knowing poverty. What did socialism mean to him then? 'A better life,' he instantly replied, though quickly going on to explain that he meant a better life for everyone. When I asked him about his subsequent career, he produced an extraordinarily wooden recitation of his successive offices and titles, talking like a Robert Maxwell biography. The one really human moment came when he described his mother's pride at his earliest successes. Otherwise, what was most interesting was just how uninteresting he was. Now, as in his childhood, having enough to eat plainly figured very high on his mental list of priorities – hence, no doubt, the *Bild-Zeitung*, and the West German book publisher. His spoken German was little better than Jakes's spoken Czech. His teeth were the only large thing about him. Little man, what now?

One can interpret the banality of Egon Krenz in diverse ways. One can say that this is a good illustration of the mechanism of negative selection (yes-men to the top) which was characteristic for communist systems, and contributed to their downfall. (But in that case, how do you account for the personality of Gorbachev?) Or one can say that this shows the strength of a totalitarian system, which can continue to function effectively even with such poor quality cogs. But of the banality itself there is no doubt.

So the first thing to note is that the new rulers of East Central Europe are quite simply of a much higher intellectual, moral and human quality than their predecessors. This is true of the Catholic intellectual Tadeusz Mazowiecki, Prime Minister of the (no longer People's) Republic of Poland, whom we saw on an official visit to Britain last month. It is true of Lech Walesa, whom we may see having tea with the Queen sooner rather than later, as President Walesa. It will almost certainly also be true of the next President of the (no longer People's) Republic of Hungary. (The likely candidates at present include a philosopher and another playwright.) Yet if Krenz might serve as an epitome of the old, Havel must be the prime exemplar of the new.

He is, for a start, an intellectual of real distinction. Of his plays, it is probably the earlier ones, *The Garden Party* and *The Memorandum*, that will actually last longest. But what will, I think, last even longer is his essayistic work, which has ripened slowly over the years. He is, in fact, the outstanding literary-philosophical analyst of the Central European experience under communism, and his work would have endured even had he never become a prominent opposition figure, let alone a President. Yet of course he did, and the second reason that he is an exemplar has to do with his whole biography, an almost perfect contrast to that of Krenz. (They are almost exactly the same age, Havel born in October 1936, Krenz in March 1937.)

'Struggle' may be too heavy a word for someone with so much laughter in his life, although years of prison and police harassment would normally qualify for that description. Initially, the struggle was forced upon him, for as a millionaire's son he was barred from higher education. In his twenties and early thirties, he was most involved in the theatre, although within the literary world his defence of the independence of writers several times brought him into conflict with the authorities. But from 1968, and at the latest from the time of his open letter to President Gustav Husak in 1975, politics − or what he called anti-politics − inexorably take the upper hand, even though he himself constantly insists that what he wants to do, above all, is just write plays. Finally, there is the fairy-tale quality of his personal transition from prison, early in 1989, to Prague Castle at the end of 1989. Czechoslovakia's revolution, styled by Havel the 'velvet' or 'gentle' revolution, is − so far − the best example of peaceful transition from communism anywhere, and he is its unquestioned symbol.

Up at the castle, they are still clearing out Husak's furniture from the presidential offices. There are square brown armchairs of super-human size, silently eloquent of endless non-conversations between totalitarian rulers. Fortunately there are still some rooms with the fittings from the pre-war First Republic: Masaryk's furniture. Husak's ghastly pictures have mostly been removed from the walls, to be replaced by large nudes and a prayer rug from the Dalai Lama. Havel, unlike Krenz, has no spare time at all. But dashing down the long back corridors to a press conference, he paused for a moment to show me a room with a huge ancient metal door. This was the starvation chamber, traditional in Central European castles. He said: 'We shall use it for talks.'

The old presidential staff go on working down below. But on his upper floor, Havel has installed a *Kolegium* or counsel of advisers. A writer, a translator, a theatre director, a samizdat editor, and so on. Professional politicians have made a mess of things, he says, so let amateurs have a go. (Even his secretary is an amateur — an actress, of course.) Moreover, as he explained in his speech to the US Congress, he feels that the time has come for intellectuals to take more direct political responsibility. They cannot, he says contentiously, 'endlessly evade their responsibility for the world and conceal their dislike of politics behind an alleged need to be independent.'

Just as the Czechoslovak revolution was, in many respects, a Havel play, so now presidential policy-making is conceived theatrically: the first dramatic gesture of flying to Berlin — with the opened Wall as prop — and then to Munich; the symbolic 'Central European' homage to Warsaw and Budapest; the grand, glittering trip to the United States, for nearly a week, with half the government, then the short working visit to Moscow, taking the defence and interior ministers; and now Paris and London. In between, he speaks to Czechs, Slovaks and (as we now have to say) Moravians.

As soon as he got back from Washington, he gave a report to 'the people of Prague' from the balcony on the old town square. It was an extraordinary, joking, colloquial little chat — like a favourite uncle recounting his adventures in America — and he ended it by raising his hand and saying '*ahoj!*', that is, roughly, 'cheerio!' Two days later he was back on the same balcony, delivering a quite different sort of speech: a brilliantly turned, witty, yet deeply serious and profound reflection on the February 1948 communist coup and its legacy. Altogether, the speeches at home and abroad are superb. His first major speech as President, the New Year's Address which we reprinted in these pages ('The art of the impossible', 27 January), is one of the great documents of his historical moment, and his speeches here will surely be interesting.

Yet I must confess that I came away from Prague less happy than I had expected to be. One can easily share the Czechs' delight and pride in their new President. But there is something slightly worrying in the sheep-like devotion of all the upturned faces, the almost messianic expectations, and the virtual cult of personality in the media. It is a new and infinitely better personality, and far, far cleaner language, but is it healthy that everyone should just be repeating the same things? 'If we have any more love and truth,' said a sharp young acquaintance of mine, 'I shall have to emigrate.' Yes, said a poet, 'newspeak has been replaced by lovespeak.' And when, on my last evening, I listened to a television report of Havel's meeting with the tennis star, Ivan Lendl, it sounded like nothing so much as an account of a meeting between some communist party leader and a hero of socialist sport. Which is precisely the kind of thing which that television reporter had probably been producing for the last 20 or 40 years.

Of course there is not much that the new people at the top can do about this. Indeed, part of the problem is that there are so few of them. Almost everyone of any calibre is already in some senior official post, but they do not reach down the hierarchy. As a result, far more has changed at the top than at the bottom. In this sense, the Czechoslovak revolution has been a victim of its own success. Moreover, there is an obvious danger in such heady adulation.

> The strongest poison ever known
> Came from Caesar's laurel crown

I must say that I saw virtually no signs of a loss of contact with reality, let alone corruption by power. (The Foreign Minister received me in unbuttoned denim shirt, cooking his own omelette as we talked.) But these are early days.

The only lasting guarantees against human weakness are, of course, the checks and balances of limited government and parliamentary democracy. The crucial question is whether these can be built fast and strong enough. There is a particular urgency here. For Czechoslovakia, like all the other post-communist states, faces a very painful transition to a market economy. Only a strong government can sustain this transition. The only way to make a strong government in a parliamentary democracy is to have strong, stable parties. The trouble is that in Czechoslovakia, as elsewhere, these are not yet in prospect. The weaker the government that comes out of parliament, the greater the demands on the presidency. There is already talk of a further two-year transition period after the parliamentary elections on 8 June, with the new parliament as a kind of constituent assembly. In that case, there would be enormous pressure for Havel to stay in the castle until 1992. And who says two years is enough?

Travelling to and fro between Britain and Eastern Europe over the last decade, there is one theatrical exchange that has constantly returned to me. It is the exchange between Brecht's Galileo and his former pupil, disgusted at the master's recantation. 'Unhappy the land that has no heroes,' the pupil cries. But Brecht's Galileo says: 'Unhappy the land that has need of heroes.'

Unhappy the land that has no Havels? Yes, but unhappy the land that has need of Havels. For you cannot count on having great and good men. Most people are eventually corrupted by power. That is one of the very few universal laws of history. The second generation is most unlikely to have the qualities of the first, even without a 'negative selection' such as happens in dictatorships. The essential thing is to create a system which will work even with Hattersleys. Or Kohls. Or Quayles. Or even Krenzes.

There are many things that intellectuals from East Central Europe have to teach us. But how to construct a durable system of controlled power is not one of them. The best is the enemy of the good. The emerging democracies of East Central Europe will be incredibly lucky if they achieve anything like the combination of strong government with real democracy which our system – with all its faults – provides. Returning to Britain, I find the country slowly winding up for the kind of general election of which Belloc wrote:

> The accursed power which stands on Privilege
> (And goes with Women, and Champagne and Bridge)
> Broke – and Democracy resumed her reign:
> (Which goes with Bridge, and Women and Champagne)

The worst possible system, apart from all the others that have been tried.

If you notice a slightly elegaic note creeping in, that is because this is the last article I shall write as Foreign Editor of *The Spectator*. I have written for *The Spectator* continuously for more than ten years, from Gdansk to Tirana and from Managua to Moscow. Now I hope to deepen my understanding of contemporary European history as a Fellow of St Antony's College, Oxford, which is neither ivory nor a tower, but all the better for that. However, I cannot promise never to return to these pages. Old *Spectator* writers only die; they do not fade away.

In the most unlikely event of anyone having withdrawal symptoms, in the meantime, a cheap and sustaining medicine is at hand. It is called *We The People: The Revolution of '89 Witnessed in Warsaw, Budapest, Berlin & Prague* (Granta Books, £4.99). It is available, as they say, in all good bookshops. And no doubt in some bad ones.

17 March 1990

BOOKS? WHO NEEDS THEM?

Martin Fagg

One journalist I know wears white cotton gloves while reading his review copies. They thus remain clean enough for subsequent flogging off to our local book-knacker. I do not go as far as that, but, knowing that Mr Herschel will seize on the slightest imperfection in a book's condition to depreciate the sum he's prepared to offer, I keep it as tidy as possible.

Usually, it is the book's contents that excite his detraction. 'I'll never sell it, my friend,' he'll say, gazing lugubriously at the instant biography of a publicity-crazed bishop. 'Who wants to read about an old gasbag like that? Who needs it? Tell you what, I'll give you a fiver for it.' As 'old gasbag' seems a mild assessment of the cleric in question, a fiver is fair enough.

Mr Herschel is never short of reasons for devaluing the books you bring him. If they are rampant best-sellers, he'll shake his head pityingly. 'It's a question of clientele, my friend. My customers are scholars and gentlemen, lecturers at the LSE' (I ponder this breathtaking bracketing). 'They're not interested in these' (a gesture of bottomless contempt) 'coffee-table books. Quality — that's what I need. Quality and scholarship — not this hyped-up tripe.'

However, when you do bring him something deeply, even impenetrably scholarly, his gear-change is effortless. '*Celestial Motions: Studies in the Ptolemaic Tradition* — I ask you, what a title! What a subject! Only two schmucks in the world know anything about it. Schmuck 1 writes the book: Schmuck 2 torpedoes it in the *TLS*. I mean — who needs it? Tell you what, I'll give you a fiver for it.'

Another of Mr Herschel's ways of deflating a book is vilifying everyone involved in its production, from author and publisher to editor and illustrator. I'd long known that few authors were touched by galloping teetotalism, but it was only Mr Herschel's confidences that informed me that well over 90 per cent were legless lushes. 'They've dried him out five times, but the last time he was in the shop, he was still falling over' is a typical reminiscence. 'I could tell you things about this lady', he'll say, sombrely tapping her latest block-busting bodice-ripper, 'as'd make your hair curl, supposing' (raising his eyes to my gleaming cranium) 'you still had any.' Another veteran novelist is, apparently, so enfeebled by five decades of obsessive sodomy that it's a miracle that he still has the strength to plug in his word-processor. As for publishers, Mr Herschel's fund of disobliging anecdotes is inexhaustible. 'I tell you what, my friend – when a publisher goes bathing, it's the sharks that want to watch out.'

Of all Mr Herschel's repertoire of practised responses, my favourite is his startled cry and recoil on glancing at the review slip of some insanely overpriced specialist work, whose sole ambition is to sell itself to a couple of hundred libraries that can't afford *not* to house it.

'My friend, I'd be ashamed to offer you what it's worth to me. You'd go out of this shop thinking such bitter things about me – and it's bitter cold out, so mind you wrap up well in that nice muffler – how much did it cost you? *Very* reasonable. Liberty's Sale, eh? Always worth it, cashmere – quality pays. As I say, you'll go out of here thinking "That old pirate" – how can I offer you four pounds for a 40-quid book?'

'Try me, Mr Herschel.'

'Tell you what, I'll give you a fiver for it.'

Despite his routine talking-down, Mr Herschel's offers are not all that ungenerous. Often I've entered his shop with a clutch of books, hoping to raise £25, knowing I'll take £20, but emerging with £30. Just as, often, the quest exceeds the goal and the ascent excels the summit, so, plainly, in Mr Herschel's case, the ritual of bargaining surpasses the bargain itself.

His pessimism is not confined to the actual books he deals in. 'A lifetime I've spent in this business, and every single minute of it wasted. One day, when I've the time – *when* – I should be so lucky – *I'm* going to write a book that's going to blow the lid off the whole rotten trade. I mean books, who needs them?' This inclusive scorn is hard to reconcile with his encyclopaedic knowledge of the very artefacts he affects to despise.

These recollections have rambled on in the present tense because, I suppose, I have not yet adjusted. I hadn't been to the shop for some time. In fact, 'flu and its after-effects had kept me away since before Christmas.

Mr Herschel had always had assistants — friendly, unobtrusive presences somewhat overborne by the personality of their boss; but when he was indisposed (he never took holidays) his place was taken by his grandson Leonard. It was Leonard I found the other day. I enquired after Mr Herschel.

'Oh, grandpa — you hadn't heard? He died on Boxing Day.'

'I'd no idea.'

'It was the 'flu. Peaceful though. He died in his sleep.'

'I'm *very* sorry. I shall miss him.'

'Yeah.'

'He must have been getting on, I suppose.'

'Ninety-one.'

'Good God! I thought he was about 70.'

'Everyone did.' Leonard smiled. 'It was the books that kept him young.'

'The books?'

'Well, you know how he loved books.'

'Oh yes . . . indeed.'

'They were his whole life. Talked about nothing else. Amazing what he'd read.'

Leonard smiled again. He is a charming young man, and I'm sure ours will be a mutually advantageous relationship. Somehow, though, I find his meek acceptance of the wares I proffer rather dispiriting. Leonard seems to have a very high opinion of authors — even of publishers. Has he learned *nothing* from his grandfather? As for the sums he offers, they work out at much the same as his grandad's — a little less if anything. It's been a painful experience.

17 March 1990

LEAVES FROM THE COMMONPLACE BOOK OF WALLACE ARNOLD

AFORE YE GO

Second to none in my appreciation of Miss (Ms!) Ann Wilson, I only hope that her new biography of C. S. Lewis will not be thoroughly overshadowed by my own first-hand account of the man, *Wallace and Jack*, to be published next week.

Ever the busy bee, Ann has been diligent in grubbing around in the mud, and, sure enough, she has discovered that Jack Lewis 'led a double life', replacing top on Parker '45 betwixt penning paragraphs on *The Problem of Pain* in order to bicycle posthaste to a Miss Marilyn Monroe, then lodging in digs somewhere beyond Magdalen Bridge, there to have his wicked way.

Such prurience in a biographer is to be roundly condemned. It may well be that there are those who wish to have their reading of *The Lion, the Witch and the Wardrobe* sullied by visions of an erotic whirlwind of discarded bicycle clips but I am not among them. My own, more personal, reminiscence recalls Jack as he was: a bachelor don, distinguished in a tremendous variety of fields, as much a friend of the saloon bar as of the common room, full of earthy good humour and (occasionally caustic!) observation, a man imbued from top to toe with Christian understanding, a theologian, a literary critic and a part-time cabaret artiste in the risqué Pussy Galore Club in Old Compton Street. My own affectionate memoir concentrates on this latter, perhaps less well-known aspect of Jack's immensely varied career, an aspect all but missing from Ann's now hopelessly outmoded effort in poison-pennery.

Toe-tapping

From Miss Monroe's digs on the far side of Magdalen Bridge, Jack would don nose-specs-and-moustache novelty mask to bicycle without fear of recognition to the railway station, there to catch the fast train to Paddington. Once aboard, he would meet his fellow Inklings – J. R. R. Tolkien (double-bass), Nevill Coghill (bassoon), Charles Williams (keyboards) and H. V. D. Dyson (maracas) — and, in the closely-guarded privacy of the guard's van they would rehearse that night's perform-ance, with Jack Lewis going full throttle on vocals.

> Oh, we think things
> 'Cos we're the Ink-lings
> And we're always wink-ing
> Yes, we're the I-N-K-L-I-N-G-S
> — INKLINGS!!!

The gusto and sheer toe-tapping bonhomie of this witty, fast-moving intro may lose a little in print but on stage the effect was electrifying, the number gaining greatly from Professor Tolkien's undisputed mas-tery of the kazoo. But alas, the days of variety were already in decline and the more glamorous and up-to-date (dread phrase!) combination of the Beverley Sisters — females all three — soon supplanted the Inklings. Of the original Inklings, only F.P.J. ('Frankie') Vaughan found fame in show business; the rest sought succour in the more dry and dusty world of academe. In ignoring this other, even more secret life, Ann has, I fear, failed to grasp the essence of the man.

10 February 1990

LIFE & LETTERS

SHOES COVERED FOR OCCASIONS

P. J. Kavanagh

The poet Pearse Hutchinson, old friend, Dubliner, has long been sceptical of my tales of the pleasant experiences that Ireland always affords; he feels he knows the place too well. It seemed a good idea to take him to the west, and prove my point. We had been lent a cottage in Mayo, long disused, and I wanted to leave Dublin first thing in the morning so that we could reach it in daylight, find how to warm the place up. Then I remembered that Pearse likes to sidle gingerly into the day, so in Dublin I telephoned to book us a staging-post, and immediately began one of the pleasant experiences, with Directory Enquiries. 'D'you mean you got *through*?' was the chorus when I returned to tell my tale. I had indeed. 'Could you tell me the number of the Anglers' Arms at Headford, County Mayo?' 'Of course I can — except it isn't in Mayo, it's in Galway. A lovely place.' 'You know it!' 'It's one of my favourite watering-holes when I'm visiting my brother Matt in the west. You'll have a great time. The new people there have done a fine job with the renovations.' That word cast me down a little, for it is always bad news when connected with a pub, but I was enchanted by the personal note, characteristic of my experience of Ireland, although I suppose it may be a reason why people get the engaged tone. Anyway, when I told the story, Pearse's face took on its usual expression of courteously suspended disbelief.

On our way to supper we passed a notice: 'SHOES COVERED FOR WEDDINGS'. Pearse and I stared up at it, puzzled, and one of our group said gently: 'It's for people with not too much money', as though fearful that I was about to make an English Marie Antoinette remark, and wonder why they did not just buy new shoes. It was good to be reminded how much poorer Ireland is than England.

Reminded, also, of how settled it is, compared to England. In the car driving west Pearse's talk was always of people, and these were given a locality — 'a Limerick man', 'a Cork man', even 'a west-Cork man' — and such origins were held to explain, in some part, their characters and behaviour. By late afternoon we had crossed the Shannon, and were certainly in a particular place, the skies widened, the fields were bordered with walls of black boulders, with white lichen on them. When the sky is seen through the gaps between the boulders these walls are like intricate lace. The cottage, on a lake, nestled, it seemed, in its own cloud of variegated birds, but it would be too difficult to warm up in time; besides, Pearse had arranged for us to read our poems to the Yeats Society in Sligo, so, at least to my regret, next day, we left the Anglers' Rest and pressed on. In Sligo we were talked to, pleasantly, by strangers in the street, Pearse's disbelief diminishing by the minute. Also, you can talk easily about Christianity in Ireland. Someone at the Yeats Society said that it was all right to love Creation, since Vatican II, because it is God's; 'the vale of tears' side is now played down. Many of us have had no difficulty with this, but it was a reminder of the importance, and danger, of words. A misplaced emphasis can ruin a life. The later Church Fathers recognised this and developed a principle of *oeconomia* (of precise formulations) and Christ was notably economical when he was allowed to be; it is easy to hear his impatience with the demands on him to be too narrowly specific, of which more later.

We heard neighbouring Leitrim called the Cinderella of Irish counties, be-laked but little visited, and so poor, 'the snipe fly over it upside down', because they know they will see nothing below worth eating, so we made our way into it. At Dromkeeran — 'slope of the rowan trees', Pearse speaks Irish — the snipe would have known there would have been no food in the pub we stopped at, but would have been wrong, for somewhere from a private kitchen a sandwich was produced, for which payment was refused, and that was before Pearse had found out he knew the barman's cousin. This young man bade us Godspeed to Ballinamore (just down the road) with such an unselfconscious Synge-song of eloquence, so lengthy, so well constructed, that we both sat for a while silent in the car, wondering if we could trust our ears. 'Can you remember *exactly* what he said?' I asked Pearse. 'I wish to God I could,' he replied. In the Ballinamore hotel a princely girl climbed two flights of stairs to ask the newly arrived visitors whether she could bring them a cup of tea. Our progress, for so it seemed to have become, was much punctuated by such princely girls, bold-eyed — so long as 'bold' does not suggest an invitation, which was certainly not there.

But Tommy Sheridan, presiding over the bar opposite, did not see this quality in the younger generation. He genially pronounced them useless. 'The young fellas, if they had to look after themselves they'd even burn the shaving-water! And the girls are no better. They may have qualifications as long as your arm, but they'd serve a dishcloth for a dinner!'

Sceptical Pearse, after a last, lengthy encounter with a woman from whom he was buying me some homemade pickle, was convinced at last. He had been told the people of Leitrim were the pleasantest in Ireland, and he found them so. There and elsewhere, he agreed, we had had nothing but good experiences. But back in Dublin, before our poetry-reading, someone said Jane Grigson had died. This shook me; she was a friend and neighbour and I had meant to ring her before I left for Ireland. 'Oh yes,' boomed the voice, 'it's been a great week for literary deaths. Rosamond Lehmann is dead too.' My mother-in-law, a central part of my emotional furniture, to say the least. The evening passed somehow, we cut the trip short and I flew home.

There I came upon something that has nagged at me since: a matter of words. Her obituary described Rosamond as a Christian. Rosamond believed many things but whether the word Christian could be elasticated to include them all, and whether she would want it to be, is doubtful. There was the same discomfort at Jane Grigson's funeral. She was not a Christian; she told me so, when inconsolable at Geoffrey's death. But the devout priest, a friend of hers, claimed that because she was brave and generous – which she was – hers was a 'Christian soul'. Well, maybe, but I had an uneasy feeling that in both cases shoes were being hurriedly crammed on feet they did not fit, shoes two thoughtful women had chosen not to wear while they were alive; or, at best, willy-nilly, a sense of, Shoes Covered for Funerals.

7 April 1990

'It was touch and go for a while. I'm lucky to be dead.'

A RIDDLE

I have a friend who, when I am alone,
Sits with me — and how intimate we've grown!
He talks, but what he says he never hears,
He is unfeeling, but he dries my tears.
He has one back, he has a hundred faces
As lovely as the spring in desert places
(Sometimes I thump him on the back — I must,
He gets half-smothered in thick, choking dust).
He talks, but soundlessly; he has to find
A clever man before he'll speak his mind.
Whenever I encounter him, his eyes
Recall the precepts of the good and wise,
And yet he's quiet till I look his way
Unlike some fools, who blather on all day.
In darkness he falls silent — which is right,
He is a Prince who glories in the Light.

                                   Naser Khosrow (1003-1088)

Translated from the Persian by Dick Davis
The Answer is 'A Book'.